TRADING TIME

Can exchange lead to social change?

Lee Gregory

First published in Great Britain in 2015 by

Policy Press   North America office:
University of Bristol   Policy Press
1-9 Old Park Hill   c/o The University of Chicago Press
Bristol   1427 East 60th Street
BS2 8BB   Chicago, IL 60637, USA
UK   t: +1 773 702 7700
t: +44 (0)117 954 5940   f: +1 773-702-9756
pp-info@bristol.ac.uk   sales@press.uchicago.edu
www.policypress.co.uk   www.press.uchicago.edu

British Library Cataloguing in Publication Data
A catalogue record for this book is available from the British Library

Library of Congress Cataloging-in-Publication Data
A catalog record for this book has been requested

ISBN 978-1-4473-1829-3 hardcover

Cover design by Policy Press
Front cover image: istock
Printed and bound in Great Britain by CPI Group (UK) Ltd, Croydon, CR0 4YY
Policy Press uses environmentally responsible print partners

Contents

Acknowledgements

As this is my first book, it is the end product of a long journey, and it is not possible to write a book about time that does not reflect back and construct a personal narrative that explains how this present point was reached. The journey started when I was encouraged to attend university, having never considered this an option before, and without that initial nudge from David Cutts, this book would not be here today. At Cardiff University, there are many people I owe thanks for the years of study I completed there. First and foremost is Mark Drakeford, who has been a supervisor, mentor and friend for the last 11 years. His advice, guidance and support have always been invaluable – it was at his suggestion that I started my research into time banking that underpins the discussion to follow. Thanks also go to Barbara Adam for her enthusiasm and insights into the social theory of time – and for persevering with me as I explored the topic and drew it into my research. Eva Elliott is also due thanks for her supervision during the PhD research that underpins this work and for her valuable insights and advice. In thinking through and developing the ideas that are presented in this text, I would also like to thank Finn Bowring, fellow time bank researchers Ruth Naughton-Doe and Liv Pearson, and Christala Sophocleous, who have all listened to and discussed my ideas with me. Thanks also go to previous colleagues at the University of Bristol and current colleagues at the University of Birmingham. In preparing the text itself, I would like to thank Ailsa Cameron for her comments on early drafts, the reviewers for their thoughts and views, as well as Ali Shaw and Laura Vickers and everyone else at Policy Press.

Special thanks also to Dan, Ste, Reena, David, Rachel, Laura, Hannah and Stu who have provided much-needed distractions and friendship over the last few years, and to my parents, who have consistently provided support.

An unpayable debt is owed to all who have contributed to the completion of this work in some way. However, errors of fact, expression and interpretation remain my own responsibility.

ONE

Introduction

> In this new social order, there is only one thing worse than
> domination by the market, and that is exclusion from it,
> since there is now no other source of knowing who we are.
> (Seabrook, 2007, cited in Bauman, 2009: 151)

The growth of capitalism and the development of social policy are
intricately linked. Industrialisation created rapid change within
societies, fostering economic progress that improved employment
opportunities, life expectancy, infant mortality, education and advances
in technology (Ben-Ami, 2012). Yet, this same process has also
generated unstable economic cycles, environmental damage and the rise
of neoliberal economic theory at the global level, promoting a particular
path for economic, political and social development, with a number
of damaging consequences (explored later). From the perspective
of the social policy historian, industrialisation and the subsequent
economic growth generated a new wave of social problems that were
gradually met with increasing levels of state provision from the 1900s
until the 1980s. At this point, an increased critique of the role of the
state led to a diversification of welfare providers, with consequences
for the alleviation of social problems. In the UK context, upon which
the majority of this book is focused, the Liberal reforms in the early
1900s through to the Beveridge blueprint for welfare provision in the
1940s and beyond centred on a debate regarding the role of the state
in relation to the market economy. Despite the ideological minefield
around which this debate has developed, the provision of welfare
services is intimately tied to the rise and fall of market growth. Perhaps
at no other time in recent history has this been more obvious as, at the
time of writing, with the consequences of the 2008 global financial
crisis. In the UK, unemployment has increased, especially among young
people; higher numbers of the poor are in work while experiencing
poverty; and popular political discourse has not only switched to
focus on the 'squeezed middle', but has come to agree on a need for
'austerity' (see Chapter Two). This focus on austerity has resulted in
cuts to welfare provision and services aimed at helping to support the
welfare of citizens and to address social problems. While there are some

signs that the UK economy is starting to recover, the austerity agenda continues apace, driven by the ideological need to reduce the state.

Financial collapse has led to a call for significant cutbacks in state spending, with welfare provision being the first target of governments seeking to navigate the fallout of the economic crash. It is possible to point to the 1940s, when, despite economic restraint, the 'welfare state' was established in the UK. Part of the justification of this activity was the social-democratic idea that markets have pernicious effects on individuals, communities and society as a whole. The role of the state was to intercede and counter the negative consequences of market activities. In a similar way, many of these views of the consequences of market activity remain, and the argument developed in this book offers a different insight into this debate. It agrees that there are negative consequences of neoliberal markets, and that the state should intervene to tackle the most severe of these outcomes. However, it offers an alternative theoretical framework through which to consider the relationship between the state and market, and between the state and citizen: one related to time.

The rise of capitalist/industrial societies in the West has generated widespread commentary on the various problems that have arisen from its expansion and practices. At the theoretical level, there are debates regarding alienation and exploitation (Marx, 1974), as well as the use of money leading to the erosion of personal bonds and interactions (Simmel, 1900, 1964). Others have argued for the benefits that industrial advancement has brought (Ben-Ami, 2012), and thus the debate between the positive and negative outcomes of capitalist growth continues. Contemporary arguments, however, have increasingly focused on the negative externalities of capitalist expansion, especially in relation to the environment (Kümmerer, 1996; Adam, 1998; Bell, 2011), which have prompted calls for alternative forms of market practices that do not fit with the broader neoliberal ideology (New Economics Foundation, 2008d). From a social policy perspective, the persistence of inequalities in health, income and wealth within and across nations remains a constant focus of policy activity to address the consequences of capitalist expansion, in a way not too dissimilar from the early Liberal government of the 1900s.

The promotion of alternatives in the contemporary setting, however, is often closely associated with a range of social movements, both within and across nations, advocating for change and reform to capitalist systems, from alternative currency systems such as Local Exchange Trading Systems (North, 2006a, 2006b) to the Idle Foundation.[1] These organisations campaign for change across a range of different elements of human life and interaction. Yet, change rarely occurs. In fact, despite consistent challenge and critique, the neoliberal ideas associated with capitalist expansion remain rooted deep in the social fabric, resistant to criticism. As will be shown in later chapters, explanations for this resistance can be found, but, here, it is important to note that the challenge to the global neoliberal order that has come to dominate national and supranational organisations has come from local communities tucked away within nation-states. From the 'global ethnography' of Burawoy and colleagues (1991) to the revived work of Saul Alinsky (Schutz and Sandy, 2011) as a means of empowering communities to self-organise for change, there is renewed focus on the possibilities of breaking the hold that neoliberal ideas have in the organisation of both the economic and social world.

Within this history of attempted resistance, however, there is a narrative to be told regarding alternative forms of production and exchange. As Chapter Four will briefly outline, this is a history that can link the social credit and 'green shirt' movement (Drakeford, 1997) with the complementary currency systems (CCSs) of the 1980s onwards. It is this latter group of alternatives, CCSs, that will be the focus of discussion here, in particular, time banking. Generally, CCSs have been linked to the 'new economics' of writers such as Ruskin (1862), and are proposed as a means by which society can reconcile the tension between finite environmental resources and economic production. Time banking is one part of this narrative, which can be associated with environmental, or green, philosophies (Seyfang, 2004a) for reordering social and economic relations in contemporary society. Yet, time banking, a form of CCS that is drawn upon as a case study for the discussion of this book, is also associated with the idea of 'co-production', which, for some, such as the New Economics Foundation, is an additional means by which to move towards zero-growth economics. For the 2010 Coalition government in the UK, however, co-production is a means for achieving the 'Big Society'. In this latter formulation, time banking facilitates individuals and communities to take on increased care responsibilities within their communities, a form of self-help that can facilitate state withdrawal. Thus, we have set up the central tension to be explored in this book: the alternatives to capitalism can often presented as both a contradiction and complement to neoliberal praxis.

To untangle this tension, the discussion in this book focuses upon the benefits that can be gained through an analysis embedded within the social theory of time. As such, Chapter Three will specifically outline this theory and its use in policy analysis to date. What is necessary here is a justification as to why to use the theory of time.

Time rather than social exchange

Complementary currency systems seek to promote alternative forms of exchange and production that lock money into the local economy. The aims of such systems, more broadly, have been described as the 'leaky bucket' economic problem (Hopkins, in North, 2010b: Foreword). Communities are represented by the bucket in this analogy, and when members of the community buy goods, they are pouring money into this bucket. However, purchasing goods in non-local stores, especially those owned by multinational corporations, results in the money being sucked out of the community. As such, it is not reinvested in the community as it would be if local stores were the recipient of such funds. Alternative currencies are suggested as a means of plugging the gaps. Using a CCS ensures that people spend their money locally and that local stores use the currency to procure their goods locally, creating a stronger, revitalised local economy. This is a proposed response to a number of problems associated with capitalist practices and values. Local Exchange Trading Systems (LETS), for example, are associated with wider environmental ideologies, and offer a sustainable system of exchange and production within local communities. The aim of such CCSs is to create a parallel currency through which members of the LETS can exchange with each other. An innovation of the theme has been alternative 'pound' currency systems, as can be seen in Bristol and Brixton (and a number of other UK localities; see Hickman, 2009; Whitehead, 2010a, 2010b). Here, members of the scheme can exchange their money for an equivalent amount of alternative pounds; thus, this alternative is underpinned by pounds sterling (unlike LETS currencies that do not have this backing). Additionally, LETS are promoted as an environmentally friendly alternative form of production compared to capitalist production. Its local focus is said to lead to smaller supply and demand chains that have less environmental impact and foster the development of sustainable living (Lang, 1994; Croall, 1997; Bowring, 1998).

Time banking, while part of the CCS umbrella, is not considered an economic endeavour, but a social one. Early research in the UK associated its practice with efforts to tackle social exclusion (Seyfang and Smith, 2002), potentially placing it within a different set of practices and values due to its exchange mechanism. Other CCSs, such as LETS, create a new currency that has equivalence with pounds sterling. This means that members can exchange with each other or with local businesses. The same holds true for alternative pound schemes. Time banking is different, as the name implies, the basis of exchange is in time. Each hour of service/activity provided earns one time credit, which entitles the holder to access a service/activity for an hour. As Cahn (2000: 6) explains: 'Give an hour; get an hour. One hour = one service credit or one Time Dollar. 1 = 1 = 1 did not seem like rocket science. There wasn't any obvious flaw I could spot.'

For some, time banking is less radical, and the question is raised as to 'how many credits for a pound of carrots?' (North, 2003: 270). Others have suggested that the success of time banking (in its earlier form of service credits) provides a model of practice that LETS should seek to emulate (Bowring, 1998), or that the focus on the social dimension offer more supportive arguments for the benefits of time banking in terms of engagement, participation and forming social networks (Callison, 2003; Seyfang, 2003b). Of course, it is possible to question if an hour for an hour is fair, as the skill required and the quality of provision all impact upon price – but these are the means by which the market determines value, which is not, as will be discussed later, the way in which time banking determines value.

However, the focus on exchange is highly significant. If CCSs are part of a wider questioning narrative of neoliberal ideology and capitalism, then offering alternative production and exchange practices is an important consideration. LETS and 'pounds' offer this alternative economic analysis, and this has been essential to the 'Transition Towns' movement (see North, 2010b).[2] Of course, the discussion of exchange leads to a consideration of exchange theory, and it is possible to argue that this theoretical framework has more to offer in understanding time banking than a framework established within the social theory of time. Consideration of social exchange theory in relation to CCSs has been provided, and it is possible to briefly outline why this is inadequate for the task at hand.

Social exchange theory has provided insight into human interaction (Befu, 1977; Lawler, 2001), although it is critiqued for its application of economic rationality to human interaction (Miller, 2005). Notions of gift exchange have been developed within this analysis (Mauss, 1950), which has been an influential idea in social policy since Titmuss's (1997) famous study on blood donation. Gifts are considered to promote reciprocity as they are inalienable in that the property right is never fully transferred to the receiver: the gift giver retains some ownership (Mauss, 1950; Gregory, 1982). However, such analysis has been critiqued for not acknowledging that gifts are actually free of obligation (Testart, 1998). Exchange theory has been drawn upon to explore CCSs (Terese Soder, 2008), and time banking specifically (Powell and Dalton, 2003), to enhance understanding of the role of exchange within such systems.

Powell and Dalton (2003) suggest that time banking can harness the value that young people associate with peer groups to facilitate behavioural change. Utilising social exchange theory, particularly the work of Blau (1964 , cited in Powell and Dalton, 2003), they explain how time bank practices engage in relevant 'steps' of social exchange. Step one is the negotiation of exchanges between individuals, while step two involves the recognition of status and power differences embedded in the exchange. The fairness of time banking, noted earlier, levels these differentials for all activity as contribution is equally valued. Steps three and four are legitimisation of exchange within its social context and the formation of larger social structures, respectively. While potentially useful in exploring how time banks develop and how credit exchange can alter institutional practices where time banking is adopted, this leaves unclear a key aspect of exchange: what is it that members value to encourage them to earn credits? Specifically, what is the source of value in time banking and what implications does this have for its growing association with government policies. If time banking practices are equated to gift giving, the value of the gift is associated with time, and this is what necessitates an understanding of time banking based upon the wider social theory of time.

It has already been mentioned that exchange is tied to the practice of an hour equals an hour credit, which entitles the earner to an hour of service in return. Here is why time becomes important as the framework of analysis. On the surface, time is being measured and related to an exchangeable credit. This relates to the clearest symbol of time in contemporary society, the clock. The clock measures how much time has passed during the day; it regulates a range of social interactions and organisations (from when we eat to when the bus arrives). This is time as a measure of duration.

When time is measured in this way, it can act as a basis of exchange: an hourly rate of pay, how much production can be achieved within a set time or how many time credits we earn. However, our philosophical, social and even scientific understanding of time is much broader than time as duration. The phrase 'time is money' represents a key development within capitalist societies. As Weber (1992: 14, emphasis in original) noted, this is found in the arguments of Benjamin Franklin, who he quotes:

> Remember, that *time* is money. He that can earn ten shillings a day by his labour, and goes abroad, or sits idle, one half of that day, though he spends but sixpence during his diversion or idleness, ought not to reckon *that* the only expense; he has really spent, or rather thrown away, five shillings besides.

As Chapter Three will outline, time can be experienced in this absolute, quantitative form, as an external phenomenon in the world around us; yet, time also has a relative conception – time exists within things. Time exists within planetary cycles, the changes of the seasons and growth in nature, as well as humans. Adam (2004) explains this best when she suggests that time in the external world moves from past, to present and into the future. However, within our minds, time moves from future actions, into the present to eventually fade into the past. Our lives are shaped by a series of future decisions that come into the present before becoming our past. At one point, you decided to read this book, which you are currently doing, and when you reach the end, it will become something you have read. Reading the book may prompt you to make new future decisions about what to read next, which soon you will do before they also become a part of your past. The same applies to your studies, your employment and your relationships: a series of future-oriented decisions that become the present before forming our past. However, this narrative can also change when we look back at how we arrived at the present. The story you tell about how you came to read this book will be different from the narratives of how you came into your current job or formed a relationship. We reconstruct our past in our minds to explain our present (and make assumptions about our future) and this varies depending upon which moment of the present we are discussing.

What I am trying to impress upon you at this stage is that time is not simply a measure of duration; it is embedded within our thoughts, actions and everything around us. Industrialisation has become dominated by the time of the clock, which, attached to a profit motive, promotes a particular set of criteria for judging the value of certain actions and activities. However, understanding the multiplicity of time promotes a range of different ways to link time and value. Thus, time theory needs to guide the discussion of time banking because it may put into practice values that do not fit with capitalist determinations of value, and an exploration of time bank activities through the lens of social exchange will overlook this.

Why time?

Engagement with time theory needs to be justified, in the first instance, by a broader approach to theory in relation to social problems and social policy. For this, there are three interlinked ideas that can be drawn upon. First, Williams (1989), in her classic text on social policy, argues that the development of the subject did not adopt a questioning stance towards the limitations of the state's capacity to solve social problems, while simultaneously unintentionally adopting state definitions of these problems. Lack of questioning of state definitions ensures that the status quo is maintained, and this can be presented as a critique of the Fabian tradition, which dominated the formative years of the subject. In similar, unquestioning fashion, absolute clock time has come to dominate in capitalist societies. Chapter Three illustrates critiques of this domination and how the multiplicity of time has been brought into policy analysis.

Second, Townsend (1976) argues that the analysis of social policy had to draw upon different concepts and theories to discover the implicit and explicit values that influence the economic management and administration of a country. Drawing upon these theories illuminates these values, exposing them to sociological analysis. Such thinking has dual relevance in the discussion of subsequent chapters. Similar to Williams, Townsend presents a case for critically examining the guiding principles embedded within society and its institutions to uncover those that guide policy formation and implementation. Again, drawing the theoretical exploration of time into such an analysis illustrates the absolute–relative time dichotomy and the dominance of the former in contemporary Western society. Additionally, this search for implicit and explicit values is relevant in establishing a case for time banking, associated with Cahn's (2000) notion of co-production. Drawing upon the analysis of time exposes implicit values embedded in time bank praxis that Cahn did not comment upon. These implicit values have serious implications for the use of time banking to offer alternative practices to those of neoliberal capitalism. Thus, like Gouldner's (1956) 'clinicians', applied research such as policy analysis cannot assume the client's (ie the state's) formulation of social problems – the starting point is the client's definition alongside other possible definitions to be sought out and explored.

The final theoretical strand that guided the formative stages of developing the analytical framework for exploring time banking was the 'utopian method' set out by Levitas (2005). Analysis of contemporary society requires the use of new tools, not those of modernity (Deeds Ermarth, 2011); these are required to understand the implicit assumptions and ideas that underpin society. Once more, a link to time-based analysis can be made as much of the research drawing upon the theory of time (see, eg, the journal *Time & Society*) illustrates the domination of the clock and time as an external measure of duration and its implicit impingement on social organisation and development. With regards to the utopian method, we can categorise such analysis as part of the 'archaeological mode' (Levitas, 2005) – which examines contemporary society and highlights its shortcomings. This is followed by two further stages of the utopian method. The second is the 'architectural mode', which outlines different institutional organisational arrangements and practices that address these shortcomings. The final stage is the 'ontological', which requires that we think about ourselves and how we can *be* different, how we can have different lives within the reformed organisation of society. Central to this, therefore, is a consideration of the 'ills' of contemporary society and what is required to rectify them.

Exploring time and time banking

In this section, it is necessary to briefly introduce the key ideas and concepts that will be explored in greater detail in later chapters. The purpose of this introductory overview is to demonstrate the importance and relevance of an analytical framework associated with time theory and what it can contribute to the wider debate: challenging and resisting the dominance of neoliberal ideology and capitalist values and practices. It is important to note that this does not seek to question the potential benefits of capitalist development; rather, it suggests that the application of its values and practices outside of the market have potentially negative consequences, in particular, pushing to one side other ways of valuing our lives, interactions and society.

A European Social Research Council (ESRC)-funded PhD studentship underpins the discussion and analysis of this book. The research sought to explore the potential contribution of time banking to fostering co-production in health care, as well as to examine wider theoretical concerns with regards to time banking, co-production (see Chapter Four) and the Big Society (see Chapter Two). The concept of co-production has received increasing policy attention and refers to public service reform seeking to engage service user inputs into service provision, alongside the activities of traditional service providers (Kiser and Percy, 1980; New Economics Foundation, 2004a; Brandsen and Pestoff, 2006; Gannon and Lawson, 2008). Combined, both sources of inputs can, it is claimed, improve the outcomes of services. The relevance to time theory links to how co-production can be conceptualised. Dividing the literature into two groups allows for a distinction between efficiency co-production and efficacy co-production to be presented (Gregory, 2012a). Efficiency co-production relates to efforts to reduce the cost of public services and to continue to maintain and improve outputs (Parks et al, 1981). Parks et al provide the example of policing to illustrate this. Co-production of community safety can be achieved by police patrols of neighbourhoods, individuals placing locks on their doors and neighbourhood watch schemes. Here, co-production need not require users and providers of services to come together to jointly produce – they can provide inputs with a degree of separation. Efficacy co-production is the term used to explain efforts to directly integrate users into provision alongside service providers. It is branded as 'efficacy' because it seeks to build up the confidence and skills of users while gradually empowering them to take more control of service design and implementation: this is the co-production of time banking. From this perspective, co-production has been integrated into economic alternatives to capitalist practices (New Economics Foundation, 2008a; Glynos and Speed, 2012; Gregory, 2012a).

The argument that time banking is associated with alternatives to capitalism can be reinforced by the argument of Cahn (2000) that there exist two economies in society: a core economy of family, community and democracy, and a market economy containing everything else. Cahn argues that the values of the market economy are used to tackle social problems in the core economy and that this is actually the wrong approach to adopt. Rather than alleviate and remove social problems, solutions based upon the capitalist values of 'competition, conquest, aggression, [and] acquisition' (Cahn, 2000: 58) exacerbate them. An explicit theorisation of time as a concept within time banking helps explore the non-market values of time banking, co-production and the core economy. This can then be mapped against wider debates with regards to contemporary social welfare provision.

Complementary currency systems, of which time banking is one type, seek to offer alternative practices to neoliberal capitalist markets. Co-production has been associated with similar 'green' philosophies and new economics (Boyle and Simms, 2009), and Cahn has explicitly placed time banking as a tool of the core (not market) economy. The implication is that time banking is part of a wider historic critique of neoliberal capitalism, and part of the search for alternative practices and values to inform reform and change within Western society. However, time banking has two potential flaws in its offer towards a challenge to capitalism. Both of these challenges relate to its foundation as a form of 'service credit' for public service use. The first is clearly articulated by Cahn and Rowe (1992: 163):

> The Time Dollar … does not fit the standard groove. It has elements that appeal to the Right, elements that appeal to the Left; and overall, it's an idea that lies in a frontal zone that is unclaimed by either side.

Here is a pragmatic concern with presenting time banks as being ideologically neutral. Owned by none and all, it is cast adrift, with unclear boundaries as to its ultimate aims, purpose and intention. A second, related problem is raised by North (2006a: 8): '[t]he less resistant ethos of the co-production of public services, and on volunteering encapsulated by Time Money was far more attractive to government [than LETS]'.

Does the association with co-production mean that it is easily adopted by governments? On the surface, this may appear true (see Chapter Four), but an analysis that draws upon the social theory of time demonstrates that this may be too quick a judgement (see Chapter Five). Rather, on the one hand, the ambiguity of time banking established by Cahn as to the values at the core of time banking means that it can be drawn into government policy, as other CCSs have (Pacione, 1997; Peacock, 2006). On the other hand, time banking by itself remains one, small-scale, initiative in the face of global neoliberal hegemony. Chapter Seven will speculate on this latter point when considering how the concept of time may be used to link a series of policies to develop a broader, progressive framework for welfare reform that questions the encroachment of capitalist language and practices into the 'core economy'.

Book structure

Chapter Two provides an analysis of 'austerity' and welfare retrenchment in the UK, which combined with the overview of the social theory of time in Chapter Three, provides material for the 'archaeological mode' (Levitas, 2005) – an analysis and critique of contemporary society. Chapter Two starts with an examination of key concepts in contemporary UK policy: 'austerity' (a term found in most of the Western world post-2008) and the 'Big Society'. These developments are linked to a general theme in policy change since the 1980s around 'responsibilisation' (Garland, 2001) and 'citizen-consumers' (Clarke et al, 2007) to illustrate how global neoliberal ideology dominates and promotes national hybrids. The chapter concludes by considering how to resist this neoliberal hegemony and the consequences it has for the UK.

Chapter Three builds upon this to consider how to foster resistance to neoliberal dogma. It begins by revisiting Tawney's (1921) idea of 'function' before outlining key aspects of the social theory of time. The first explores the theoretical critique of capitalist society; the second demonstrates how policy analysis has sought to draw upon this theory to explore policy formation. Chapter Three concludes by linking time, the 'utopian method' and the suggestions that CCSs, including time banking, offer alternative practices to capitalism and a potential source for rethinking key concepts such as citizenship. Chapter Four outlines time banking to examine its development, its key values, theoretical insights and the links between theory, practice and the contemporary UK policy context. Through this discussion, it will also be necessary to explore some of the wider global developments of time banking to illustrate similarities and differences at both theoretical and practice levels.

This allows for Chapters Five and Six to reflect upon time banking through the analytical lens of time. Drawing upon the analysis from the PhD research, explicit attention is given to the central debate regarding the ability of time banking to promote an alternative to capitalism or its co-option into neoliberal ideas. Chapter Five outlines much of this discussion by drawing upon research data. Chapter Six places this analysis into the wider context of resistance to 'austerity' and draws upon insight from analysis of third sector/voluntary organisations to explore the potential of time banking to offer a starting point for the architectural and ontological stages of the utopian method – can time banking provide a new set of practices and values to inform living different lives to those that we have in contemporary society? Part of the answer is presented in the final chapter, with a reminder of the importance of time not only in offering a critical lens through which to examine society, but also for providing a narrative that threads together a number of policy options for promoting change. Thus, as explored in the final pages of this book, 'time' is not just a source of analysis; it also links with a view of social policy that not only describes policy mechanisms and impact, but also questions both of these aspects and offers alternative possibilities to inform the debate regarding future policy action.

The opening quote to this chapter is from Bauman's (2009) contribution to the Joseph Rowntree Foundation's examination of contemporary social evils (Utting, 2009). In his conclusion, Bauman argues that the roots of these contemporary social evils can be found in sociocultural and political transformations over the last few decades. As will become clear in the subsequent chapters of this book, the potential of time as a concept in policy analysis allows for a critique of these changes and provides insight into alternatives that may create new ways of knowing who we are that need not be tied to the market. However, as will also be demonstrated, this potential has a number of barriers that need to be broken down before such change is possible.

Notes

[1] See: http://idlefoundation.org/ (accessed 22 May 2014).

[2] Transition towns are a community-led movement seeking to develop stronger, happier and locally sustainable communities.

TWO

Austerity and its alternatives

> We are not doing this because we want to, driven by theory or ideology. We are doing this because we have to, driven by the urgent truth, that unless we do people will suffer and our national interest will suffer. (Cameron, 2010: 5, cited in Clarke and Newman, 2012: 304)

The previous chapter suggested that market values guide solutions to social problems despite resistance from other value positions. This chapter starts to explore this claim in detail by focusing upon how market values have come to dominate in social policy. Particular attention is paid to the idea of 'austerity' promoted by the UK and other governments across the Western world in the wake of the 2008 financial crash. By articulating a view that austerity is required to address the consequences of the financial crash, the scope for policy solutions is drastically shrunk. As will be explored, this shrinking results from the influence of neoliberal economic doctrine on political debate. Drawing on the argument of Jamie Peck and others (Peck and Tickell, 2002; Peck, 2004; Peck and Theodore, 2012), the chapter explores the notion of neoliberal hybridity, outlining its development under previous Conservative and Labour administrations in the UK since the 1980s. Setting out this context establishes the wider ideological reformation of welfare provision and normative assumptions of citizenship that inform the Coalition government (henceforth, Coalition) formed in May 2010. Exploring the Coalition argument for and policy development towards implementing the 'Big Society' and the need for austerity, the chapter explores the current neoliberal hybrid constructed in the UK (Gregory, 2014). The final part of the chapter outlines the challenges to resisting this current neoliberal hybrid and the policy agenda of the Coalition.

Neoliberal hybrids: market values in the wrong place

Academic debate since the Thatcher government has drawn attention to the influence of neoliberal economic theory, promoted on the global stage by a range of global actors and by various political parties within specific national geographical boundaries. The argument often found in the political arena is that the nation needs to compete in a global economic market and must pursue a series of economic (and welfare) reforms that allow for this competitiveness to flourish for the national good. Such a view was expressed in the UK by Tony Blair (1995) and when he was prime minister, whilst, post-2010, Prime Minister David Cameron has focused on the 'global race' (Beckett, 2013). Such developments have led to the suggestion that neoliberalism is a global paradigm that interacts with different national contexts to form a specific hybrid within the boundaries of those nations, and it is this hybrid that informs economic and social policy.

Building neoliberal hybrids: 1979–97

To understand the aetiology of the Coalition's own neoliberal hybrid, policy propositions and barriers to alternative policy agendas requires an examination of the Conservative and Labour governments that preceded 2010. In particular, it is important to consider how the hybrid forms of neoliberalism that developed during this time reshaped the provision of welfare and normative assumptions of citizenship. This section examines the period of 1979–97, the Thatcher and Major administrations.

The integration of neoliberal thinking within the New Right in the UK has been well documented (Boyle, 1988; Johnson, 1990; Savage and Robins, 1990; Waine, 1991; Wilding, 1992). Under Margret Thatcher and John Major, Conservative administrations pursued a wide range of changes in the way in which welfare was provided (a shift from state to market provision) and a re-conceptualisation of citizenship (as consumers). In particular, the break from the post-war Keynesian consensus and a shift towards neoliberal economics lies at the core of these changes. With regards to social welfare, market principles provided an effective narrative for critiquing state provision. It was argued that states failed in provision because they were occupied by self-interested bureaucrats seeking to expand their budgets and power while operating monopolies of provision that stifled efficiency and innovation (the argument being that these could only be fostered by competition). Additionally, political parties could secure success by accepting the never-ending demands of the electorate, which further facilitated state growth. This latter was seen to blur the distinction between 'needs' and 'wants' (Langan, 1998) and to drive the never-ending growth of state activity and interference in market operations.

Such a situation was said to have developed since the 1940s' welfare settlement in the UK and was perceived as dangerous because large states interfered with free market operations. Furthermore, Thatcher, as a signed-up advocate of the ideas of Hayek (Ranelagh, 1991: ix), subscribed to his view outlined in the *Road to Serfdom* that large states are a small step away from the authoritarianism of Nazi Germany. Consequently, the Thatcher and Major governments sought to reform the role of the state under a broader neoliberal economic agenda: the privatisation of key utilities, the Right to Buy to increase owner-occupation and the introduction of quasi-markets in health and education were all examples of the utilisation of economic thinking within social reform (Le Grand, 1991).

However, the suggestion that these administrations were neoliberal hybrids makes us aware that this economic agenda was not the only influential philosophy on policy and welfare reform. As Levitas (1988) notes, a tension exists in New Right thinking between its small state neoliberalism and its moral authoritarianism. This latter was influential in government perceptions of welfare claimants. During this time, the 'underclass thesis' and 'culture of poverty' arguments started to permeate government thinking and public debates, influencing public opinion as a consequence (Macnicol, 1987; Murray, 1990; Bagguley and Mann, 1992). Focused on individual behaviour, not social and economic changes caused by a new economic paradigm, social security reforms became increasingly punitive. The British Social Attitudes survey[1] records that while 81% thought that the government's responsibility was to provide a decent living for the unemployed in 1985, this had reduced to 59% by 2012. The promotion of behavioural explanations and the idea of dependency on state benefits reinforcing work-shy behaviours facilitated social security reforms that suited both neoliberal economics and the social authoritarianism exhibited by the Conservative administrations (Hall, 1988; Becker, 1997).

The changes to social security combined with reforms across welfare provision led to a number of commentators articulating a defence of the welfare state amid concerns that it was being dismantled (Bean et al, 1985; Wilding, 1986). Pierson (2006), however, suggested that the welfare state was not, necessarily, being dismantled, but systematically changed. Such concerns were expressed with regards to the Labour Party as it sought to reform its own ideology and policy offer in the build-up to the 1997 election. While some have argued that a new consensus was developing that favoured neoliberal economics and a small welfare state (Rutherford, 2007), Powell and Hewitt (1998) argue that as the Conservatives left office and New Labour took over, it was too early to suggest that a new consensus had developed. Rather, New Labour policies could be summarised as falling into three categories: 1) continuity, 2) reversing and 3) extending Conservative policies. Despite this, when asked of her view of her greatest success in government, Thatcher is said to have replied 'New Labour'.[2]

Building neoliberal hybrids: 1997–2010

Drawing links between the New Labour ideology of the 'Third Way' and the values of the New Right has been another preoccupation of academic thinking (David, 2000; May et al, 2005). This reflects a continuation of the broader neoliberal economic paradigm and the promotion of markets and the private sector as one, among a number, of welfare providers within the broader mixed economy of welfare (Powell, 2000; Taylor, 2000). A number of accounts demonstrate this continuation and extension of (and some differences to) Conservative policy within a number of domains: education, health, housing and social security (Powell, 1999b, 2002, 2008). The focus here, however, is on the integration of neoliberal economics into a hybrid form with social democratic thinking.

Gilbert (2004) argues that New Labour represents a second wave of neoliberal hybridity and presents the Thatcher/Major governments as the first wave. In line with Levitas (1988), Gilbert suggests that the mix of social conservatism and neoliberal economics creates a hybrid presenting a particular ideological narrative. This is a divergence from Hall (2005), who argued that New Labour is the first hybrid consisting of a dominant neoliberal agenda mixed with social democracy as the junior partner. Hall suggests that this hybrid is formed through the modernisation and reform agenda, which subordinates the social democratic ideology to the requirements of neoliberal economics. In part, this reflects Weiss's (1998) argument regarding the influence of globalisation on nation-states. Rather than be passive recipients of the global leviathan that is neoliberalism, state actors are actively choosing to adopt and purse this agenda and integrate it into their locally constituted ideologies. Thus, for Hall (2005: 21), New Labour's welfare reforms must meet a range of criteria that place economic concerns as paramount to social concerns (such as opening up provision to private investment to blur the public–private divide, embracing the ideas of value for money and efficiency, and promoting a range of workforce disciplining policies and practices). Hall has been criticised by Jessop (2004) for neglecting political economy in his analysis, as well as Labour's efforts to promote extra-economic conditions. Yet,

Jessop does agree with the idea of hybridity, although he views New Labour as pairing neoliberalism with Christian socialism as the junior partner rather than social democracy.

The consequences of this hybridisation have also been commented on by Clarke (2004). Although not specifically mentioning hybridity, his argument overlaps and therefore supports this view. Clarke argues that policy has continued to shift the provision of public services to the private sector, as well as the not-for-profit, voluntary or 'third' sector. Alongside this, a shift in social responsibilities from the public sphere (government) to the private sphere (individuals and families) has occurred, echoing Drakeford's (2000) argument regarding privatisation under the Thatcher and Major governments. Clarke (2004: 30) suggests that 'neo-liberalism tells stories about the world, the future and how they will develop – and tries to make this come true', in this case, through welfare reforms that reduce the role of the state as a provider of welfare in favour of the private and voluntary sectors. This dominance of the economic discourse reshapes debates about welfare to 'what we can afford' – a reminder that unlike political and civil rights, enshrined in law, social rights are tied to fiscal policy. Under New Labour, Clarke (2004: 35) suggests that '[g]ood fiscal housekeeping became an obligation that (supposedly) governed the behaviour of prudent customers, corporate managers and national governments alike'. It is the application of these ideas to the notion of citizenship to which attention now turns.

Changing citizenship

The adoption of neoliberal ideology into Labour Party thinking created a shift in the framing of social policy debates. Definitions of need, politicised under the previous Conservative governments (Langan, 1998), are further modified through a focus on the risk society discourse. The suggested privatisation of social problems from the government to the individual/family (Drakeford, 2000; Clarke, 2004), focuses policy increasingly upon the responsibility of individuals for addressing the problems and difficulties they face. Before coming to office, Labour articulated a new ideological position and subsequent policy agenda, built around the idea of a Third Way (Blair, 1996; Mandelson and Liddle, 1996; Giddens, 2003). This position accepted neoliberal economic thinking and used this to reposition government action to facilitate competitiveness in the global economy. This required welfare reforms that sought to invest in human capital rather than provide economic maintenance (Giddens, 2003: 117). Certain forms of welfare expenditure were considered 'good' (such as education and health), while others (such as social security) were labelled 'bad' (Powell, 1999a). Such spending is bad because it is used to support people who should be working – in Blair's words (cited in Powell, 1999a: 21). These welfare reforms required a new view of citizens that developed the consumer narrative established by the previous Conservative administration.

The Third Way ideology integrates the idea of reflexive individuals (Beck, 1992; Giddens, 2002) into its conception of citizenship. Combined, the expansion of choice, new risks in contemporary society and disillusionment with traditional norms and social boundaries require a move towards reflexivity, where individuals manage their risk choices. Welfare is subsequently reformed to facilitate the development of positive risk-taking, as is most evident in social security reforms pursued by the previous Labour governments, from the New Deals to increasing conditionality (Dwyer, 2004). The aim of such reforms is to create positive risk-takers and to promote greater responsibility on the part of citizens. Similarly, the theme of responsibilisation has been noted in relation to wealth and assets (Rowlingson and McKay, 2012). Thus, in the example of pensions, Langley (2004, 2006, 2008) explores the issue of financialisation, illustrating the promotion of the assembly of 'investor subjects'. He suggests that:

> the making of financial subjects and financial self-disciplines more broadly plays on freedom and security as central features of (neo)liberal governmentality … prudence and thrift are displaced by new moral and calculative self-disciplines of responsibility and entrepreneurially meeting, managing and manipulating ever-increasing obligations. (Langley, 2008: 134)

Thus, the neoliberal hybrid pursued by New Labour facilitates a shift in policy discourse regarding citizenship.

Thinking of citizens as active agents was evident not only in financial/income policy reforms, but also across other welfare reforms. Building on the Major government's idea of citizens as consumers of services, New Labour rephrased this debate with a communitarian twist (Dwyer, 2002). Rights are tied to responsibilities; thus, certain obligations must be met if the state is to continue to provide certain services. This offers a moral framework within which duty is placed over rights within the social sphere in order to strike a balance between personal autonomy and the common good. The concept of 'active citizenship' encapsulates the wider shift from a passive rights-based to an active, participatory view of citizenship (Coffey, 2004). Influenced by communitarian thinking, responsibility is towards oneself and others which changes the normative sense rather than legal framework of citizenship (Hall et al, 2000), with these responsibilities coming to overshadow other dimensions of citizenship (Coffey, 2004).

Yet, this focus on participation is not linked to participatory citizenship; rather, it is defined within the notion of the 'citizen-consumer'. Needham (2003: 14) suggests that the promotion of choice as part of wider welfare reforms and the shift towards the mixed economy of welfare suggests a conceptualisation of citizenship that is 'individual, instrumental and transactional'. The citizen-consumer is self-regarding, has reflexive preferences and market accountability, uses voice to complain, is exposed to promotional advertising to secure loyalty to the political community, and has an instrumental attitude to politics. For Needham, this citizen-consumer rested at the core of New Labour reforms of welfare services, although this is not to say that this is exactly how citizens view themselves (Clarke et al, 2007). Therefore, under New Labour, citizenship came to reflect a mix of consumer characteristics when accessing certain welfare services (the good areas of welfare spending, such as education and health), but for others (the bad areas of spending, such as social security, but also in matters such as pensions), citizens have individual responsibilities for provision to which they must conform. This resulted from the introduction of neoliberal economic ideas into Labour's social reforms. Similar developments can be traced in the Coalition's own policy agenda.

Austerity: constructing the neoliberal response to the financial crisis

Hybridity suggests that 'neoliberalism' is an overarching ideological framework that is drawn into national contexts, where it is mixed with a number of specific local ideas, values and practices. For Peck (2004), this qualitatively and geographically transforms state–market relations and necessitates an analysis of the process of institutionally specific state rollback to explore how neoliberal discourse 'converses' with other national discourses and processes (Kingfisher, 2002). Consequently, Larner (2005: 12) suggests a need to place political struggle at the centre of the analysis of neoliberalism so as not to assume that 'new political configurations as monolithic projects [are] imposed on passive victims'. The articulation of austerity, as outlined later, draws upon this global neoliberal ideology, which helps develop a discursive space in which the notion of austerity gains popular support in order to facilitate the cuts agenda and the reform of welfare provision (Clarke and Newman, 2012).

The financial crisis: creating austerity

The financial crisis of the summer of 2008 started when mortgage-related securities within the global financial system suddenly collapsed. This rapidly moved from a mortgage to a financial crisis as banks withdrew lending in order to build up reserves (Kotz, 2009; Farnsworth and Irving, 2011). Gough (2011) argues that the bailout of financial institutions by nation-states transformed the crisis in 2009, shifting the crisis into a fiscal or sovereign debt crisis, resulting in a tightening of fiscal/welfare policy. Consequently, '[g]overnments have thus emerged from 2009 with gaping holes in national finances, which are to be filled ... by increasing taxes on middle- and low-income groups and by making swinging cuts in public expenditure, primarily social welfare' (Farnsworth and Irving, 2011: 20). Such a response is perhaps unsurprising if one accepts Galbraith's (1958) suggestion that the public sector is blamed for private sector collapse and failure.

As Clarke and Newman (2012: 300) explain, in the UK context, the response to the crisis moved:

> from an economic problem (how to 'rescue' the banks and restore market stability) to a political problem (how to allocate blame and responsibility for the crisis): a reworking that has focused on the unwieldy and expensive welfare state and public sector.

This reworking of the crisis into one of public finances presents a key policy challenge for efforts to promote alternatives in UK policy debate and across the Western world. Prime Minister Cameron has called for austerity to be a permanent feature of UK policy to ensure a leaner state, while German Chancellor Merkel has argued for continued economic restructuring and imposing 'austerity measures' in nations such as Greece (BBC News, 2012; Morris, 2013b; Wearden and Elliott, 2013). Globally, therefore, the policy terrain has drastically shrunk to focus on austerity policies. However, as noted in the opening quote to this chapter, this is presented as necessary in order to prevent the suffering of individuals or the nation.

Presented as an 'urgent truth', this view of austerity is reflected in the media narrative, which supports the 'Westminster consensus': the global financial crisis has generated a need to reduce public spending and reform welfare services. In the UK, the presentation of the debate in these terms has resulted in an intensified neoliberal agenda (Grimshaw and Rubery, 2012) that seeks to withdraw state provision in favour of a 'Big Society' (see later). It is the view of Grimshaw and Rubey that this is likely to be successful as, historically, the Thatcher governments were capable of transforming the labour market with little long-term resistance and the Coalition were successful in winning the argument about the need for cutting public expenditure. Essentially, the financial crisis can be seen to have resulted in the entrenchment of neoliberal economic theory as the dominant ideology in the UK (and potentially the Western world) within political debates.

Farnsworth (2011) suggests that the Coalition is following a specific approach to the economic crisis from a centre-right perspective and he hopes that resistance will prevent the imposition of cuts. Taylor-Gooby and Stoker (2011) note that not only are cuts being made to welfare provision, but the state is also being significantly restructured in how welfare is provided to meet needs. Such changes will prevent the re-emergence of a larger state in terms of both spending and the direct provision of services. This change to welfare provision reflects the continuing neoliberal-influenced changes found under previous Conservative and New Labour governments from 1979 to 2010. Under the Coalition, this effort to change welfare provision has taken the form of the 'Big Society'.

The Big Society

During the build-up to the 2010 general election in the UK, the Conservative Party started to develop its policy agenda around the idea of a 'Big Society'. This has been viewed as a continuation of the concept of active, responsible citizens promoted by New Labour (Lister, 2011; Davies and Pill, 2012). The origins of the 'Big Society' are found in the work of Blond (2008a, 2008b, 2008c, 2008d, 2008e, 2009a, 2009b, 2009c, 2010). Blond offered a critique of the state and the market, claiming that both support each other's monopoly interests, consequently eroding civil society. Challenging these monopolies, Blond argued, requires a series of reforms that roll back the welfare state, redistribute wealth and reinvest in local economic activity (Blond, 2010; see also Jordan, 2010a, 2012). The economic crash offered a window of opportunity to challenge the current economic orthodoxy and provide space for new paradigms to establish influence over social and economic affairs (Blond, 2008a, 2008b, 2008c), though Hill (2011) is less certain that paradigm change is likely to occur. Limiting the chance of a more radical paradigm shift, David Cameron, when leader of the opposition, soon drew the idea of a 'Big Society' into his own political narrative, and here is the start of a new neoliberal hybrid.

Cameron (2009) adopted Blond's critique of the state in his Hugo Young lecture, arguing that the big state generates a paradox. He suggested that collective responsibility within state action fosters selfishness and individualism while removing individual power and responsibility. Mixing this view with the explanations of poverty and vice offered by the Centre for Social Justice (established by an ex-Conservative Party leader), 'Broken Britain' (Centre for Social Justice, 2006b) was to be repaired by a 'Big Society', which decentralised power and responsibilities from the state to the individual. Nowhere in Cameron's analysis is there are shared view of the market with Blond, Cameron's critique is on the role of the state only. He is careful not to claim that the state will be dissolved; rather, it is to be reformed to enable and empower local communities and to release the power that the state has assumed to itself. Here, Cameron (2009) quoted Fukuyama:

> [t]here is a certain assumption that civil society, once having been damaged by the excessive ambition of government, will simply spring back to life like brine shrimp that have been freeze dried, and now you add water to them and they become shrimp again. It is not something that can be taken for granted.

The state has to maintain a role in engineering social action through a number of policy reforms (Department of Health, 2010; Cabinet Office, 2011; Great Britain, 2011). This has been facilitated by a reduction in the role of the state to provide welfare and an increase in the role of other sectors, as seen with regards to New Labour. Increasingly, welfare-to-work initiatives, disability assessment centres, school provision and hospitals are being opened up for other providers to step in to the vacuum left by the state (Whitty, 1997; Malpass and Mullins, 2002; Wright et al, 2011; Hall et al, 2012; Rees et al, 2013). While voluntary and community organisations are to become the 'first sector' in Cameron's terms (Ainsworth, 2009) , the evidence shows private sector and social enterprises stepping into the gap, leading to concerns about the increasing privatisation of welfare provision (either in terms of increased providers or, drawing on Drakeford [2000], relocating social problems onto the individual; see Pollock and Price, 2011; Hodkinson and Robbins, 2013; Wright et al, 2011), with links being made with the previous Thatcher governments, One Nationism and Burkean conservatism (Bochel, 2011; Ellison, 2011; Wiggan, 2011).

This development of a Big Society narrative has been linked to a new neoliberal hybrid (Gregory, 2014). This seeks to overcome the tension in New Right ideology, noted by Levitas (1988), between economic theory requiring a small state and social authoritarianism necessitating a strong state to re-establish moral authority. This is achieved by linking both arguments to the ideas of self-help. Here, the economic demands to reduce expenditure and a concern for appropriate citizen behaviour overlap: first, advocating self-help reduces welfare budgets; while, second, the use of self-help prevents the breakdown of social cohesion (Burns and Taylor, 1998; see also later). The 'Big Society' achieves both these because the state is reformed to act as a facilitator of self-help rather than to provide services directly, reconciling shrinking welfare budgets with the narrative of 'austerity', which is drawn upon to cut public spending. There are, of course, criticisms of the 'Big Society' that are relevant here.

One argument is that focusing on individual responsibility and behaviour will only address symptoms and not the (structural) causes of social problems, reflecting a move that retains the dependency culture explanation of poverty (Davies and Pill, 2012). Alcock (2010) adds that there is no evidence that withdrawing the state generates an automatic expansion of provision in other sectors. Additionally, cutting funding available from the state reduces the provision of local facilities for people to meet and act collectively (Cattell, 2011). Jordan (2010b: 202–3) adds that the 'Big Society' ignores the need for time to be invested to foster cultures of self-organisation, as well as the historic erosion of wider solidarities which mean that new self-organised units are likely to be homogeneous in their membership, reflecting fragmentations in society. Freedland (2010) notes that there remains a contradiction between economic and social aims. The 'Big Society' requires people to invest their time in their communities, but neoliberal economics demands a flexible, mobile workforce able to move as job demands dictate. Finally, there is no account of how the policies for promoting the 'Big Society' overcome the trends noted under New Labour's community initiatives. On the one hand, New Labour policy was designed to 'nudge' community decisions towards the government's favoured policies (Fussey, 2004). On the other, the form of activities that localities seek to engage in need not always fit government expectations of the form that community activism should take (Mooney and Fyfe, 2006).

Despite these criticisms, the 'Big Society' has been promoted as a form of community self-help to be promoted by the 'enabling state' in a process of localism and decentralisation. What happens to the state once decentralisation has been completed, or what safety nets exist under community-based services, remains unclear. Rather, the 'Big Society' brings together neoliberal economics and a brand of self-help that fits with the government's view of active, responsible citizens. There remains, however, a fault line in this argument, which relates to the concept of self-help.

The purpose of self-help

The challenge for the 'Big Society' argument rests upon why self-help initiatives should be pursued as a good goal of social policy. A theme of this text is that ambiguity rests in a number of concepts, allowing ideas to fit into neoliberal political narratives as easily as the narratives of other ideologies: self-help is one such idea. Jordan (2010a: 191) argues that social policy has been 'hijacked by a version of individual self-realisation which subverts the whole basis of a viable collective life and social order'. Furthermore, to resist this hijacking, social policy must find ways to support the mobilisation of citizens to provide services for families, districts and communities that complement government programmes: 'a politics which motivates [citizens] to take collective action for change' (Jordan, 2010a: 197). An overlapping focus on localism and associations as the core of empowerment and reviving collective life can be found in debates around health (Cattell, 2011) and community organising (Schutz and Sandy, 2011), but also in a much longer historical narrative of cooperativism and mutualism (Birchall, 2001). Many of these themes have been associated with the political Left but have also been articulated within New Labour policy (Kellner, 1998; Jowell, 2009) and now by the Coalition under the auspices of the 'Big Society' (Elliott, 2010). This results from ambiguity in the concept of self-help.

Self-help is defined as activity carried out by individuals and/or communities for themselves or others in their locality (Burns and Taylor, 1998). Such activity is reciprocal as it is carried out by citizens, drawing on their skills, knowledge, labour and power. Taylor (2011: 10) suggests that the term 'self-help' is a reinterpretation of community by thinkers within neoliberal ideologies, which accommodates a wider narrative of pluralism in welfare provision that gives individuals the capability to take control of their services. Reflecting Burns and Taylor, the suggestion is that changes in the mixed economy of welfare and ideology promote self-help as a viable policy option for delivering welfare services. Criticism of such trends suggests that it facilitates the residualisation of services, reinforces the construction of citizens (not wider structural forces) as the authors of their own misfortune and results in a postcode lottery: not only are services no longer universal, but different communities will have different skills and resources to draw upon, with the most disadvantaged communities having fewer of these to utilise in service provision.

Burns and Taylor (1998) suggest that self-help solutions are drawn upon by policymakers in order to: 1) reduce demands on welfare budgets; 2) counter the breakdown of social cohesion (both of these points relate to the Big Society); and 3) soften the impact of poverty. They also suggest that different roles for self-help exist that alter governments' perception of self-help activity. Self-help can be established as a 'solution' to social and economic disadvantage, providing community coping strategies. Self-help can also be a 'springboard' to move beyond subsistence and integration into mainstream society. Finally, self-help can be an alternative way of organising social activities that challenges neoliberal market values and practices. Under the 'Big Society', self-help is the solution, and potentially a springboard in some arguments. However, in anarchistic writing, it is a challenge to this neoliberal practice (Ward, 1996). Self-help can facilitate the creation of local support networks and revitalise social relationships, and is therefore an alternative to market individualism, gathering people around a common social purpose (Leadbeater and Christie, 1999; Jordan, 2010a). Such support for self-help/mutualism overlaps with Jordan's arguments, as outlined by Taylor (2011: 61): self-help has 'aspirations to transform society, defining membership in ways which are not confined to the upper or aspiring middle classes, and offering an alternative to the emergent private capitalism'.

As such, two views of self-help have been briefly sketched. Self-help as a neoliberal concept reduces state services and changes the notion of citizenship to focus on individual/private responsibility for addressing social problems (Drakeford, 2000) – which results in the management rather than elimination of social problems (Freeman, 1992). This is supported by changes in the mixed economy of welfare (Powell and Hewitt, 1998) and the politicisation of definitions of need (Langan, 1998; Dean, 2010). Self-help as an alternative to market forces and neoliberal values has been expressed in a range of policy contexts (Williams and Windebank, 2001a; McKillop and Wilson, 2003;

Seyfang, 2003b, 2004b; Williams, 2011), but has had little impact on the wider policy debate. The next section of this chapter starts to explore why challenging the dominant neoliberal hybrid remains a substantial difficulty.

Challenging 'austerity' and neoliberal hybridity

This final section does not outline the challenges that have developed in response to the economic crisis and the policy pathways pursued by governments, but, rather, sets out, initially, the barriers that these alternative policy prescriptions face and explores why it is necessary to examine local practice in the search for alternatives. This sets up the following chapters, which do explore alternative values and practices that may offer a starting point for challenging the austerity package of policies implemented by the Coalition.

Preventing change

The quest for a post-capitalist world has prompted a range of arguments and policy prescriptions that have sought to offer alternative frameworks for meeting human welfare and supporting social relationships (Gibson-Graham, 1993, 1996, 2006; Cameron, 1996; Chatterton and Pickerill, 2010). Such theories often draw upon a particular critique of capitalist production/exchange or the consequences of industrial growth as the justification for implementing alternatives. Yet, despite the cycle of boom and bust ensuring a frequent experience of recessions, evidenced by the 2008 financial crash, and a growing concern with the environmental damage caused by unrestrained capitalist growth, alternatives tend to find no purchase in public debate. Part of this resistance to change, as outlined earlier, results from a shift in how welfare is provided and citizenship is defined so that market values and practices are carefully integrated into social relations and the relationship between citizens and the state. Neoliberal thinking has come to dominate despite the existence of alternatives practised within families and communities on a daily basis. The existence of such alternatives has been considered by Gibson-Graham (1993, 1996), forming part of an analysis as to why change does not occur.

Gibson-Graham (1993, 1996) argued that the existence of alternative forms of production in capitalist societies (such as community currencies, informal working and other forms of production and exchange outside of the market) demonstrates that alternatives are lived in day-to-day life. Yet, capitalism is presented through discourse as the only form of economic provision, despite these multiple forms of production existing on the fringes of the economic sphere. Gibson-Graham explains how capitalist hegemonic discursive practices present capitalism as a singularity. Exhibited as having no peer or equivalent, capitalism exists in a category of its own and becomes the dominant mechanism for production and exchange. Such a presentation of capitalism as having no peer may depict alternative forms of production as pre-capitalist: as both inferior and consigned to the past. Household production illustrates this point. Capitalism developed as the economy became a distinct sphere within society, distinct from the household, which is consequently cast as a pre-capitalist form of production and exchange unable to compete with contemporary capitalist production. Entwined with this view is the presentation of alternative forms of production as being dependent on external support in order to operate. Capitalism, however, needs no such support, so it is argued, as its internal laws of continuous growth promote its reproduction and expansion. Thus, non-capitalist production is dependent upon external sources of funding and, as such, can be depicted as existing in a state of crisis, one where its own sustainability is under question, emphasising its inferior status. The economic crisis of 2008, however, is treated differently. This is not presented as weakness by its architects, but, rather, as part of the process of renewal, feeding into the claim of capitalism's superiority. Consequently, community currencies may exist as alternatives, but are portrayed as inferior forms of production and exchange.

A final discursive practice outlined by Gibson-Graham (1993, 1996) is the presentation of totality. Capitalism colonises all productive spaces, presenting any production as ultimately capitalist reproduction. As such, household production or community currencies can both be perceived as forms of capitalist reproduction as they help to ensure that the means by which capital is able to reproduce itself are maintained. These discursive practices establish capitalism as unable to coexist with alternatives and push alternative practices into unrealisable futures. Efforts to promote change must address the whole system as fringe practices do little to overturn the totality (as well as unity and singularity) of neoliberal capitalism. However, Gibson-Graham (1993, 1996) suggests that while these powerful discursive tools are deployed under capitalism, the alternative forms of production exist and thrive in ways that are distinct from capitalist mechanisms. Capitalism provides a blanket view of productive practices when, in reality, diversity flows throughout transactions. One illustration of this can be found in relation to informal work (Williams and Windebank, 2001a; 2001b), which demonstrates non-profit motives behind exchange activities. Perhaps implicit in the work of Gibson-Graham, but articulated by Chatterton and Pickerill (2010), is the fact that the resistance offered by alternative production is on the micro-scale and there is a challenge of transforming this into something substantial and suited to the global stage. In part, the global ethnography of Burawoy et al (1991) offers some insight here into how the local can influence theoretical development to inform the global debate (see later). Following on from Gibson-Graham, however, is a need to explore how capitalism resists alternatives in practice.

Examples of 'resistance'

One example of an alternative to the capitalist mode of production and exchange can be found within CCSs. Various academics and campaigners have located these practices within green/environmental ideologies (Lang, 1994; Fitzpatrick and Caldwell, 2001; North, 2007), with contemporary accounts making links between currencies and the 'Transition Town' movement (North, 2010b). Generally, it has been suggested that schemes such as Local Exchange Trading Systems (LETS) and time banking offer a means by which non-capitalist values are practised. Additionally, they facilitate a rethinking of economic exchange to question the damaging social and environmental effects of continued economic growth and expansion pursued under neoliberal economic theory. Yet, despite a few decades of practice in the UK, and beyond, these alternatives have had little success in challenging mainstream economic narratives. The work of Gibson-Graham (1993, 1996) has been drawn upon to explain this limited impact (Leyshon and Lee, 2003; Peacock, 2006).

Of particular interest, and demonstrating how alternatives are integrated into dominant capitalist ideas, Pacione (1997) argued that changing social trends in the early 1980s not only weakened the moral economy of family and neighbours, but also saw the development of a policy narrative around welfare retrenchment and an emphasis on individual self-help. LETS were therefore presented as a potential framework for 'relocating interpersonal social and economic relations in the face of the hegemonic power of a global political economy' (Pacione, 1997: 180). Such a framework allows LETS to respond directly to unequal power relations by acknowledging the hegemonic power of the capitalist economy but without challenging hegemony outright in order to develop 'a parallel complementary form of social and economic organisation within a local context' (Pacione, 1997:

1180). Thus, a social and economic identity is fostered locally that, while separate from the global economy, does not upset the mainstream economic order. Rather than challenge, community currencies are co-opted into neoliberal capitalist practices. Under New Labour, Williams et al (2003) suggest that LETS fitted into the 'employment first' narrative as these community initiatives can be set up to help individuals to develop employability skills and experience in order to facilitate a return to work.

State uses of CCS can, however, be viewed negatively. North (2006b) highlights left-wing critiques that these complementary currency initiatives facilitate the dismantling of the welfare state and provide a minimalist welfare safety net based upon voluntary organisations (a theme that could be reflected within the 'Big Society'). These organisations bypass the state, consequently reducing the rights of citizens (North, 2006b: 32), a view supported from experience in New Zealand, where these initiatives stepped in to fill the void left by state withdrawal from welfare provision (North, 2007). Alternatively, articulations of community currencies suggest that they offer a 'deeper and more inclusive polity', rather than facilitating neoliberal inequalities, environmental damage and wasted lives (North, 2006b: 32). Consequently, community currencies become a tool for green alternatives to capitalism (Fitzpatrick and Caldwell, 2001). However, not all environmentalists would agree with this argument and would claim that community currencies actually clash with their own aims because they cause the commodification of actions and networks that worked better through reciprocal, money-less exchanges (North, 2006b). It is this ambiguity and tension between the use and purpose of community currencies that makes them a fascinating focus of study.

Why locality matters

As Larner (2000, 2003) has argued in relation to hybridity, we must put political struggle at the centre of any investigation into the formation of 'neoliberalisms'. Useful here is Burawoy's (1991b: 9) view that '[r]ather than treating the social situation as the confirmation of some theory, we regard it as the failure of theory … [which] leads not to rejection but rebuilding theory'. The argument in this book starts from a particular mix of theories. It considers the overlap between the arguments of neoliberal hybridity discussed earlier and the suggestion by Gibson-Graham that alternatives in production and exchange exist but are blocked from contributing to wider political debate. Illustrated by community currency systems, it has been shown how resistance to neoliberalism can lead to potential co-option not into neoliberalism *per se*, but into the national hybrid that has formed. Offering a potential route to articulating alternatives, the aim of the following chapters is to explore the co-option of another community currency system, time banking, into the 'Big Society', and through the use of the utopian method (Levitas, 2005) combined with the social theory of time (Adam, 1990), to provide an analysis of time banking that offers a route to challenging the imposition of market values onto social relationships. Chapter Three pays particular attention to the theory of time before Chapter Four outlines time banking theory and practice. At this point, it is then possible to draw upon the research data that underpins this study (in Chapter Five) to extrapolate what Burawoy refers to as internal contradictions (between the theory and the cases being explored) and theoretical gaps and silences. As such, the aim is to reconstruct theory around time bank practice in order to draw out implicit assumptions that critique the imposition of market values onto social relationships within community relationships and welfare provision.

Burawoy labels this approach the 'extended case method' (ECM) and it seeks to elucidate the link between the micro- and the macro-levels of reality; thus, it constitutes the social situation in terms of the particular external forces that shape it. In practice, this form of analysis seeks to problematise rather than dismiss that which does not fit with theory and to develop a situational analysis that draws out the specific historical context. As Burawoy (1991a: 281) explains:

> In constituting a social situation as unique, the extended cases method pays attention to its complexity, its depth, its thickness. Causality then becomes multiplex, involving an 'individual' (i.e. undividable) connectedness of elements, tieing the social situation to its context of determination.

Furthermore, as Gamson (1991) and Schiffman (1991) illustrate, ECM allows for an exploration of social movements and how they challenge society's use of resources and how society legitimates inequality and its imposition of needs. Such an approach fits with the wider argument in this book: neoliberal hybrids in the UK have legitimated, maintained and to some extent expanded a number of social problems and reconstructed the proposed policy solutions to fit with market values and mechanisms, including reframing the normative view of citizenship. This view has been established through the presentation of three potential barriers to alternatives: first, the construction of neoliberal hybrids fuses together dominant economic ideas with national political ideologies and shifts how welfare is provided; second, this process also alters the normative view of citizenship and consequently impacts on the citizen–state relationship; and, third, localised resistances are seeking to challenge ideologically driven practices on the global stage. Consequently neoliberal capitalism itself is presented in a way that resists the influence of alternative practices found in communities and households. Starting to explore and challenge these barriers, and the imposition of economic values outside of the market, requires embracing the first stage of Levitas's (2005) utopian method – the archaeological. In introducing the social theory of time, Chapter Three provides a continuation of this archaeological stage, which was started here in the overview of neoliberal hybridity, the starting point of this archaeological mode.

Conclusion

This chapter has sought to trace the development of neoliberal hybrids in the UK and outline the consequence that this has, first, on welfare provision and, second, on the normative view of citizenship. Influenced by neoliberal ideology and, under various governments, social authoritarianism and communitarianism, the citizen has become viewed as a reflexive, active individual and the author of their own choices and (mis)fortune. This conception of citizenship has introduced 'economic theory [into] society, politics and public administration' (Jordan, 2010a: 196) to reshape social policy in terms of its values and methods. Jordan subsequently argues that these changes represent the introduction of market and contract-based practices into welfare provision. Market values have moved from the economic sphere into other aspects of social life, which consequently erodes collective life and collective action. Similar arguments have been presented in relation to excessive individualism as the new 'social evil' (Utting, 2009). It returns attention to Seabrook's quote in Chapter One: engagement in the market becomes all important and, as such, market activity is the only way in which we can know ourselves. Jordan (2004, 2010a) argues that the aim of social policy should be to support social relations, the quality of life and civic culture – to invest value in the interactions between family members, neighbours, associations and other citizens. The argument in later chapters (Chapters Three, Five and Seven) is that drawing on the social theory of time, it is possible to articulate other ways of knowing ourselves and to use these to inform a policy agenda that supports social relationships outside of the market. The challenge rests on whether such arguments can find purchase in political debate and overcome the discursive practices of actors within capitalist systems that, as outlined earlier, limit the potential of alternatives to impact on policy development.

Notes

[1] See: http://www.natcen.ac.uk/our-research/research/british-social-attitudes/ (accessed 22 May 2014).

[2] See: http://conservativehome.blogs.com/centreright/2008/04/making-history.html (accessed 22 May 2014).

THREE

Time for an alternative

> We are so immersed in a money environment that we can no more perceive how it shapes or affects our perception than a fish can imagine that water might distort the world it perceives. But each of those characteristics creates a special dynamic, alters the world in which we live and breathe and have our being. (Cahn, 2000: 60)

The argument in Chapter Two developed the following themes: first, that the construction of neoliberal hybrid ideologies by various governments in the UK over the last 30 years has altered welfare provision and the normative conception of citizenship; second, that this has introduced market values into how welfare is delivered and how citizens interact with each other; third, that this excessive individualism makes market inclusion all important, eroding other ways of knowing ourselves and each other; fourth, that there exists an argument for non-market values to underpin social relations that should be supported by social welfare provision; and, finally, that non-market values face a number of barriers to engaging in debate and facilitating change in welfare provision. As Cahn notes in the opening quote to this chapter, we must also consider how the dominance of market values within the capitalist system has altered our perception of the social world and the interactions that we engage. Illustrating this altered perception requires a focus on time, as outlined in Chapter One.

Consequently, this chapter sets up a broader theoretical argument for developing a narrative of non-market values. These ideas are then refined through a discussion of the social theory of time. How to assess the function of activities can be facilitated by this time-based analysis, and after outlining key aspects of the theory, the chapter outlines how social policy analysis has already engaged with the concept of time before outlining how the theory can facilitate a rethinking of the normative assumptions regarding citizenship.

Value and time

Developing a discussion of values and alternatives requires building up an argument of what alternative values are to be sought out, pursued and developed in social activity and supported by social policies. Before drawing on the social theory of time to articulate a view of value that underpins the analysis in the subsequent chapters, there is first a need to discuss this in relation to the notion of 'function'. It may be possible to use this term to overcome the suggested challenge outlined at the end of Chapter Two: presenting the argument for non-economic values in publically convincing terms.

Function

The discussion of neoliberal hybrids suggested that the global ideology of neoliberalism interacts with local political contexts to form national variations of the ideology. Alternatives to this narrative exist within the local community context, which practices different production and exchange relationships that do not fit with the values of capitalism, but are disregarded as outdated or inefficient. Such views of alternatives reflect Lee's (2006) argument regarding circuits of value. Economic geographies consist of a number of circuits of value that promote and sustain their own notions of value. These can draw upon social and economic relations, but value emerges from the practice and performance at the local level. The suggestion is that economic and social values interact in the construction of production and exchange within local geographies. In particular for the discussion in later chapters, Lee et al (2004: 597) suggest that a complementary currency system known as Local Exchange Trading Systems (LETS) represents one such circuit of value, which is 'independent of mainstream institutions and processes'. This overlaps with Zelizer's (1994, 2005) theory of money, which suggests that money has social, political, economic and contextual restrictions on how and to what purposes it is used, an argument supported by North (2007) in his analysis of complementary currencies.

Accepting that within localities, alternative, non-capitalist practices can be constructed illustrates the existence of judging the value of activities outside of market criteria. Efforts to explore alternative values have been pursued by academics in considering the construction of value in post-capitalist societies (Soper, 2008; Arvidson et al, 2013). Here, however, the argument will be presented that we need to reconsider the normative assumptions of citizenship promoted by neoliberal hybrids. To achieve this, the starting point will be the argument presented by Tawney (1921) in *The Acquisitive Society*, which critiques industrial society. He suggests that industrial development obscures the concept of 'function' in determining the worth of social activity. Tawney (1921: 8) defines 'function' as:

> an activity which embodies and expresses the idea of social purpose. The essence of it is that the agent does not perform it merely for personal gain or to gratify himself, but recognizes that he is responsible for its discharge to some higher authority.

He suggests that as the Industrial Revolution developed, the utilitarian argument that rights are derived from utility became a guiding principle for activities across the economy and society. This allows for the pursuit of self-interest in a way divorced from any notion of service: individual gain takes precedent over societal improvement. Gradually, this notion of rights relegates the 'public' to a secondary and contingent position. Consequently, rights are presented as not requiring social justification.

Industrialisation resulted in the development of an 'acquisitive society', where the acquisition of wealth becomes paramount, and due to the separation of rights from function, this accumulation of wealth occurs undeterred by social consequences. To counter this development, Tawney argues in favour of a notion of function, arguing that functions reflect social purpose. Utilising the concept of function to guide social actions and obligations would bring collective rather than individual motives back into social activity. For social and economic activity, it would become important to start from a position of what people can 'make or create or achieve', not what they possess, which would establish the foundations of a 'Functional Society'. As Tawney (1921: 29) explains, 'in such a society the main subject of social emphasis would be the performance of functions', rather than industrial society's pursuit of destructive, functionless activities. Underpinning social and economic activity with the idea of function would mean that only socially justified actions are permissible.

The idea of function can be implicitly found in much contemporary debate concerning the environment, sustainability and anti-productivist critiques of capitalism (Boyle and Simms, 2009; Jordan and Drakeford, 2012). It is a fundamental argument found in debates about the usefulness (or otherwise) of certain activities to society (New Economics Foundation, 2009; Turner, 2009). For example, the New Economics Foundation suggests that for each £1 that an investment banker creates, they will destroy £7 of social value, whereas a child carer creates between £7 and £9.50 for each £1 that they are paid. The intention of such an example is to seek to highlight how different activities in the economy are given a monetary value, which is perceived as the main measure of activity in neoliberal economic theory, and to then contrast this with a monetary value of the social contribution that the 'function' of different activities have. Such arguments have been used to develop the concept of social return on investment (SROI), which is an attempt to measure the creation of social value that different activities have (Millar and Hall, 2012; King, 2014). Essential here is that a notion of 'function' allows us to develop a framework of alternative values for judging social and economic activities. It becomes important to fully articulate how a notion of function can be developed to provide a means for judging social/economic activities. This needs to be distinct from market valuation criteria, and the social theory of time is relevant to the analysis here.

Time and contemporary society

Time is implicit in all that we do; yet, rarely has time been made explicit in our analysis of society. Time can be found within our interactions, our social organisation and cultures. Adam (1990, 1994/95, 1996, 1998, 2001, 2004; Adam and Groves, 2007) has explored time across a number of academic disciplines to show how time flows though human history, and her work is influential in the discussion that follows. Noteworthy, Adam suggests that time is generally conceptualised dualistically, distinguishing between 'absolute' and 'relative' time, but that this dualism prevents a complete understanding of time. Inevitably, this section must work with this dualism to outline the theory, but surmount the dualism when conducting analysis.

'Absolute time' is typified by Newtonian notions of time, which hypothesise time as duration between events, unimpeded by the alterations that it describes and therefore external to humans. As Adam (2004: 30) explains, time is, 'as a quantity: invariant, infinitely divisible into space-like units, measurable in length and expressible as a number '. Time measures motion. Time remains unaffected as the speed of an object increases or decreases. A distinction can therefore be made between the measurement/laws of things in motion in time and 'absolute time within which motion and change are thought to take place' (Adam, 2004: 30). 'Absolute time' is independent of human beings and their world, with its externality reinforced by the clock as a tool of measurement and expression of time. This emphasises time as both measurable and controllable and establishes a link to how society determines the value of goods and services in social and political domains (see later).

In contrast to this, 'relative time' is theorised as being internal, integral to the human mind, body and soul, and embedded within planetary seasons and the workings of the cosmos. Past, present and future are intricately linked within human minds as time is not a measure of duration, but how we compare what remains fixed in memory against our expectations (Adam, 2004: 51–4). The external world travels from past to future, but from the position of the self, 'life involves an unbroken chain of future-orientated decisions that bring the future into the present and allow it to fade into the past' (Adam, 2004: 54). Consequently, 'relative time' illustrates subjective, internal time. Refining this discussion, Adam (2004) explains how the construction of the present is a horizontal flow containing impressions and perceptions of the now, extended through retentions and protentions (anticipation of future events). Speech illustrates this idea, for retention is required so that we know what we have said but protention is necessary to know what we will say next. 'Relative time' contrasts with 'absolute time', for it is internal and contextual: the process through which past, present and future are entwined and defined in relation to each other.

This theorisation of time has facilitated an analysis of contemporary Western societies and the conceptualisation of time in capitalist societies. Indirectly, such commentary engages in the archaeological mode of the 'utopian method' set out by Levitas (2005). As such, it has been suggested that the development of capitalist societies has promoted and utilised 'absolute' over 'relative' definitions of time: emptying time of social meaning (Thompson, 1967; Adam, 1990, 1994/95, 2004; Glennie and Thrift, 1996; Bauman, 2000; Westenholz, 2006). In this regard, attention has been given to work practices, tracing a shift towards practices where time as an external measure is utilised to ensure that predefined levels of production are achieved within set work hours (Thompson, 1967). As illustrated by Weber (1992), time becomes a quantitative resource for economic exchange. Adam (2004: 45) writes that 'time emerges ... as a tool for the regulation of conduct. This of course required as pre-condition an externalized, universal time, abstracted from events and emptied of all content.' The advent of the clock facilitates the rationalisation of conduct and the harnessing of time for economic goals and profit creation with a future-focused orientation: time is money.

Adam (1990, 2004) makes explicit the theoretical arguments that underpin the time-is-money argument in her analysis of the work of Marx. She suggests that his labour theory of value draws on the notion of 'absolute time', for it requires the control, regulation and exploitation of labour time, which relies on time as an abstract exchange value disconnected from the value of goods and services. This forms a precondition of capitalism as labourers can be paid for their *time* rather than their *labour*. This is an important development for 'clock time', as Adam (2004: 38) explained: '[t]he common, decontextualized value by which products, tasks and services can be evaluated and exchanged is time.... Time is the decontextualized, asituational abstract exchange value that allows work to be translated into money.' Here, time is quantifiable as money is quantifiable. The UK minimum wage at the time of writing (for over 21 year olds) is £6.31 and this is an hourly rate. Employees on this pay are expected to complete X amount of work in each hour for this wage. The value of the activity, its function and the profit it produces for the employer are not reflected in the wage. Rather, it is a quantitative measure of time that is brought and sold, which is seen to reflect the 'worth' of the hour – not the activity. Employers could easily require more output per hour and not increase the wage to reflect this despite the increase in profits that this would generate. Additionally, as illustrated by the New Economics Foundation (2009) regarding SROI, outlined earlier, different jobs can have different impacts on society that are not reflected in the wages paid. Time, in these examples, has been decontextualised as a means of exchange. Disembedded, time consequently becomes one object, subject to bounding, exchange and transformation, which, expressed through the clock, has permeated the key institutions of industrial society: political, scientific and economic. Time is colonised by 'absolute', clock time.

This colonisation has been critiqued through an examination of the extreme consequences of the process to the environment (such as unforeseen impacts of the genetic manipulation of crops). Such arguments seek to emphasise the need to reconsider the ascendency of absolute time and its false notion of reversibility (Kümmerer, 1996; Adam, 1998).[1] A number of theorists have sought to expand these critiques of the dominance of clock time and to promote a more nuanced understanding that draws upon both 'absolute' and 'relative' conceptions of time. Such analyses critique the adherence to clock time and the consequence that this has on understanding and living social interactions in contemporary capitalist societies. These often highlight the gendered divisions in the lived experience of time within social interaction (Leccardi, 1996; Gunning, 1997b; Zucchermaglio and Talamo, 2000; Oechsle and Geissler, 2003; Brannen, 2005; Kremer-

Sadlik and Paugh, 2007; Bouffartigue, 2010), but also explore how within our daily lives, different times are experienced and woven together (Davies, 1990, 1994; Nowotny, 1992; Urry, 1994; Darier, 1998).

Time and lived experience

The analysis of time within contemporary society has sought to demonstrate the resulting damage generated by the colonisation of time as an external measure of duration. In particular, it seeks to highlight that this imposition of clock time throughout the political, economic, social and cultural aspects of social interaction has altered how we value social relationships. Efforts to counter this domination by the clock start from the position that time exists in events and will not readily fit the steady flow of the clock (Nowotny, 1992). One particular focus has been on the existence of various different temporalities in which activities take place, for example, evolution is immensely long and imperceptible – thus making us aware of non-anthropocentric times (Urry, 1994; Darier, 1998). Others have demonstrated that our lives can contain measured quantities of time as 'time out' for holidays or family activities, which rely upon the same temporal rhythms as work and the same sense of experienced pressure and speed. However, spontaneous moments of time, freed from the shadow of the clock, reflect true moments of quality that are woven into other times within our daily lives (Elsrud, 1998; Kremer-Sadlik and Paugh, 2007). Recognition of different times within our personal and work lives has also been reflected in analysis of social interactions in order to demonstrate how different community groups in one locality can live different temporal cycles (Kenyon, 2000). Additionally, time has been linked to forms of exchange that emphasise cooperation and solidarity over precision measurement, reflecting the complete opposite to time in the Western world (Raybeck, 1992). What such analysis demonstrates is that time is not just a measure of duration; it has a qualitative dimension that influences how we experience and value a range of different social interactions.

Interest in different times has drawn attention to two important ideas: 'process time' and 'task time'. Davies (1990, 1994) develops the idea of 'process time' in relation to care work. She argues that caring activities cannot be measured by timed segments as it is impossible to calculate how much time will be 'consumed' in care work. Distinguishing specific periods of caring activity to be timed by the clock is challenging because such activity involves the moment of providing care, but also non-direct caring moments, for example, in our thoughts (planning, thinking and worrying about caring responsibilities and duties). Caring is interwoven with other times to 'weave intricate patterns in the work carried out by carers and in our lives more generally' (Davies, 1994: 281). Along similar lines rests Thompson's (1967) suggestion that industrialisation in Western societies facilitated a move away from 'task time'. Pre-industrial societies saw workers control the length of their working hours, which reflected the time needed to complete the task. However, within the time-is-money framework, employers' control of time enhances economic performance as increased production is sought within smaller time frames to increase profitability (Adam, 1994/95). Increased profit rather than a job well done becomes the key focus of work, with the result that unremunerated work in the household or school is considered 'unproductive labour' and rendered invisible. Such practices can be found in the noticeable shift within domiciliary care services, where staff have shorter time frames within which to carry out caring duties.[2] Such production has been referred to as the 'shadow economy' of work (Adam, 1994/95) and is considered of less worth by dominant capitalist notions of 'absolute time'.

The argument to be presented at this stage is as follows. We cannot accept the domination of clock time in our work or social relations. To do so pushes aside our comprehension of our social life through relative notions of time. We live both absolute and relative time simultaneously, although we cannot always comprehend both at the same time (Adam, 1990). Knowing time in its relative conception offers a means of questioning the domination of capitalist values within our social interactions: family time and caring time treated as segmented allocations of clock time experience the same pressures and anxieties as are experienced in work. This damages not only our well-being, but also our social structure, as the time-is-money framework promotes the use of clock-time mechanisms to tackle social problems that are incompatible with the times of the environment and social life, consequently generating future unforeseen problems from present solutions (see Kümmerer, 1996; Adam, 1998). 'Process time' and 'task time' illustrate alternative sources of value for social and economic activity that are integrated into different experiences of time, not just the dictates of the clock. As will be demonstrated, this can become a source for questioning and challenging the dominant temporal order in Western society. Before it is possible to do this, however, it is necessary to provide an overview of how the notions of 'absolute' and 'relative' time have been drawn into social policy analysis.

Time and social policy

Some efforts have been made to draw the social theory of time into analysis of social policy. Such analysis can be divided into two groups: those that treat time as a resource and those that draw upon the wider theory to explore different times. This section will explore these two groups before paying particular attention to Tony Fitzpatrick's (2004b) discussion of time and social policy in order to set a foundation for making time explicit in policy analysis and within concepts such as citizenship.

Time as a resource

The analysis of time as a resource brings the concept into discussions of need, income and wider welfare debates. Here, efforts seek to demonstrate the complex interplay between the competing time demands of employment and non-paid work. In reference to the latter, the concern is with the subsequent effects of such demands on the individual's availability for employment and the consequences that this may have for their income. How individuals are able to allocate their time use depends on their income. Individuals have to weigh up decisions between employed work and other activities, with each having implications for the other. Thus, time spent in work, earning, results in less time for caring and other activities; while allocating more time to the latter (either by choice or need) will reduce time for employment and impact on income. Burchardt (2010) suggests that these allocations of time can generate time poverty, income poverty or both time and income poverty. Treating time as a resource to be divided up and allocated to different activities requires that social policy make time a more explicit resource in welfare calculations (Piachaud, 1984; Burchardt, 2010). As with income, time constraints should become an accepted idea for policymakers and social scientists concerned with poverty.

Noteworthy here are discussions of how government policies can impact on time allocation and the suggestion that policymakers develop 'time targets' similar to poverty targets. For example, Goodin et al (2004; see also Goodin et al, 2008; Goodin, 2010) distinguish between time that is free 'discretionary time' (time over which you have autonomous control) and time to be allocated to securing a minimal income, unpaid household labour and the minimum necessary personal care. Focusing on 'the poverty style question: how much is strictly necessary' (Goodin et al, 2004: 38), Goodin et al argue that the tax and benefit systems of different governments impact on the allocation of time without this being a distinct aim of policy. Goodin (2010) develops this argument by establishing the idea of 'temporal justice'.[3] However, this notion of temporal justice is based upon the narrow conception of time as a measurable quantity. Along similar lines, Piachaud (2008) has focused on 'time burdens', which reflect inconveniences for different groups of people. His example of these burdens distinguishes between getting the central locking fixed on the car or the rush between town and country house (for the middle-class family) and the burden of someone using the bus because they cannot afford a car (for the unemployed/low-income family). Here, available income can result in different lifestyle choices (or lack of choice), which lead to different demands on individuals' time.

Furthermore, treating time as a resource has also underpinned analyses of social services. Access and use of services will have different demands to the service users' time, and in the wake of service privatisation in the 1980s, this has resulted in increasing time costs required to access welfare services (Lee and Piachaud, 1992). Additionally, this overlaps with issues of equity and efficiency and has an inbuilt gender bias regarding divisions of time use in society (Pascall, 2012: esp ch 7).[4] Consequently, Lee and Piachaud (1992: 29) argue that the time consequences of service access need to be a consideration in service design and implementation in order to 'shift from the blinkered balance-sheets of financial accounting towards the broader concept of social accounting'. Yet, such accounting remains wedded to 'absolute time' as time is a measure to be counted and monitored.

Policy and multiple times

Moving beyond the focus on time as a resource, a number of academics have sought to draw on a range of different concepts of time to develop a more nuanced understanding of social policy and welfare provision. Building on a discussion with direct links to the work of Adam (1990), Coffey (2004) suggests that time can be explored in terms of timing (as a schedule within which policy is made, implemented and practised, and the timing of welfare payments) but also in terms of a more complex interplay of present and future: 'care packages address *present* caring needs, and anticipate *future* caring needs' (Coffey, 2004: 102, emphasis in original). This complexity between past, present and future plays out in policy discussions of the life course and lifetime transitions but also in key concepts such as social justice, need and equality. Thus, Coffey (2004: 107) claims that '[s]ocial policy and social welfare can thus be reconstructed in terms of pasts, presents and futures, transitional movements, cycles and rhythms, time to and time for, making time and taking time'. This overlaps with the work of Dey (1999), who suggests that policy often neglects time by focusing on the instant (the current moment of need) and the eternal (generalised need over time and place). Such discussion broadens out the analysis of time in policy analysis.

In particular, Dey (1999) suggests that a range of temporal frames need to be considered in relation to social policy, with careful consideration of structure and the agency of the welfare user. It is inaccurate to assume that users are a bundle of needs; rather, they should be considered as agents involved in developing strategies for tackling the social problems that they experience. Time is relevant here as it facilitates a discussion of 'desert' and investment in the analysis. Essentially, this seeks to make explicit the relevance of time invested by users into welfare provision in order to establish entitlement, against which a benefit can be claimed, that is, social security based upon insurance principles. This theme of multiple expressions of time in social policy was also explored by Bussey (2007). The suggestion here is that the dominance of 'absolute time' within capitalist society has blocked the natural relationships that exist and excluded other forms of knowing (through other times). Bussey subsequently developed a typology divided between individual and collective time against layered and linear time to map different temporal experiences (eg memories are individual and layered, but policy is collective and linear). From this, Bussey advocates for understanding different times within social life and argues, in line with the critique of clock time offered earlier, that instrumental time develops a temporal order that renders invisible the systems of social reproduction while defining the individual as isolated, autonomous and responsible for their own life (similar ideas reflect the impact of the 'risk society' on social welfare; see Kemshall, 2002). Thus, the dominance and imposition of clock time at the expense of other forms of knowing and experiencing time leads to a social policy that is a knee-jerk, present-centred reaction, and blind to other ways of living and experiencing time. Bussey argues that policy must articulate and engage with all forms of time, creating messy policymaking processes that require new tools of community engagement. Time banking, explored in Chapters Four and Five, may be one such tool for achieving this.

Moving beyond the 'absolute' and 'relative' time discussion, Fitzpatrick (2004a) offers a conception of time based on 'absolute', 'relative' and 'relational' times. 'Absolute' and 'relative' times have been outlined earlier. Fitzpatrick suggests that 'relational time' refers to the collective space in which debates about meanings and values of time take place. This considers how the value of time impacts on the organisation of society and its institutions, and how people engage with time. Fitzpatrick (2004a: 201) believes that '[m]eaningful time is therefore a positional good, a mobile site of conflict as society "makes itself" through the endless reconfiguration of who possesses the most control over the meaning and distribution of time'. Consequently, 'relational time' is political and social, and it is within this space that debate occurs about the role of welfare in (re)creating the social world and the vision of how that world should develop and operate. Thus, within this space, a prescriptive ideology developed an outline of the world that political actors seek to create. It is here that Fitzpatrick starts to form links to radical politics as this style of politics engages actors in shaping their environment, which, in turn, shapes them. Consequently, time becomes a key concept in how we rethink social organisation and social interactions, which is associated with the second and third stages of Levitas's (2005) 'utopian method'.

Temporal reordering and citizenship

Developing links between radical politics, time and social policy tends to consider how the dominant temporal order, the dominance of clock time in capitalist societies, influences social organisation. In particular, many of the arguments that explore this debate reflect upon the role of citizens and their ability to participate in activities outside of paid employment. This begins with a discussion of time as a resource to be allocated to certain activities, but, more broadly, questions the dominant idea of time-is-money. This questioning of the decontextualisation of time to facilitate exchange with money suggests that non-market activities are of equal, or greater, value; however, in the functionless, acquisitive society (Tawney, 1921), we do not appreciate this value because time spent outside of paid work is seen as wasteful. Time invested in profit, not functional activities, dominates. This view is perpetuated in capitalism by neoliberal theory on the global stage. Building on the foregoing discussion, which is critical of how time has been colonised by the clock, a number of theorists have adopted the multiplicity of time into their analysis in order to suggest a range of reforms to be sought in policy that would change the normative conception of citizenship and the welfare institutions that seek to support citizen activities.

Time in leisure societies

One policy reform that has required rethinking the value of time and how citizens use their time has been associated with citizen basic income schemes and moves towards a leisure society. Darier (1998), for example, explores how time (specifically busyness and speed) interrelates with work, the environment and modern subjectivities. He argues that work as duration rather than task-focused no longer follows natural rhythms and contradicts other times found in environmental processes. He suggests that there is a need to redistribute employment and non-work time rather than to create more jobs, within a framework of a minimum income for all, in order to reconsider how we construct our social organisation, daily activities and subjective selves: from the busy-self to the lazy- or green-self. Drawing the multiplicity of time into our analysis leads to a critical consideration of how we value a range of activities in our daily lives, which aligns with analysis critiquing the dominance of work in contemporary society (Gorz, 1999; Russell, 2004; Frayne, 2011).

Fitzpatrick (2004b) develops a specific analysis of time in relation to leisure societies, likely building on his own interest in a basic income (Fitzpatrick, 1999). He suggests that one of the key challenges to rethinking the temporal order of society results from Rawls' theory of justice. Rather than challenge the dominant way in which time was treated and used in industrial society, Rawls augmented the commonplace by accepting the eight-hour working day as the norm. Subsequently favouring neoliberal arguments promoting materialist and possessive individualism, it becomes possible for governments to demand that we spend our time working and consuming as the primary duty of citizenship; as the Seabrook quote (cited in Bauman, 2009: 151) opening Chapter One reminds us, consumption in the marketplace has primacy as the only means of creating an identity. As a brief aside, it is interesting to note that Van Parijs actually justifies a basic income using Rawls' theory of justice (Van Parijs, 2009).

Building on this, Fitzpatrick (2004b) explores the arguments for valuing non-employment activity in the work of Goodin (1999) and Gorz (1999). While Goodin and Gorz write from different philosophical foundations, Fitzpatrick seeks out commonalities in their arguments, which he then presents in the following terms. First, there is an argument for time to be accepted as a resource to be treated in the same terms as income and wealth when seeking social justice. Second, there is a need to 'democratise time' so that citizens have increased capacity to engage in social dialogue to consolidate just distributions of time, income and wealth. Third, there is agreement with feminist and environmentalist arguments for reforming employment-based societies. This requires an uncoupling of time from employment and its associated income to recognise the valuable contributions made by non-employment activities, and therefore the need for a basic income to support such activity. Finally, this rethinking of time within contemporary society to facilitate a move towards a leisure society requires a new localism in order to create sites for new political and social formations. However, Fitzpatrick does distinguish his general approach from that of Goodin et al (2004; see also Goodin et al, 2008). Goodin, Fitzpatrick suggests, has developed a negative conception of free time: time free from employment. Rather, a positive conception based on informal, civic engagement should be promoted in order for theories of social justice to facilitate an equalisation of time between people to increase their opportunities to engage in meaningful and deliberative participation. For Fitzpatrick (2004b: 355), welfare reform should seek to develop 'Such strategies [that] involve making greater room for egalitarian redistributions of time from advantaged to disadvantaged groups and evolving a politics of post-productivism and post-employment by allowing political economies of care, sustainability and democratic deliberation to emerge.'

'Time wealth'

The suggestion for post-capitalist societies to be built around notions of care, sustainability and deliberation requires a rethinking of time within contemporary society. In part, as outlined earlier, this requires a consideration of 'absolute time', time as a resource to be distributed fairly across society, but also breaking away from the time-is-money calculation. Developing frameworks for this debate, Reisch (2001) offered the concept of 'time wealth'. Modern society is founded upon money-based and property-based wealth. Subsequently, time is viewed as an input factor or constraint. People rarely feel that they have enough time at the right time. Reisch outlines the environmental implications of this perception of time as a clash of different timescales: the timescale of modernity is acceleration, which collides with the biological time of the earth. Promoting alternatives in order to build sustainable consumption requires a new temporality built around the idea of 'wealth in time'. This requires: a focus on different time horizons (essentially, a concern for future generations, not just our own); a move towards sufficiency, sustainable lifestyles and informal work (here, making links to LETS); accepting the limitations of production and consumption: and an integration of the plurality of timescales into society.

Biesecker's (1998) suggestion that time-as-money is an economic resource that damages social life and the natural environment's reproductive cycles is reflected in this argument. In contemporary society, time is perceived as a scarce economic resource and this necessitates acceleration within production: the more time you can save in order to increase production, the greater the profit generated. Sustainable consumption requires a 'new economy of time' and a re-conceptualisation of economic rationality. This new economy will require cooperation and self-organisation between businesses, traders, producers, consumers and private households. Each exists within different temporal frames and these must be 'interlaced' with each other, which is achievable only through cooperation. Here, links start to form with the work of Fitzpatrick (2004b) as this cooperation is established through communication between cooperating partners, as Biesecker (1998: 85) explains:

> [c]ommunication requires time, and this contradicts the understanding of time efficiency within a modern market economy.... [Consequently, t]ime efficiency would no longer imply reaching a goal in the shortest possible time, but rather reaching a goal through agreement of all those associated with it, or affected by it [expressed as 'agreeability efficiency'].

Fitzpatrick's call for a more equitable distribution of time between people in society to allow citizens to engage in deliberate activity overlaps with 'agreeability efficiency' to develop a new economic model which emphasises agreement, responsibility and cooperation. It embraces different multiple timescales that exist within different practices and institutions in society, and as coordination occurs through discussion rather than money, the latter becomes less important, thus dissolving the time-is-money mantra of capitalism.

Consequently, Reisch's (2001: 373) argument for personal autonomy – to be able to work according to one's own pace and to organise tasks according to one's preferences and rhythms – becomes important here. Whether we use the term 'leisure time', Goodin's notion of 'discretionary time' or Reisch's notion of 'time sovereignty',[5] the focus is on the distribution of time as a resource with greater equality than exists in contemporary society as part of a broader societal change towards sustainability and new ways of conducting our lives. Such change requires a time-based wealth model and a communicative strategy for tackling the negative consequences of the acceleration of life on our lives, our society and the environment in which we live. One potential route for achieving such change is now explored in detail.

Uchronia

Bryson (2007) develops an analysis of Western society that offers a similar critique of the dominance of the clock as that outlined earlier. She then progresses from this to explore the potential reorganisation of society. On the one hand, time is a resource; on the other, it is generated and lived experience. Bryson suggests that 'disposable time' should be viewed as a 'primary good' and a political resource: time is required by citizens to contribute to communities and express views and interests through the deliberative processes recommended earlier. The focus on local participatory politics can overlap with the discussion of self-help in Chapter Two; however, here, the focus is on the radical and alternative conception of self-help suggested by Burns and Taylor (1998).

As with other academics explored in this chapter, Bryson argues that capitalism develops an unjust distribution of time, particularly in terms of gender (see also Pascall, 2012), and promotes long hours of paid employment as the norm. Bryson (2007: 2) paid particular attention to inequalities in time, arguing that:

> [i]nequalities in the way that time is used and valued are therefore part of a vicious circle that leaves many women economically dependent and vulnerable to exploitation and domestic abuse, whilst lack of free time makes it difficult for women to gain a political voice and express time-related expenses and needs.

These developments are damaging to individuals, families and society, and create a care deficit, a decline in economic effectiveness and a reduction in civic engagement. The solution is to find a healthier balance between paid work and other aspects of our lives.

Developing a framework to challenge these inequalities and to engage in political debate, Bryson (2007) outlines a feminist 'Uchronia'[6] – a temporal utopia – not a blueprint to be imposed, but the start of a debate about the sort of society we wish to live in and how to achieve it. The welfare state has a key role to play in addressing these inequalities as it can reinvigorate values in productive labour and caring activities outside of employment, and dissolve the link between time and money. Subsequently, all aspects of life would no longer be reduced to considerations of cost efficiency. Rather, time is perceived as both a collective and individual resource, and, as such, its distribution is accountable to principles of justice and subject to state regulation. Rethinking the value of time provides a foundation for determining the function of an activity and its importance to society. The welfare state facilitates this change by supporting the ways in which time is organised and rewarded, and by reconfiguring normative assumptions of citizenship.

Thus, central principles developed within this 'Uchronia' include ensuring that citizens spend time caring for others and ensuring that care becomes a normal responsibility of all citizens in the same way as employment has been presented in modern society. Additionally, citizens must be able to participate in voluntary, community and political groups and competent adults must be responsible for their own domestic work. Consequently, citizenship involves a combination of earning, caring and participating in community and political activities. For Bryson, this would require the duties of citizenship to place care work before employment activities, a change supported through both the welfare state and industrial relations.

The dominance of clock time, for Bryson (2007), is not inevitable, and indications of alternatives do exist in her analysis. The most noteworthy of these is the suggestion that LETS and time banking challenge the time-equals-money culture at both national and international levels. These self-help schemes will be the focus of Chapter Three. Here, Bryson argues that combined political, social, attitudinal and legislative developments have provided a powerful impetus for change in society and how it must integrate multiple times and competing values into social life. Implicitly, therefore, Bryson has essentially drawn upon the 'utopian method' (Levitas, 2005). The first step, the *archaeological* mode, provides a critique of contemporary society, highlighting its shortcomings, such as the dominance of the time-is-money perception in organising social life (Adam, 1994, 2004) and, more broadly, market values guiding welfare provision (Jordan, 2010a). Furthermore, the *architectural* mode can be found in Bryson's work, which outlines different institutions and practices that critique contemporary society and practise new ways of fostering social relationships and interaction: here, Bryson has suggested LETS and time banking, others discuss basic incomes. Thus, the final mode, the *ontological*, is outlined in the concept of citizenship that Bryson introduces us to: a consideration of how we can *be* differently.

Conclusion

Drawing on the theoretical framework outlined earlier, it is possible to suggest that time is not simply a measure of duration monitored by the clock, or just a resource through which increased productive output can be pursued. Time cuts across a vast number of experiences in our lives and is woven through social institutions and the interactions that take place within them. Rethinking time can offer new insights not only with regards to how we 'spend time', but also with regards to the meaning and value that such time has. It offers insight into the interrelationship between past, present and future (not explored here). The argument, therefore, is that exploring the multiplicity of time exposes different ways in which time is valued at the local level, as will be explored in greater detail in Chapter Five. This offers a way of conceiving of value in social activity that does not fit into the time–is–money calculation. Rather, it allows us to rethink actions in relation to 'functions' (to draw on Tawney, 1921) in order to ask what activities and contributions we want citizens to make to the well-being and advancement of society. Time provides a tool for analysing activity; function provides the language to bring this analysis into policymaking and ideological debate. Pierson (2006: 233) has previously suggested that 'within the envisageable future, the "real" issue is not going to be whether we have a welfare state ... but what sort of welfare state regime it will be'. This debate has been renewed in the UK since 2010 and the Coalition government's austerity policies. This neoliberal hybrid offers one narrative about the possible future development of welfare and the influence that this will have on social relationships. An analysis of time potentially offers an alternative to this. The remaining chapters start to explore this alternative narrative in relation to the policy tool of time banking in order to consider what alternatives it offers and its potential to resist the co-option of policy into neoliberal thinking suggested towards the end of Chapter Two.

Notes

[1] Newtonian theory states that time is reversible, for it is an external linear measure and, as such, we can go forward or backwards along the line. The relative notion of time critiques this based on the view that it is not possible to reverse time and therefore to undo things once they have been done.

[2] See: http://www.bbc.co.uk/news/health-18347303 (accessed 4 August 2012).

[3] This term is used in an attempt by Goodin to bring time into considerations of distributive justice alongside money.

[4] Referring to the gendered distribution of employment, domestic care and personal care times.

[5] Some overlap here could be suggested with Goodin's discussion of temporal justice and discretionary time; however, Reisch is not limited to only discussing time as a measure of duration and as a resource.

[6] 'Uchronia' is a political challenge to existing practices promoting a set of criteria against which to assess contemporary society, while simultaneously encouraging debate around the form of the 'good society' and the temporal values that this would require.

.

FOUR

Time banking

> LETS [Local Exchange Trading Systems] was attractive to many precisely as it did not involve capitalist labour discipline – consequently it proved to be a poor tool for helping the socially excluded get work. The less resistant ethos of the co-production of public services, and on volunteering encapsulated by Time Money was far more attractive to government. (North, 2006a: 8)

The preceding chapters have examined the development of neoliberal hybrids in the UK and the potential space to resist these narratives through drawing on the social theory of time to underpin value in citizen activities outside of the marketplace. Both offer insight into how citizenship can be conceptualised and the role of self-help initiatives in developing local practices that enact deliberative activities in order to develop 'agreeability efficiency'. This relies on appreciating the value of time invested in activities outside of employment and supporting the growth of practices that support these activities. This chapter explores one particular example of such a practice already mentioned in earlier chapters: time banking. As a form of complementary currency, time banking is part of a wider history of such initiatives, which will be explored later. The chapter explores the theory and practice of time banking before accounting for its global development. Finally, the discussion in this chapter returns its focus to the UK and the current political theories of the Coalition government and the Labour Party – the main opposition in Westminster and the government in the devolved Welsh Assembly (at the time of writing) – in order to consider how time banking, as a form of self-help, may fit within these political narratives. This allows us to begin to consider the tension between Bryson's (2007) view that LETS and time banking offer a means to erode the association between time and money (see Chapter Five) and North's view in the opening quote to this chapter that time banking is less radical than other complementary currencies and will consequently work within the dominant government narrative.

Time banking: origins and theory

Time banking is often presented as a new innovation for generating community participation and engagement. However, the practice builds upon a longer history of alternative thinking and practice with regards to production and exchange. In part, this is contained within the wider history of complementary currency systems (CCSs), but it also shares a historical narrative with other practices, such as social credit and basic incomes, as part of a broader narrative of alternative policy options to secure human welfare. These wider origins are initially explored before specific consideration is given to the development of time banking by Edgar Cahn (1986, 2000), an American civil rights lawyer and activist who is attributed as the founder of time banking. After outlining the development of time bank exchange and practice, the discussion focuses upon the theoretical argument of time banking, which returns attention to the imposition of market values onto the social sphere and introduces the concept of co-production.

Pre-time banking

Before exploring CCSs, it will be beneficial to examine the broader range of alternative economic practices in order to inform the discussion. The most relevant of these to this discussion is the idea of social credit developed by Major C.H. Douglas, a British engineer. Douglas (1920: 6) argued that 'Systems were made for men, and not men for systems, and the interest of man, which is self-development, is above all systems, whether theological, political or economic.' His idea developed during the First World War, when he noticed that the total cost of goods produced was greater than the pay outs in salary, dividends and wages. This contradicted the Ricardian economic theory dominant at the time: that all costs were distributed as purchasing power (the number of goods/services purchased with a unit of currency). Douglas demonstrated that consumers lacked enough income to purchase back what they had made, leading him to develop his 'A + B' theorem. As Hiskett (1935) outlined in his critique of the theory: 'A' is the payment to individuals while B is the payments made to other organisations for raw materials and so on. 'A' is therefore purchasing power, the money used to buy goods/services, but the price of goods and services cannot be less than 'A + B'. Douglas, however, argued that all output should be purchasable and as it is not possible for 'A' to purchase 'A + B', some part of 'B' had to be accessed through alternative purchasing power. Finlay (1972: 107) states that this explanation is ambiguous to the extent that it does not claim that there is an increasing inability to consume the goods being produced; nor did it claim that the system was breaking down. Rather, the system could be maintained by using alternative purchasing power that was not only equal to 'B', but also not made up of the forms of purchasing power in 'A'. Finlay (1972: 108) goes on to explain:

> It was an argument devoted primarily to showing the inevitability of servility, for since the people could never buy the whole product, the plant owners retained power … [while] the continuance of the system depended upon the whim of those who controlled the supply of B payments, in other words, the financiers. Capitalism had given way to cretinism, the objectionable to the diabolical.

The intention here is not to explore the theory in detail, or its criticisms, but to note that part of the advocacy for social credit is based on the argument that through labour, workers still lack sufficient purchasing power within markets founded upon neoliberal economic theory. The aim, therefore, is to alter practice in order to realise that production's only purpose is to consume and that this must serve the freely expressed interests of consumers – these interests direct production policy, not the interests of capital. Production must service and be accredited by a democracy of consumers (Douglas, 1921). Consequently, the aim is to change the basis of production and exchange.

The argument for social credit was noted by Keynes (1936) in a footnote in his *General Theory of Employment, Interest and Money*, and has influenced political parties and social movements in Australia, Canada, Ireland, New Zealand and the UK. While these groups have experienced mixed success in developing social credit policies, they form part of a bigger alternative economics movement. This wider narrative adopts a different economic critique by drawing upon the work of John Ruskin (1862) and E.F. Schumacher (1974) to argue that money is not an accurate measure of success. Despite two centuries of economic expansion, poverty persists to the extent that people go to bed nightly across the world malnourished, children die of preventable diseases daily, wealth inequalities continue to grow, the well-being of people in the richest countries has stalled, while continued economic expansion is creating an ecological crisis (Boyle and Simms, 2009). The New Economics Foundation's (2008d) analysis thus claims of the financial crisis of 2008 that it represents a 'triple crunch': a credit-fuelled financial crisis, accelerating climate change and soaring energy prices underpinned by encroaching peak oil. This warrants the need to develop alternative economic practices, just as the social credit movement argues for alternative forms of purchasing.

One proposed alternative that is based upon this alternative economics is the 'Transition Towns' movement (O'Rourke, 2008; Scott-Cato and Hillier, 2010; Smith, 2011; Taylor, 2012; North and Longhurst, 2013). The Transition Towns movement seeks to address, in part, the 'leaky bucket' theory, outlined in Chapter One, by rebuilding local economies through a specific local currency. However, the justification used for developing the movement is based upon two global concerns (North, 2010b): first, localised production and consumption will generate lower quantities of the greenhouse gases that fuel climate change; and, second, accessible stores of oil are running low and once we pass the peak, production will start to decline and this, combined with the first, requires adopting low-carbon production. To achieve this transition from the current to the new modes of production/exchange requires the use of CCSs to facilitate a change in lifestyles and the economy (North, 2010b).

The history of complementary currencies, however, pre-dates the Transition Towns movement. CCSs are local currencies usually not backed by national currencies (henceforth, money). Early examples include stamp script (Gesell, 1918) – tokens of exchange – each stamped with a date indicating when they expire. The intention behind the stamp is to facilitate rapid/continual consumption and so encourage individuals to use the token by the date indicated, which is then renewed when exchanged. Examples of this initiative were developed in Austria in the 1920s as *Wörgal* and *Wära*. The *crédito* used during the recession in Argentina in the 1990s was an alternative form of credit/CCS developed to encourage exchange and maintain economic activity (Pearson, 2003; Ould-Ahmed, 2010). The most visible examples in the UK have been the development of LETS. This currency was developed in Canada and spread globally as an alternative to capitalist production and exchange (Lang, 1994; Lee, 1996; Croall, 1997; Fitzpatrick, 2000). LETS, however, sought to match the value of services/goods to the market, allowing the complementary currency to interact with businesses in the formal economy (Bowring, 1998). Boyle (2000) explores a range of currencies that seek to do the same thing, such as Ithaca Hours, where portions of an hour have an equivalence to money (Herrmann, 2006). Other recent innovations include local 'pounds', such as the Brixton and Bristol pounds (Hickman, 2009; Whitehead, 2010b; Rodgers, 2013) – but these require a deposit of money to be exchanged for an equivalent of local pounds, as well as the electronic currency bitcoin (McGee, 2014). Most of these currencies seek to promote localised production and consumption chains, reflecting market exchange (and value) but with a non-capitalist philosophy underpinning practice. Time banking, however, does not seek to match its currency with parity to money. It does not seek to measure the value of an activity in the same way as the market economy. Rather, it facilitates trade through an exchange in hours, and it is this practice to which the chapter now turns.

The development of time banking

Initially, time banking was devised as a form of 'service credits' (Cahn, 1986). Essentially, service credits sought to engage users of welfare services to assist in the achievement of expected service outcomes. For example, a teacher may deliver a lesson or a GP may prescribe medication, but without the effort and contribution of the pupil or patient, the student will not learn and the patient's health will not improve. Service credits were therefore established as a means of encouraging this effort from the welfare user. Cahn (2000) later refined the idea in an effort to create a new kind of 'money' in order to achieve this same aim, thus relabeling the currency system time banking.

Rather than develop a currency that sought to reflect money in its valuation of activities, as other community currencies have done, time banking utilises a credit system based on time. For each hour that a member gives to their community through voluntary activity, the member earns one time credit. These time credits can be redeemed for an hour of service or activity offered by other members of the time bank. This system pays no attention to the level of skill in determining the 'worth' of the activity. Rather, the amount of time that the activity requires determines how many credits are paid to the supplying member. Criticisms of this approach highlight concerns over the quality of services offered and the proficiency of members in discharging services. Two important counterclaims exist.

First, Offe and Heinze (1992) offer three counterarguments to the objection that the quality of unskilled labour supported by time banking will be inferior to that of the market. They suggest that activities are often of a low skill level and, as such, can be quickly learned. Alongside this, training courses and conduct agreements can be provided to ensure the quality of services. Additionally, they also offer the view that this form of practice challenges the traditional monopoly of power held by professionals. To this, Cahn (2000) adds that time banking engages people's innate skills, talents and services. Babysitting, companionship, dog walking, basic DIY, gardening, homework help, music lessons, art classes, language classes, knowledge of local history, the ability to drive and word processing skills are all some of the services and skills that can be exchanged via time banking. This starts to illustrate how time banking exchange operates. Joe spends two hours working on Adam's garden, earning two time credits. He uses these credits to access two one-hour computer classes from Alice each week. Alice uses one of her credits to have Zack help her paint her fence and the other to have piano lessons from Audrey. Zack uses his credit and another he earns by helping Gillian with her shopping to take part in a French class offered by Adam for two hours a week, while Audrey is saving hers so that she has five credits for the time bank member day trip.

In this way, a network of exchanges are developed that Alford (2002) refers to as 'generalised exchange'. This differs from exchange in the market, which he labels 'direct exchange'. Essentially, in a direct exchange, Person A wants something that Person B can provide, to access this, Person A pays Person B. The exchange is therefore between these two actors. In generalised exchange, A still wants what B has but rather than offer B money, B offers the good/service based on the knowledge that when they require something, Person C will be able to provide the good/service in return for something from Person D. Thus, generalised exchange creates a series of exchanges between multiple people. Within time banking, however, this exchange is facilitated by a time broker. This individual oversees the operation of the time bank, often building up relationships with members in order to encourage their participation and engagement in time bank activates. The broker will introduce members by arranging the exchange and maintain records of hours exchanged (some systems of time banking do this electronically to forgo the need for a broker). Facilitating such exchanges can take place: in a person-to-person (P2P) model, where exchanges are between individual members; through person-to-agency (P2A) models, where an organisation operates a time bank to engage local people in their work/activities; or through an agency-to-agency (A2A) model, where organisations share resources through a time bank exchange (New Economics Foundation, 2008c). The majority of time banks tend to operate a 'hybrid' model that incorporates elements of P2A and P2P exchanges, as outlined in the preceding illustration of practice: members can spend credits accessing services from each other or to gain access to group activities/services offered by an organisation while earning credits through offering services to members or to the organisation. This generalised exchange is linked to the idea of co-production by Alford (2002), and is a concept found in the work of Cahn.

Time bank theory: co-production

Co-production has already been briefly mentioned in Chapter One. At its most basic, it is a term used to refer to an approach to service provision that combines inputs from producers and consumers to enhance outputs (also illustrated in Cahn's argument for service credits outlined earlier). The US literature uses the labels of 'traditional producers' and 'prosumers' (consumers also involved in production). Here, however, we will maintain the UK distinction between the producer and user of welfare services for ease and clarity. While Cahn (2000) argues that time banking is based upon the idea of co-production with a social justice element (although it is not clear how he defines social justice), Chapter One suggested that there is a distinction between efficiency and efficacy co-production, with Cahn's argument falling into the latter category. The former is associated with earlier literature around co-production that Cahn does not make any clear links to.

The notion of efficiency co-production maintains a specific form of user involvement in public services to produce services. Here, the focus is primarily upon involving users to enhance the cost-effectiveness of services in achieving outcomes, and is less concerned with the issues of participation and empowerment found in notions of efficacy co-production, discussed later (Kiser and Percy, 1980; Percy et al, 1980; Brudney, 1984; Kiser, 1984; Percy, 1984). Ostrom (1997) suggests that co-production can therefore take two forms: either as direct engagement between service provider and users or as additional work outside the remit of services (some may refer to the latter as parallel production; see Boyle et al, 2006). Illustrating this distinction, Parks et al (1981) provide the example of community safety, suggesting that the responsibility for producing safety can reflect co-production in Ostrom's first form when local people engage with the police to form neighbourhood watch-type schemes. Yet, it can also follow Ostrom's second form when the police operate patrols but local people put locks on their own doors. The first approach to safety requires that both providers and workers operate together, while the second requires that each acts independently. The justification for their development rests upon whichever is cost-effective.

The literature tends to focus upon the role of co-production in enhancing the effectiveness and efficiency of local government (Lovelock and Young, 1979; Kiser and Percy, 1980; Percy et al, 1980;

Whitaker, 1980; Parks et al, 1981; Brudney, 1984; Kiser, 1984; Percy, 1984; Lam, 1997). This argues for a co-production relationship to be integrated into local government services as successful production relies upon the resources, motivation and skills of consumers (Parker, 2007a). Such perspectives can be positioned beneath the umbrella term of 'efficiency co-production' as it seeks to incorporate service users into service production for economic and performance gains and to enhance the efficiency of the services offered. The rationale for this approach relates to changes in the role of citizenship, and economic recession necessitating the need to find new models of service delivery at a time of fiscal constraint and welfare cuts. This need to see citizens as central to ensuring public service efficiency is a theme mirrored in contemporary policy debates (Cabinet Office, 2011).

One key means by which efficiency and efficacy co-production are defined rests on the association between the former and 'nudge' behavioural economics (Thaler and Sustein, 2009). This is an argument that people should be free in the libertarian sense while it is simultaneously legitimate for governments and other organisations to shape the choices that people make and to influence their behaviour to foster longer, healthier and better lives. Leaving to one side the debate about how to define 'better lives', the relevance of nudge economics to co-production can be found in the typology offered by Whitaker (1980): citizens' request for assistance; citizens' provision of assistance; and citizen–agent mutual adjustment. This final type is focused on the modification of clients' behaviour through both persuasion and coercion. Thus, Whitaker (1980: 246) argues that:

> Co-production is especially important for services which seek transformation of the behaviour of the person being served. By overlooking coproduction, we have been misled into an over-reliance on service agents and bureaucratic organization of human services.... We have too often come to expect that agencies can change people and have forgotten that people must change themselves.

Utilising time bank mechanisms to engage service users, credits may act as an incentive, or nudge, to change behaviour and therefore co-produce. What remains central to the efficiency notion of co-production is the view that individuals who use services are important contributors to efficient service outcomes. This is a theme shared with efficacy co-production, associated with the work of Cahn (2000).

Efficacy co-production

Cahn (2000: 24) begins from a set of principles of co-production rather than a definition: assets, redefining work, reciprocity and social capital:

1. Assets. The real wealth of this society is its people. Every human being can be a builder and contributor.
2. Redefining work. Work must be redefined to include whatever it takes to rear healthy children, preserve families, make neighbourhoods safe and vibrant, care for the frail and vulnerable, redress injustice and make democracy work.
3. Reciprocity. The impulse to give back is universal. Wherever possible, we must replace one-way acts of largesse in whatever form with two-way transactions. 'You need me' becomes 'We need each other.'
4. Social capital. Humans require social infrastructure as essential as roads, bridges, and utility lines. Social networks require ongoing investments of social capital generated by trust, reciprocity and civic engagement.

The intention of co-production, therefore, is to utilise the assets that people can contribute to their community through 'generalised transactions' (Alford, 1998, 2002), allowing people to contribute in a wide variety of ways (based on skills and a redefined notion of work). This, Cahn suggests, builds up social capital within their community.

As noted earlier in relation to time bank practice, time brokers facilitate exchanges between members. In doing so, this fosters a form of linking social capital between members and the broker (Gregory, 2012a). This is an essential part of practice as time brokers engage members in a range of activities in the time bank, building up the number of exchanges that they participate in and gradually being drawn into a wider range of exchanges: building up their capacity to co-produce. Gregory (2009a) suggests that this is the political goal of time banking and it is the foundation of efficacy co-production. This idea of efficacy draws upon Bandura's (1994: 71; see also 1977) concept of self-efficacy: 'a strong sense of efficacy enhances human accomplishment and personal wellbeing'. Time banking (and, potentially, co-production) seeks to develop this approach by building up the skills and capabilities of service users over time in order to improve their self-efficacy and ability to co-produce services (Gregory, 2012a), and can be associated with wider work on social learning theory (SLT) and the health belief model (HBM) (Janz and Becker, 1984;

Rosenstock et al, 1988). The argument within the health literature is that the concept of self-efficacy facilitates changes in health behaviours as it encourages actors to change through enactive/performative acts, vicarious experience, verbal explanation and/or physiological state changes. Time banking engages the first three of these, as through participation members engage in performative acts – often those who run time banks will spend time building up member activity and participation, vicarious experience can come from participation in group activities, observing others whilst verbal explanation also occurs in group settings where members share advice, information and experiences (Gregory, 2012a).

This approach to co-production shares ideas and justifications for reform with a wider analysis of the potential for co-production to reform the delivery of public services (New Economics Foundation, 2004a, 2004b, 2007, 2008a, 2008c; Boyle and Harris, 2009; Horne and Shirley, 2009; Boyle et al, 2010a, 2010b) and health services in particular (Simon, 2003; Dunston et al, 2009; Hunter, 2009; Glynos and Speed, 2012). Here, the focus of co-production shifts from a primary concern with efficiency towards the empowerment and participation agenda in relation to welfare service provision (Beresford and Croft, 1993; Pithouse and Williamson, 1997; Beresford, 2001, 2002b, 2010) as a means to develop the new economic thinking outlined earlier (New Economics Foundation, 2004a, 2004b, 2008a, 2008c) and to enhance democratic participation (Parker and Heapy, 2006; Pestoff, 2006; Parker, 2007a, 2007b; Prentis, 2007). Thus, efficacy co-production relates to the wider debates outlined in previous chapters. On the one hand, it focuses upon a change in the conception of citizenship and the role of citizens in the delivery of welfare; on the other, it is concerned with activities that may create deliberative spaces and a framework for valuing work outside of the market economy suggested by some of the theories of time outlined in Chapter Three (Reisch, 2001; Fitzpatrick, 2004a, 2004b; Bryson, 2007).

While some of this work conceptualises co-production practice as being 'to engage and involve the beneficiaries of a service in the delivery of the service itself' (New Economics Foundation, 2004a: 5), others have explored the potential role of co-production in developing effective citizen engagement with public services. However, these have not drawn upon the core concepts set out by Cahn (2000), preferring to relate to participation in its own right (Needham, 2003; Parker, 2007a, 2007b). Furthermore, the time bank literature *per se* claims improved outcomes in terms of health and social exclusion (Seyfang and Smith, 2002; Seyfang, 2004a, 2004b; James, 2005) but offers no clear understanding of the specific qualities of time banking that generate such outcomes. While the New Economics Foundation (2008b) have outlined two forms of co-production – 'generic' and 'institutional' – giving an impression of how services could be designed and delivered, the distinction between efficiency and efficacy co-production goes further to suggest that the latter should seek to transform welfare provision, not be an addition to existing practice (Glynos and Speed, 2012).

Global developments

As noted earlier, time banking was initially conceived as 'service credits' (Cahn, 1986), but the story told of how the idea developed has been tied to Cahn's personal history (Cahn, 2000). This section explores the development of 'Time Dollars' in the US before moving on to explore the transfer of the idea to the UK specifically and then outlining some developments in a range of other nations. It is important to highlight here, however, that the discussion relies upon a non-academic, 'grey' literature in places. Sources of information on time banking are predominately non-academic as research into this area is only gradually developing. Often, there is a need to draw upon the evaluations, reports, newsletters and websites of time banks and national organisations alongside the growing academic research. The former must always be treated carefully as they form part of documentation used to advocate for the development of time banking and, as such, contain a greater potential for bias. That said, in an effort to illustrate time bank development, the information from this 'grey' literature drawn upon here is historic, and where evaluative comments are made, these have been drawn out of academic research.

Furthermore, it is unclear how many time banks actually exist. The online directory of time banking[1] lists 452 time banks across the globe,[2] the majority of which were in the US (397), followed by 27 in New Zealand, 15 in Canada and one each in Argentina, Australia, Bermuda, Costa-Rica, Germany, Guadeloupe, Israel, Monaco, the Netherlands, Panama, the Philippines, the UK and Uruguay. There is a problem here, however, if we just take the UK figure of one; in 2008, the New Economics Foundation (2008c) noted that 109 time banks existed, with 48 in development, while the Timebanking UK (TBUK) website states that there are 250 (as of June 2014),[3] 67 of which are in London.[4] Counting time banks is only achieved where they formally register with an organisation. In relation to the online directory, this is a record of those time banks using the specific online exchange software associated with the directory. The UK figure is based upon those organisations registered with TBUK. Among this development, there is a central spine to the activities of time banking that very much rests upon the work of Cahn, despite slight variations within national contexts, which this section sets out.

Time banking in the US

In the narrative offered by Cahn (2000), the idea for time banking came to him during his period of recovery from a heart attack in the 1980s. Phrased in a way that argues against labelling people as 'burdens' or 'useless' because they are unemployed, disabled or old, it is possible to see that these people are able to contribute, in Cahn's (2000: 5) words: 'I realised that a new fight had begun. It was the fight over being declared useless.' Initially established as 'service credits', the focus of activity found its niche in elderly care in the US and this soon became a key motivation behind its development. Cahn's own account discusses the development of these credits and their cautious welcome in the US. Here, US economists argued, was a form of barter as the main organising principle and, as such, it was an inferior form of exchange to that found in the market. Yet, while visiting the London School of Economics (LSE), Cahn (1986) discovered an alternative economic narrative that offered a definition of cost and benefit outside of orthodox economic thinking (Cahn, 2000: 8–9). Through the contributions of the academics assembled at the LSE, Cahn explains, he discovered that 'benefit' could also include personal satisfaction and self-esteem. Furthermore, here, he developed a new argument in favour of service credits associated with money. Now, his core argument was that money contains specific characteristics that produce certain results, but if you change those characteristics, you change the results. From this, Cahn developed the new name, Time Dollars.

There is an important aside to explore here in relation to money. Simmel (1900) suggested that money facilitated the objectification of subjective value, a view later critiqued by Zelizer (1994), who suggested that money reflects social, political, economic and contextual restrictions on its purpose and use. North (2007) argues that CCSs relate to the work of Zelizer, and this is suggested by Gregory (2012a) in relation to time banking (see also Chapter Five). Time credit use is restricted, which, for Cahn (2000: 62–70), reflects a different purpose and character in his exchange system. Money can buy guns, drugs or be used in bribes, and money can be sucked out of a community; the same cannot be said for time credits. Relating back to Cahn's argument about the core economy, time banking seeks to promote a different set of values in human interactions and so cannot use the same symbol of market value. Furthermore, Pacione (1997) suggests that LETS put into practice Dodd's (1994 , cited in Pacione, 1997) argument for a re-evaluation of the role of money in society, and similar claims could be made with regards to time banking. The intention is not to replace the market economy, but to work towards tackling social inequality. The focus is not upon credits to facilitate exchange; rather, they are an additional reward for investing time within the community. The aim is to provide a symbol of the values of the core economy, which, as noted in Chapter One, have been defined in ambiguous ways. Consequently, there is a need to develop a clearer theoretical account of the values of the core economy as an alternative to those of the market, and the associations to be made between time, function and money offer this.

Money developed to facilitate exchange and measure value, reflecting a number of important functions in contemporary society, but also overcame the inefficiencies of barter by generating a form of trust, thus reducing transaction costs (Ingham, 2000). Money generates a focus on quality and monitoring of the supply of money (Ingham, 2000), but the current form of money is specific to contemporary capitalist systems, implying that money may look and act differently under different economic systems (Ingham, 1999). Cahn's time credits are one alternative form of money that looks and acts differently, as do many currencies in the CCS spectrum. Efforts to draw upon the sociology of money and explore the diversification of money, including community currencies (Dodd, 2005; Zelizer, 2005) and paid informal work, demonstrate the inconsistent use of money in relation to market values (Williams and Windebank, 2001a, 2001b). This has led to the suggestion that the analysis of money should consider how its meaning is created, transformed, transported and possessed (Carruthers and Espeland, 1998). In his interview with David Boyle (2000: 11), Cahn explained:

> As I see it, there is a real function of time dollars. It is to provide value in a world where the market economy defines the work which the majority of people do … as useless. All those tasks are work which will never be adequately valued in a market system which must devalue what is common and universal. To give adequate value you just have to step outside the system.

Cahn is not explicit enough in his discussions of the values underpinning time banking as a form of exchange; the argument set out in Chapter Three and explored in more detail in Chapter Five is that the analysis of time banking within the wider theoretical consideration of temporality allows for an explicit account of value to be articulated.

Returning now to the development of time banking in the US, promoting the growth of practice required funding, which was initially received from the Robert Wood Johnson Foundation. This provided resources to fund initiatives in Miami, Boston, New York City, Washington DC, St Louis and San Francisco (Boyle, 2000). In 1985, the states of Missouri and Florida both passed 'service credit' legislation to authorise these programmes and they were made tax exempt by the regional Internal Revenue Service (IRS) office (Cahn, 2000: 7). Elderplan, a health maintenance organisation in the US, was one of the first to develop time banking within its services, which facilitated the growth of the currency. Time credits were used as part payment of premiums in order to ensure that older people remained part of the community through earning time credits. Additionally, a Member-to-Member programme was established to provide home care services to the elderly, which not only sought to overcome the stigma associated with 'claiming welfare' or social care support, but also offered members a chance to contribute in order to earn credits and to feel socially useful and valued. Befriending activities were also facilitated, and have proven to be the staple of much time bank activity across the globe.

Time banking in the UK

While starting in the US, the ideas of time banking soon transferred to the UK. As Gregory (2012c) explains, time bank learning in the UK initially reflected the ideas of emulation found in the comparative literature. Here, a number of fact-finding investigations facilitated the discovery of the initiative and the support of time bank practice in its US form within the UK context (see Boyle, 2000). Thus, in 1998, the first time bank was developed in Gloucester, England, within an organisation called Fair Shares, supported by a national association: TBUK. TBUK focused its efforts on England and Scotland, whereas in Wales, the development of time banking resulted from a partnership between TBUK, Newport University and Valleys Kids (a youth organisation in the Rhondda Cynon Taff valley, South Wales), which established the Welsh Institute of Community Currency (WICC) during 2003. WICC has since divided into two separate organisations:

Timebanking Wales (focused upon developing time banking practice across Wales within the third sector) and SPICE (focused on developing practice with public services across the UK). Since 2010, there has been an increase in organisations claiming to offer time banking, resulting from UK government support for the initiative as part of its efforts to build the 'Big Society' and to reform health and social care (Department of Health, 2010; Cabinet Office, 2011). Consequently, from the early development in the late 1990s until 2014, there are now a number of organisations seeking to promote time bank development, often competing against each other for limited resources.

However, the initial emulation of time bank practice facilitated the replication of exchange practices and the adoption of principles and values outlined by Cahn (2000). This transfer, however, was facilitated by a number of modifications to practice to fit with the UK context. Initially, time banks were established as part of the person-to-person (P2P) model, in line with Cahn's ideas. Yet, the adoption of time banking was gradually modified by practitioners. Consequently, in Wales, time banking practice engaged people with specific organisations/agencies (Gregory, 2012b): referred to as the person-to-agency (P2A) model. Subsequently, different models of time banking have developed, including a third model, Agency-to-Agency (A2A), established to encourage the sharing of resources between public and voluntary agencies (New Economics Foundation, 2008c). This third model seeks to promote exchanges between organisations, so that when organisation 'A' requires the use of a minibus to which organisation 'B' has access, time credits provide a way for the first organisation to access the minibus by providing credits in return that organisation B may use at a later date to access resources that they require but do not possess.

Further differences have developed due to variation in policy contexts. In the US time credits can be used to purchase goods such as refurbished computers; this is not possible in the UK (Cahn, 2000: 128–131). As Seyfang (2006b: 8) stated, a ruling by the Department of Work and Pensions (DWP) considers any time credits used to 'purchase' goods as counting as earned income, which will affect benefits negatively. This is a key difference with LETS in the UK, which have not been granted a disregard by the DWP.[5] Along similar lines, there has been a general concern among UK time bank members that the DWP will perceive participation in time banks as an indication of ability to work, with consequences for benefit entitlement. Should such a view become official government policy, this would be at odds with the potential use of participation in complementary currencies as a route back into employment (Williams et al, 2003; Gregory, 2012a).

Predominately, time banking has been developed within community development settings (Seyfang and Smith, 2002; James, 2005; Gregory, 2009a, 2009b), with particular attention paid to a whole range of related concerns: from the development of reciprocity and altruism, to citizenship, community ownership and local economic development. However, arguments have been made to widen this focus to public service delivery (New Economics Foundation, 2004a, 2004b, 2007, 2008a; Boyle et al, 2006, 2010a; Drakeford and Gregory, 2010a, 2010b). This illustrates the application of time banking to a broad range of social problems rather than just one. Complementary currencies are promoted as one means of addressing the perceived defects of neoliberal capitalism (Seyfang, 2001b, 2004a, 2006a; Richey, 2007; Seyfang and Longhurst, 2013a). However, it is important to note here that for Cahn (2001 emphasis in original), time banking is different from other complementary currencies because:

> Time Dollars are not an attempt to create an *alternative* to market. They are designed to rebuild a fundamentally different economy, the economy of home, family, neighborhood and community. And there is nothing *alternative* about home and family and neighborhood. Home, family and neighborhood are *not* an alternative economy. They are the Core Economy.

As such, the UK development of time banking has focused on the argument presented by Cahn (2000) around co-production. The aim here is to foster the view that citizens are able to contribute to public services and, as such, are not just a bundle of needs that services seek to provide for. Thus, the use of time banking is located within the empowerment and participatory literature seeking to alter the delivery of welfare services to empower service users and enhance service outcomes. While early evaluations have illustrated the potential benefits to citizen self-perceptions of well-being and the use of time banking to tackle social exclusion (Seyfang and Smith, 2002), later research developed a more cautious note about the political interest in the use of time banking, which this book seeks to explore (Glynos and Speed, 2012; Gregory, 2012a, 2013b, 2014). As such, a number of themes highlighted in this brief overview of the UK development of time banking (the use of the mechanism to reform public services and to address a wide number of social problems, and the uncertain ideological intentions behind the development of time banking by governments) can be reflected in global developments of time banking.

Time banking in Europe and beyond

Time banking research is still a developing field, and, as such, there is a very limited amount of research beyond the US and UK. While evaluations of and research into time banking in other countries is currently developing, the following discussion must rely upon the 'grey literature' – that is, literature that has not been through the same scrutiny as academic work, but can still provide an insightful account of the development of policy and practice within local settings. The intention of this section is to draw out a brief overview of the development of time banking in countries where some of this grey material has been produced. Thus, the discussion will start with a focus on Europe (in particular, Greece, Estonia and Finland) before considering developments in non-European countries (New Zealand, Australia, Japan and Senegal). This will not be a comprehensive picture. Earlier in this chapter, it was stated that 452 time banks could be counted using the online exchange monitoring software available to time banks but with a cautionary note that this is not an accurate count – many time banks do not use this software as the cost can be prohibitive. This review demonstrates two key issues in relation to time banking. The first relates to the preceding discussion about the fact that time banking is being used as a means to reform welfare service provision towards co-production and that there is a consequential need to consider the ideological basis of this: self-help as empowerment and change or self-help as a means of maintaining the neoliberal status quo (Gregory, 2013a, 2013b, 2014). The second relates to the development of time banking as part of a wider focus on isolation in contemporary society and the need for policy responses to this social problem (Boyle and Bird, 2014). These two points are not mutually exclusive as, in part, the concern with isolation reflects the view of inclusion through the market outlined by Seabrook in Chapter One, which translates into a wider concern about the effect of neoliberal ideology and practice on social relations – essentially, on the core economy, which time banking is intentionally seeking to support.

The European development of time banking reflects similar issues discussed earlier in relation to the UK. One country where time banking exchange has been exposed to some academic focus is Greece (Sotiropoulou, 2012). Of the community currencies operating in Greece, the Athens Time Exchange (ATX)[6] is one of the oldest. Established in 2006 by a European network of women, individuals within the network are offered time credits to facilitate exchanges in the usual way. However, Sotiropoulou notes one key difference of the

Greek context in comparison with other systems: the time credits have a six-month expiry date. Following the practice of stamp script, discussed earlier, the aim of time-limiting credits is to ensure that the currency is in constant circulation and, as a consequence, that exchanges are frequent and maintained over time. This approach has been adopted to ensure that credits are not accumulated by members as a form of 'savings', but actively used to maintain economic exchanges. Here, therefore, it might be possible to suggest that the Greek model seeks to support economic over social exchanges – although without a more in-depth study of the uses of credits and the underpinning ethos of the currency organisers, this is only speculative.

Yet, this economic focus may be unsurprising considering the impact of the economic crisis on Greece and the severe withdrawal of welfare services experienced since 2008 (Papadopoulos and Roumpakis, 2012). Yet, Sotiropoulou states that ATX provides a collective space for redefining value, reflecting a political-economic effort to create a new discourse for exchange and creating a new material environment for implementing these alternative, non-neoliberal practices. Thus, from reading across the available information, there is a similar tension to Greek time banking as noted in the UK (and discussed in greater detail in Chapters Five and Six): credits can be used in an economic sense to support the market economy but also offer a counter-narrative to neoliberalism, creating a tension between practice and rhetoric. Here, Sotiropoulou offers a familiar argument for CCSs: the currency is tied to locally created rules of transactions and measurements of value.

A similar theme is picked up in a discussion of Estonia's 'Bank of Happiness' (Ahuja, 2009). Although not strictly a time bank, this initiative follows a number of similar efforts to promote the engagement of and social exchanges between isolated citizens but with an added focus on the consequences of austerity resulting from the 2008 economic crash. As Ahuja explains, the economic recession has reduced the availability of money and weakened social cohesion in Estonia. Although it is not clear how social cohesion has weakened, there is a comment on the 7000 people who protested in Vilnius, in Lithuania, to demonstrate 'social unhappiness', with members and organisers of the 'Bank of Happiness' suggesting that their activities keep people busy and socially engaged, thus avoiding such dissent. This bank uses an online system that lists who is engaging in what exchanges and seeks to facilitate exchange in a similar fashion to the time bank online software. Exchanges must take place within the specified code, which determines how different goods/services equate to each other (so there is no clear time link), and there is a paper note representing the currency. Each note is stamped with the word '*Tanutaht*', which means 'Thank you' – this reflects Cahn's own discussion of time banking as offering an additional 'thank you' for volunteering activity.

In Helsinki, Finland, time banking was established in October 2009, initially known as *Kumpula Vaihtupiiri*.[7] By 2010, the Helsinki time bank had 650 members and had spread to 18 different locations. Forming part of the broader Finnish Community exchange system, the exchanges are recorded through an online system, and so it is not clear, as with the discussion of Greece, what role, if any, a time broker will play in facilitating exchange. One key issue to note is that the time banking system has a very clear code of conduct for members known as the '*Tovi Etiquette*' – '*Tovi*' being the term used for time credits. This reiterates the responsibility of members for the exchange agreements that are made and for the actions that are carried out. It lists a long series of suggestions in relation to conduct that members should follow. These include: keeping a clear online record of requests and updating this information when the request has been met; clear guidance on how to arrange and conduct the exchange; and clear guidance on suitable practice post-exchange. There is also a note on the exchange of goods for *Tovis* (knitted items, organic food, etc) and commentary on how these should be traded, but also a note that 'goods' exchanges remain an issue of discussion between members. The *Tovi Etiquette* also highlights how the costs of materials required for an exchange should be paid (in money) by the individual requiring the good/service but that the 'labour' of should be paid in *Tovis* – this reflects a discussion of some practice in relation to local economic development in the UK noted by Gregory (2009b), but this can become problematic. In the UK context, the use of credits in this way may fall foul of the DWP ruling as this starts to reflect exchange found in the mainstream economy and, therefore, as with LETS, may have a tax liability. This is exactly what has happened in Finland, where the government has decided that credits should be taxed. Once again, it is clear from the information available that the economic and social agendas that Cahn (2001) attempts to distinguish are blurred in practice – although personal correspondence with a key worker within the Finnish time bank movement stressed the social economy perspective of time bank development.

The preceding discussion gives some insight into the variation of practice within time banking, but offers less commentary on the development of time banking within those nations as can be found out about the US and UK context. With regards to New Zealand, Australia,

Japan and Senegal, it is possible to find out a little bit more about the development of time banking practices and their development.

For example, Senegal time banking originated with a vocational training centre established in 1995. The aim was to improve the economic freedom of women via the development of basic skills. From the outset, there was very little engagement and participation by women due to continued household duties and also conservative attitudes within the community. Since 2005, however, the use of time banking to engage women has increased the numbers of participants (Shah and Samb, 2011). Time banking proved to be a useful mechanism because credits were not equated to money and so did not generate internal family disputes over resources and the control of money. The expansion of vocational training through time banking has resulted in the establishment of 13 centres, the gradual introduction of men into training schemes and support by religious leaders, who started to support the credit system as members were able to earn credits by completing work for these community figures. However, the review by Shah and Samb does not outline what these figures give back to the community as part of the exchange; rather, this seemed to tie into the previous system of obligation to the religious leader, who would use this to have labour carried out by the community. This might jar with some readers as an antiquated system of obligation and one that does not fully reflect the reciprocity embedded in Cahn's (2000) model of time banking. However, the time banking model adopted in Senegal has delivered a number of benefits, as outlined by Shah and Samb (2011: 1–2):

> As of 2009–2010, nearly 50,000 individuals have completed nutrition, health, and HIVAIDS [sic] awareness training; almost 500 students have completed the day-care program and received a foundation in numeracy, French, and Arabic. The literacy program has graduated 900 students, while nearly 52,000 individuals have received business skills and product development training. For 1,250 graduates of the three-year course in tailoring, the average increase in monthly income has been from $20 per month to $100–$200 per month. Some 500 jobs have been created.

While this discussion provides an account of time banking that focuses upon the social dimension of exchange, it does provide some account of the specific contextual development of time bank practices. This starts to be made more explicit in the discussion of Australian and New Zealander time banking.

With regards to Australia, Smith et al (2013) discuss the broader history of a time bank trial as part of the New South Wales government volunteering initiative. The headline figures illustrate this method of time banking as an online system of exchange with administrative support from the New South Wales office of community and regional volunteering. In total, 7724 hours of volunteering and 4004 members were recorded between 2012 and 2013. The initiative was established in May 2012 with a cabinet endorsement of the New South Wales Volunteering Strategy, and soon after this, time banking was identified as a means of delivering the strategy. This led to a tendering processes and AUD300,000 eventually being made available for the trial. By October 2012, testing of the online software had begun. The evaluation drew on a range of the international literature (again, predominately US and UK) to discuss the potential of time banking, in particular, highlighting the role of time brokers in facilitating time bank growth (Gregory, 2009a), but also suggesting that involvement in time banking would change community perceptions of volunteering. While there is no clear breakdown of the activities exchanged, there is a general list of the type of trades that have taken place (horticultural activities, tutoring, sales and rental, office administration, food preparation, etc), with office and administrative support and horticultural activities forming the majority of trades (the former being significantly higher, at just over 500 trades, compared with the latter, at just under 200). The evaluation is generally supportive of a number of claims found in the literature: time bank participation has benefits for health and well-being, employment, and social capital generation. Yet, as has been noted in relation to health and well-being, there is now a need for a more nuanced account of how participation relates to these perceived benefits by members (Gregory, 2012a).

Similarly, with regards to New Zealand, there is a clearer account of the development of time banking. Here, there is an easily identifiable history of CCS use tied into the development of LETS. Williams (1996: 327) discusses how the government overcame the challenges outlined with regards to taxation and benefits (discussed earlier in relation to the UK and Finland), explaining how, in New Zealand, the:

> Inland Revenue argues that only activity undertaken on green dollar exchanges which is part of one's main occupation should be taxed, whilst the social security authorities have adopted an enlightened view and foreseen

the benefits to the unemployed of allowing them to engage in such activity. Green dollars are not considered as deductible from benefits unless they are regular and sustained.

However, Williams also notes that the ruling was not applied consistently at the local level, leading some potential members to be wary of joining a LETS. The focus of green dollars, however, was community-building and a strong anti-capitalist, pro-environment agenda. This focus has also underpinned the development of time banking in New Zealand, for example, the time bank set up in 2005 by Project Lyttelton.[8] Ozanne (2010) notes how time banking has developed quickly in the area, showing how in the first year, 58 hours were traded, but by 2010, when she was writing, there were 250 individual members and 12 organisational members trading 16,054 hours (an average of 444 hours a month, with an average of 20 traders per month). According to Ozanne, this development is linked to the presence of a paid coordinator from 2006. A national network of coordinators has also established itself in the area, although with no formal body. This was initiated by Skype calls and led to a 'national hui' taking place in order to allow time bank participants to meet up and exchange ideas and practices. This network is now facilitated online and provides a supportive and learning resource for time bank coordinators.[9]

Research into New Zealand time banking supports the claims that time banking fosters social networks, and as Ozanne's (2010) research highlights, this need not be limited to previously socially excluded groups, but can also include more affluent members. There are a number of barriers to the development of time banking that rest upon the limitations of new members' understanding of time bank practices. This, Ozanne suggests, is in the form of a psychological barrier, which may be overcome through the efforts of the time broker:

> Time Bank participants may need assistance in helping to frame their notions of value. For those who do not ask for help, helping them to recognise that by asking for help, you help someone else see that their labour is valued and of value . To fail to ask for help, is to fail to acknowledge the value of other's labour in the community. In addition, members may need to be assured that asking for help is not a sign of vulnerability but a normal part of being human. (Ozanne, 2010: 13)

Such barriers were also noted by Gregory (2012a), who also offered some insight into how time brokers seek to manage relationships with members to overcome these challenges.

However, reflecting a slightly different development, Miller (2008) explains that Japanese time banking has developed in three phases, coinciding with decades: the 1970s, 1980s and 1990s. This instantly demonstrates the development of time bank practices before Cahn's work, and has been associated with changing attitudes towards older people in Japan. These time banks have grown out of the efforts of four organisations (the Volunteer Labour Network [VLN], Nippon Active Life Club, Japanese Care System Association and Sawayaka Welfare Foundation – although the first three have been through name changes over time), which established the nationwide networks that support time bank development. In 1973 in Osaka, a Japanese housewife established the first time bank for the VLN – which Miller states is also the world's first time bank despite the lack of recognition that Teruko Mizushima (the housewife who established the time bank or *taimu banku*) receives for this. The intention behind the time bank was to establish a currency that would help Japanese people survive hardship and personal insecurity, which was an idea derived from Mizushima's experiences during the Second World War. Over the 1950s and 1960s, Mizushima disseminated the idea across Japan that members should give at least two hours volunteer time a month, although active work was restricted to people under the age of 60. The work offered was to be provided in elder person institutions.

According to Miller (2008), this changed in the 1980s and 1990s, when a new form of time banking developed to offer care services in the home rather than an institution. This also incorporated service payments through a mixture of money and hours – although this generated controversy. During this time, the number of time banks being established increased, alongside the growth of organisations that helped develop the nationwide network in the early 1980s, with the combined payment of hours and money being introduced in 1985. This change to include monetary payment was defended on the basis that it would make it easier for volunteers to relate to senior citizens. The development of small groups of women committed to offering services via time banking during this decade coincided with government concerns about population growth and the additional demands being placed on families no longer able to bear caring responsibilities. In 1987, 121 such groups existed, increasing to 452 by 1992 (Kamiyoshihara and Yosikawa, 1996, cited in Miller, 2008). Further changes in the volunteer demographic started to occur in the 1990s as retired men started to enter the volunteer pool – this was to start a change in recruitment to include older citizens and to recognise that men could also be carers, thus challenging traditional norms. Here, the intention was to provide a new sense of purpose in life for retired men, which overlapped with national concerns about maintaining the quality of life during the economic downturn. Thus, by the early 21st century, the key major time banks had developed and attitudes towards older people as active carers and the role of men had started to change – although time bank provision remained focused on meeting the care needs of the older population.

This focus of time banking on elder care gained interest in the UK post-2010 as the Coalition government sought to reform social care (BBC News, 2010; Department of Health, 2010). As noted earlier in relation to the *Giving White Paper* (Cabinet Office, 2011), the intention was to reform services to reflect the idea of the Big Society. The use of time banking became one possible option for this, with significant media attention on the possibility of learning from the Japanese experience. Not only does this overlap with the interest in time banking within health and social care provision already visible in the UK, but it also provided an example of how global developments of the local schemes can influence global learning about practice (see the discussion later). However, despite the government's support for the idea in reforming social care, investigations into the use of time banking to meet the needs of older Japanese citizens suggest that time banking was not as successful as the Coalition government claimed. Rather, the picture presented by Hayashi (2012) shows that the demands to satisfy needs far outweighed the provision offered by time bank systems, thus requiring increased state provision to meet care needs. There is, therefore, a potential mismatch between the government's ideological commitment and the evidence base, which requires a more systematic investigation into both the ability to meet need, the type of engagement offered to members and the health consequences of participation (for a discussion of some of these issues, see Gregory, 2012a).

What this discussion has highlighted is that despite some practice differences resulting from political and policy context, time banking values and ideas have been adopted in a uniform way across the globe. In part, this results from global learning, which has facilitated the growth of time bank practice. Thus, it is important to consider this development before considering how time banking relates to some of the wider themes identified in Chapter Two (changed notions of citizenship in relation to self-help). This discussion needs to draw upon Gregory (2012c) in order to highlight how time banking has never fully been applied to one particular social problem, but has been offered as a solution to multiple problems. This has supported the development of the initiative outside of direct government policy, firmly locating time banking within local, community-level innovations – although these contexts are shaped by political and policy choices that are nationally constructed. What this shows us is that while the time bank movement has been successful in promoting its ideas, there is a growing need for more systematic, comparative research to explore local/national contexts and the global development and transmission of policy to better understand the variability in practice, the shared challenges across national contexts and the practice/policy solutions to address these. In part, this may offer insight into how different political ideologies interact with the idea of time banking (see the final section of this chapter). As a precursor to this future body of work, the following outlines how the time bank movement potentially established an international network that supported policy transfer in order to support and encourage shared learning. As Gregory (2012c: 202) explains:

> ... the international network becomes important, as time banking organisations and interested think-tanks generate the momentum for this local development. Through innovation and evaluation this experimentation and shared learning facilitates time-bank promotion, adopting some characteristics of an epistemic community (Adler and Haas, 1992; Haas, 1992): promoting innovation internationally, developing ideas independent of government and forging a network on a shared core-belief (co-production).

The label of 'epistemic community' does not quite fit with the network of learning that has developed within time banking. Rather, the role of think tanks as agents for sharing learning and fostering development outlined by Stone (1999, 2000) seems to be a better fit in explaining the development of the international network that has facilitated the expansion of time banking. Here, the innovation has taken place between the movement's advocacy organisations and think tanks, which then seek to bring time banking into government policy. Thus, time bank development across the globe shares the universal principles of time banking through mimicry, rather than through synthesis, emulation and inspiration (Stone, 2000). Sharing practice and ideas within the global network allows national organisations to develop new ideas and practices within their national context and then promote the development of time banking as a means of addressing nationally identified social problems to their respective governments.

Conclusion

This chapter has sought to introduce the reader to time banking, outlining the key debates with regards to the core and market economies and the suggestion of the different values practised through time bank activity. The chapter has linked this, as did Cahn, to the idea of co-production and shown that while practice may vary across the globe in terms of time banking, there is a consistency in a commitment to the market–core economy dichotomy and the belief that core economy values must be protected and practised to ensure social cohesion. What the chapter has also illustrated, and central to the discussion in this book, is that time banking is ideologically promiscuous. It fits into a number of different ideological positions, each of which is able to draw upon a different aspect of time bank theory and/or practice to make use of the exchange mechanism in order to achieve political goals. Building on the preceding discussion of alternative narratives, what Chapters Five and Six highlights is that the concept of time demonstrates that time banking cannot be seen as a tool for neoliberal hybrids. The theory and practice of time banking contradicts dominant neoliberal ideas in too many ways for the two to coexist. Thus, as will be discussed in relation to other CCSs, time banking is co-opted into neoliberal thinking and hollowed out of its alternative narrative of social relations and citizenship. The concept of time offers a means of resisting this co-option and offering time banking as a transformative tool for reforming public services – not an addition to existing practice.

Notes

[1] See: www.community.timebanks.org

[2] These figures were accurate on 29 May 2014, when the author went through the directory to count the time banks.

[3] See: http://www.timebanking.org/about/

[4] According to personal communications with Timebanking UK staff.

[5] See: http://www.timebanking.org/?resource=useful-articles

[6] See: http://athenstimeexchange.blogspot.co.uk/

[7] See: http://stadinaikapankki.wordpress.com/in-english/helsinki-timebanks-abc/

[8] See: http://lyttelton.net.nz/timebank

[9] See: http://www.timebank.org.nz/resources

FIVE

Repositioning time bank theory

> LETS [Local Exchange Trading Systems] … and time
> banks, through which people can trade skills and time
> rather than money, are emerging as a significant new form
> of cooperative organisation on a national and international
> scale.… These developments all challenge the 'time is
> money' culture. (Bryson, 2007: 179)

It is now possible to consider the relevance of 'time' as a concept in
policy analysis and debate. In Chapter Two, the argument presented
examined the notion of austerity as part of a neoliberal hybrid in the
UK that, linked to the idea of self-help (part of the 'Big Society'),
provides a narrative for cutting back welfare services. This chapter forms
part of the 'archaeological mode' of the 'utopian method' outlined
by Levitas (2005) – an analysis of contemporary society. A further
element of this was offered in Chapter Three, which outlined the social
theory of time. This provides a critique of the dominance of 'clock
time' in capitalist society and the consequences that this has for social
organisation and the value placed on different activities. Exploring the
arguments of relative time provides a critique of this dominant notion
of clock time that can be drawn upon to find alternative values to those
of the market. In Chapter Four, time banking, its theory and practice
were introduced as the final part of the archeologically mode; however,
as can be seen from the opening quote by Bryson, time banking has
also been presented as an example of practice with non-market values.
As such, it leads to a discussion of the architectural and ontological
modes within the 'utopian method'. Here, the focus of inquiry is to
find alternative ways of organising society and of living our lives.

Yet, as was shown in Chapter Two, the experience of complementary
currency systems (CCSs) has illustrated how these alternative initiatives
can be incorporated into neoliberal theory and practice. Consequently,
this chapter starts with an exploration of time banking in relation to
co-option and the appeal that it holds for those who pursue neoliberal
ideas within various hybrid forms. The discussion then explores the
alternative values of time banking, drawing on the concept of time
to illustrate key distinctions from neoliberal practice. This leads to a

concluding discussion of how time bank theory can be repositioned to offer a more explicit account of the alternative values of the core economy through the concept of time, and how this can form part of a broader policy narrative. To explore these issues, it will be necessary to draw upon interview extracts from the research discussed in Chapter One and reported in full elsewhere (see Gregory, 2012a).

Time as a resource: active citizenship and self-help

The mechanism of time banking, developed by Cahn (2000), is associated with exchange. Consequently, time is a resource that underpins the credits that symbolise time bank exchange and allow members to access services; as such, time credits can be seen to have an 'exchange value'. Yet, this is different from exchange value in the market because one hour is equal to one hour. Other CCSs seek either to reflect an equivalence to currency or, as in the case of local 'pounds' (such as in Brixton and Bristol), to be directly exchangeable with sterling. It is this exchange system that reflects market practices (although not necessarily value) but is essential for time bank operation. The development of time banking rests upon the actions of the time broker to develop and facilitate exchanges between members (Gregory, 2012b), which were identified as the 'technical goals' associated with time bank operation. It is these technical goals that appeal to those who pursue neoliberal ideas, for not only can this be associated with self-help within the broader neoliberal ideology, but it also offers a means of nudging citizens to act in a certain way while monitoring and recording their volunteer activity. Thus, the use of time as a resource in time banking practice allows its co-option into neoliberal thinking, as was illustrated in relation to CCSs in Chapter Two.

The use of time as a resource is not unique to time banking. Ithaca Hours is another form of time currency that seeks to establish parity with money (Boyle, 2000; North, 2010b) to facilitate exchanges with the formal economy. Consequently, hours are transformed into a money equivalent and can come in various denominations, such as one eighth of an hour. Thus, the hour for hour is a distinct factor of time banking within broader 'time money' narratives that reflects a form of exchange that cannot easily be connected to the market economy (Gregory, 2009b). Yet, the credit still generates a useful resource for organisations operating time banks, and for members:

> "But the other thing time banking is, in that case, [it] is a tool for measuring active citizenship in the community,

all the hours they contribute and they don't want credits, that's fine because we don't want to take away that goodness. But I think their hours can be counted, and those people aren't about counting hours, but I'm sure they would like service providers to know what is being invested in their community by local people. Some of the people who might argue with that in the local community, if they're giving a thousand hours a year to a local education project, it would be really, really good if local education providers could see what investment was coming from local people." (Janice, Person-to-Agency [P2A] staff)

This is the first way in which time banking acts as a resource. Here, for time bank staff, it is a counting/monitoring tool to measure participation in order to help in the writing of funding bids to support time bank activities. This cannot be ignored, for it is an important function of the technical goals of time banking to ensure that credits are flowing as an indicator of a successful system. Thus, on the surface, this quantification of time within time banking is parallel to the counting of money in the market economy (Adam, 2004). Yet, note how Janice states that this is 'the other thing' that time banking offers, stating earlier in her interview:

> "I think the purchasing power of the credit is limited, but it is good for self-confidence as they can use it or give it away, so they can be included and not excluded from a residential,[1] for example. But being part of the community and knowing people around them is hard to put a price tag on, it's hard to measure, but it's huge." (Janice, P2A staff)

This is an issue discussed in more detail later; here, it is important to emphasise that while the monitoring of time has benefits, it is not seen as the main value of time exchanges. Continuing with a discussion of time as a resource introduces the way in which members themselves make decisions to participate in time bank activity, providing insight into the way in which members determine the time costs of participating in time banking (Kiser and Percy, 1980; Rich, 1981; Harrison and Singer, 2007). For many of the members, participation is possible because of either retirement or unemployment: "I can slot it in fairly easily as the rest of my life isn't especially rigid, even though I am usually busy with other things, I can usually fit it all in together" (Euan, Person-to-Person – P2P member).

Members fit time banking into their day-to-day lives with some ease. The types of activity that people participate in can impact on members' use of time. For some members, their participation is flexible, allowing them to participate around other demands on their time. For others, their participation takes a more regular form, be it attendance at a weekly tea and chat meeting (where lack of attendance without prior warning can cause concern among other members) to involvement in delivering classes:

> "I have to divide my day so I can work out my commitment to time bank. So I write it all in my diary so I know when I have to be there and when I can't make it. And we all ring each other anyway and ask if we are coming next week." (Poppy, P2P member)

As Poppy is an active member of the community as well as the time bank, she has to tightly manage her scheduling and time allocation decisions. For other members, such decisions are easier because they have fewer demands on their time, for example, due to unemployment/retirement. Such time allocation decisions are also influenced by how members earn time credits: "Well, of course, the website and stuff can be done at home, and the video editing. So I don't have to get out much, unless there are special events" (Harry, P2P member). For others, time bank participation diminished with returns to employment, such as for John, although he sought to continue to participate when he could:

> "At the moment, yeah, particularly at the winter time, with the short days, I can't really do much outdoor stuff for anybody at the moment. So it will improve going forward. So there was the community garden I signed up with before Christmas but we're not in a position to do anything at the moment as we need money to secure the land. In the past, I would have whole weekdays free, but now I don't so I … generally it's Saturdays to be honest, most of the time." (John, P2P member)

While time banking offers a similar time structure and activity as employment, which underpins political support for such initiatives, it is clearly not seen as an alternative to or more important than employment, as found with LETS (North, 2005; Peacock, 2006). Employment is given priority over time bank activities because the time costs of employment offer greater reward than the same amount of time given to time banking. If time banking is to offer an alternative set of values and practices, as Bryson (2007) hopes, there is a need to develop this practice as part of a broader narrative – which is discussed later.

Yet, members' discussions of time banking illustrate differences in their perceptions of their activities – and this may be gendered. John offers gardening services while also participating in the befriending scheme. During his interview, he emphasised how the latter had led to a good friendship with another time bank member, but when asked questions about his activity and participation, he predominantly spoke of gardening activities. This relates to the theory of time, which suggests that there are various uses of time in our daily lives that we view differently (Raybeck, 1992; Darier, 1998; Elsrud, 1998; Kremer-Sadlik and Paugh, 2007). Thus, for John, one is active service provision, the main contribution he makes, while the other is a social engagement that benefits both participants. There is, potentially, a reflection of market practices here as the provision of a service is seen as a contribution that defines his membership to the time bank exchange network. The latter is a social activity and is not given as much significance in his narrative about his participation. However, while there is a need to explore this in more detail, similar patterns can be found in Euan's and Harry's own discussions (see above) of time bank participation: creating and maintaining the website and producing the newsletter. This may also illustrate a difference by gender:

> "Because I am only involved now once a week for two hours. Because I am knitting for them, I can do two or three hours a day because I've got nothing else to do. So when it comes to half past 10 and I have done a bit I can, and I am aching, so I need to sit and put my feet up, but I can't sit still. I have about six things on needles waiting to be done. But it gives me pleasure, a lot of pleasure, and fortunately I have not stopped working. I did the art class and am doing the quilting but that is all. I can do no more. That is enough. I do always do tea and chat and if someone is missing, we ask around if anyone knows if you're alright. So you know to let someone know or you'll get a phone call." (Sara, P2P member)

Despite Sara working on time bank activities at home, an individual, production-based activity, she does not discuss this in the same way as social, group activities. Value is clearly being placed upon the interaction that time banking generates as only this time with others is presented as 'time bank time'. It is important to note that these differences by gender were found in the person-to-person time bank, which was explicitly designed to tackle social isolation and depression. However, the time given is usually perceived as 'spare' time:

> "At first, it was said it [time banking] was only for those out of work and the kids and that. But now everyone is getting involved, now that they are getting that little pound an hour, just for an hour of their time. There is always somebody out there who has a spare hour." (Gwenda, P2A member)

> "It's not just for the kids, it's for the older people as well, if you've got a spare hour come and give us a hand, that's all we're asking." (Mike, P2A member)

First, these extracts suggest that members need to have 'spare' time for time banking, and reflect discussions of time allocation in relation to co-production (Parker, 2007a, 2007b). This time is distinct from employment time (and, we can assume, personal care time) (Robinson and Godbey, 1997; Goodin et al, 2004, 2008). In line with the preceding discussion, therefore, this time is given less priority than other time demands, but where it is seen as having a low cost to members, they will engage with time banking. Second, as illustrated by Gwenda, there is an association of time credits with money. As the member stated, they get a "little pound an hour". While this was not meant in the literal sense, it demonstrates a perceived equivalence between credits and money.

One appeal of time banking to governments, especially at present, when the austerity narrative is promoting cuts in financial provision to welfare services, is in the use of volunteering and credits as a replacement for money:

> "In a way, it could be perceived, yeah, as people do say it's another form of money. But the other side of that is actually it is a form of money, but what we do on a smaller budget, for instance, if we had 15 young people access cheerleading, say they went out the estate, they would have to each pay £3, which for people on this estate is a lot. But here, they don't. In terms of actual money, say we have a £10,000 budget, we could actually get £30–40,000 out of it, from volunteering. Does that make sense? What we manage to

do on a small budget, if we put into real monetary terms, would be a much greater budget, so it's not the same as money. Does that make sense? If we were to price what we do on a small budget and their time, there is not a parity." (Lisa, P2A staff,)

This illustrates a key reason why politicians advocating a narrative of austerity and public sector cuts may find time banking a 'cost-efficient' way of delivering services (Knapp et al, 2010). Yet, such analysis does not support the political goals of time banking: efficacy co-production and the promotion (and protection) of the core economy through activities based on non-market values.

While it is thus possible to treat hours and credits within the time-is-money calculus of the market economy (Adam, 2004), this would overlook the second element of time found within time banking. When discussing what is valued in time banking and its credits, members and staff consistently raised the same themes – time and the person – and these will now be explored. In Chapter Two, it was shown how the debate surrounding CCSs often sees the systems as being co-opted into a neoliberal narrative. For time banking, this possibility rests upon the surface presentation of time exchange discussed earlier. Here, credits facilitate local community activity and provide a reward for those citizens who engage with the initiative. Time banking can therefore be presented within a version of self-help that is integrated into prominent government ideologies to fit with the neoliberal hybrids of the UK (discussed in Chapter Two). To start illustrating this tension and thus discuss the relevance of the concept of time to policy analysis, it is necessary to explore how time banking has been associated with different ideological arguments. It starts with a discussion of the New Labour government (1997–2010) before considering the Coalition government (post-2010). This will demonstrate how the use of time banking to measure active citizenship is promoted within a tokenistic participatory framework attached to co-production (Pemberton and Mason, 2008).

Time banking and New Labour

The New Labour government was presented as a post-ideological, pragmatic, political platform that, it was claimed, bridged the divide between social-democratic and conservative thinking (Blair, 1996; Mandelson and Liddle, 1996; Rawnsley, 2001; Giddens, 2003, 2004). Developing the previous Conservative government's reworking of citizenship to reflect consumerist practices, the New Labour government brought a communitarian strand of thinking into the construction of citizenship, which emphasised self-help (Social Exclusion Unit, 1999). Combined, a specific articulation of citizenship developed, which saw the establishment of a range of community-based initiatives (Foley and Martin, 2000; Powell and Moon, 2001; Alcock, 2004) associated with the ever-increasing prominence of 'active citizenship' (Lawson, 2001; Jochum et al, 2005; Brannan et al, 2006). With regards to time banking, this created favourable conditions for offering the exchange mechanism as a tool of promoting active citizenship (Seyfang, 2003a), thus leading Seyfang and Smith (2002: 52) to suggest that time banking 'is an idea whose time has come'.

Levitas (1998, cited in Seyfang, 2004c) later made links between New Labour's approach to exclusion and time banking. Drawing upon Levitas's typology of social exclusion, she suggested that time banking fitted with the social integrationist discourse (SID) of New Labour, where inclusion and integration of the excluded is achieved through engagement in paid employment. Third Way ideology viewed the state as 'an enabling force, providing – as a right – equality of opportunity, whilst insisting on the individual's responsibility for their own welfare and future' (Blunkett, 1999 , cited in Seyfang, 2004a: 57). Thus, time banking and other CCSs can be viewed as a route back into employment (Williams et al, 2003) as members gain work experience and new skills through participation, but also, potentially, the daily routine and structure associated with employment (Gregory, 2012a). However, this develops alongside a narrow definition of social exclusion that links inclusion with employment, rather than a wider conception that views inclusion through a range of activities, not just employment (Williams et al, 2003). Within the New Labour approach, time banking may have lost sight of the core economy values as surface measurements of active citizenship and its recording of time took precedence as a tool for developing active citizenship.

On the one hand, time banking fitted into the narrative of social inclusion; on the other, it reflected, in practice, New Labour's active citizenship agenda. The focus here is upon the responsibility of individuals and communities to be socially (and individually) responsible for their own needs and behaviour, while also seeking to secure the needs of the least fortunate. Engagement in local, community activity becomes essential to the participation and inclusion in society promoted through government policy, but also a requirement of social rights attached to citizenship. Reflecting wider changes in the construction of needs and citizenship in order to reflect an increased politicisation of needs and a focus on the individual (Langan, 1998), this articulation develops a narrow view of time banking. For some, this reflects the 'dark side' of the exchange process because the currency becomes a useful tool for monitoring transactions – essentially, counting citizen volunteering. For practitioners, however, this is useful when applying for funding as it provides a clear indicator of engagement with local community members. Subsequently, Labour's attention to the ideas of social exclusion and active citizenship created a space in which time banking could be practised to support the policy aims of the Third Way. This established a particular view of the use of time banking that lends support to North's (2006a) quote at the beginning of the chapter: 'time money' is less resistant to neoliberal praxis, and this results from an association with co-production.

In a Cabinet Office paper, Horne and Shirley (2009: 12) discuss the concept of co-production in order to facilitate its use within government policy. They do make an explicit link to Cahn's (2000) core values of co-production but they rephrased the 'redefinition of work' as broader social contributions which are to be encouraged within the citizenry. Here is a subtle shift in language that can have significant consequences to the theory and ideas of time banking. In altering the wording, this value better fits New Labour's promotion of employment first as it does not contain the implicit critique found in Cahn's work on time banking of only seeing work as being important. Rephrasing in this way removes the more radical implications wrapped up in the idea of redefining work and the wider ideological and political agenda associated with this (Gorz, 1999; Bryson, 2007). This offers a critique of capitalist practices, ideas and the related construction of citizenship to argue for increased leisure time and the recognition of other forms of work as being of equal, or more, importance than employment to the maintenance and functioning of society. As argued later, rethinking time bank practice through the concept of time facilitates this alternative narrative (see also the discussion of Bryson in Chapter Three). Rather, New Labour maintained neoliberal market values within its hybrid form and promoted these values in public sector reforms (Jordan, 2010a).

To link back to Chapter Three's discussion of time, this reflects the maintenance of time-is-money thinking, the dominance of the clock at the expense of the alternative expressions of time embedded in time banking (see Chapter Five), which offer an alternative articulation of citizenship and a challenge to neoliberal hybrid ideologies: a challenge to the employment-first discourse around citizenship. As a result of this subtle shift, the core economy is recognised as important and of merit while its values are obscured in order to promote active citizenship within the rights and responsibilities agenda, limiting wider potential for reform. Time banking and co-production become an addition to existing services rather than a catalyst for transformation.

Time banking and the 'Big Society'

As discussed in Chapter Two, the 'Big Society' has influenced Conservative Party thinking since 2008, shaping rhetoric around policy in a range of policy domains (Grice, 2009; Alcock, 2010; Evans, 2011; Grimshaw and Rubery, 2012; Levitas, 2012b; Sloam, 2012). Here, two themes identified with New Labour have been continued: the first is a link to co-production (Ellison, 2011; Lister, 2011); and the second is a continuation of the rights and responsibilities and active citizenship agendas (Lister, 2011). Examining links between the 'Big Society', time banking and co-production permits consideration of the adoption of time banking as an addition rather than transformation of public services (Glynos and Speed, 2012). Time banking has been adopted into a neoliberal hybrid narrative as a form of self-help to forward both New Labour and Coalition government ideological aspirations. Consequently, the values and practices of the core economy associated with the political goals of time banking are removed in favour of the technical goals.

As outlined in Chapter Two, the 'Big Society' thesis has been presented as a key aspect of reform in public services. While a prominent theme in the lead-up to the 2010 general election, it soon faded into the background as the public failed to engage with the concept (Bochel, 2011). Post-2010, the idea has had several relaunches[2] and the idea has been incorporated into the 'localism' branding of government policy, underpinned by the *Giving White Paper* (Cabinet Office, 2011). This White Paper made explicit links to time banking, discussing the initiative as a new form of mutualism that helps to put into practice the self-help ideas embedded in the 'Big Society'. Emphasising community activism and the local control of services, this is firmly embedded in similar rights/responsibilities and active citizenship rhetoric as found with New Labour. Consequently, time banking remains as a form of self-help associated with Burns and Taylor's (1998) 'solution' role. Preceding the Big Society narrative, when the Conservative Party were still in opposition, one of their ex-leaders, Iain Duncan Smith, established a research think tank that examined a range of social problems within society, which argued that the UK's most disadvantaged communities contained people whose lives were blighted by social breakdown and poverty. This breakdown was linked to five pathways to poverty – family breakdown, educational failure, economic dependency and worklessness, addition to drugs and alcohol, and severe personal debt – each able to cause poverty but in combination creating a 'perfect storm'. Protecting people from these paths into poverty required government policy that supported five core necessities: strong and stable families; inspiring education; a welfare system that rewards work, not benefits; effective drug and alcohol prevention, enforcement and treatment; and efforts to prevent unmanageable levels of personal debt (Centre for Social Justice, 2006).

The 'Big Society', in part, developed as one solution to these problems. It was argued that to respond to this breakdown, there was a need to: decentralise responsibility and power to individuals, communities and civic institutions; reduce bureaucracy; influence behaviour, not issue commands; and design smart incentives rather than imposing blunt regulation. Upon this foundation, the 'Big Society' developed as the policy response as utilising time banking as a form of self-help offers a 'solution': time bank exchanges offer new opportunities for social interaction, create a sense of control over personal and community circumstances in order to prevent dependency upon the state, and generate new networks and resources in order to foster community and individual resilience (see Chapter Six). However, this seems to pay little attention to how these disadvantaged communities will lack the skills and resources necessary to facilitate this form of community activity, which can often be found in abundance in more privileged communities.

A range of research supports the use of time banking to provide a self-help solution to a range of social problems (Seyfang and Smith, 2002; Collom, 2008; Warne and Lawrence, 2009; Ozanne, 2010; Shah and Samb, 2011; Hayashi, 2012; Madaleno, 2012; Smith et al, 2013), although with some mixed success. What remains present under the surface discussion of new resources and networks is the use of time banking as a measure of citizen volunteering, but also as offering incentives to act in certain, state-approved, ways. The measurement of exchange through credits allows time banking to development without efficacy co-production in relation to local services. The dominance of technical goals offers a tool for the accounting of active citizenship for monitoring and surveillance purposes, but pays scant attention to the unequal distribution of resources and skills across communities. For both New Labour and the Coalition, time banking was never really about promoting the core economy; rather, it was an addition to the mechanisms that serve the purposes of the market economy and help to discipline citizens (both the work ethic and fostering moral behaviour within communal life). Such uses may reflect a form of co-production as compliance (Alford, 2002) and link with the nudge-style behavioural economics found in the Coalition government's thinking (Cabinet Office, 2010). This nudge approach, as discussed in Chapter Two, only ever presents the illusion of choice as the choices you can make have been constructed to meet a predetermined objective. In a similar way, time bank development has brought citizens into 'invited spaces' (Cornwall, 2008) where the terms of participation are predetermined by the service providers and the credits are used as an additional incentive for (accepted forms of) participation. Resulting from this position of time banking as a form of self-help, some wider implications of the alternative values to be found in time bank practice are lost. Rather, it becomes an acceptable tool for promoting the responsibilities of active citizens, as articulated by the neoliberal hybrid ideologies that have been dominant within the UK since the mid-1990s. Cahn's (2000) implicit argument that non-work activities are worthy and that the core economy has its own values is lost. Yet, before looking into some alternative articulations of this (see Chapters Five and Six), there is some scope within ideological debates for building an alternative interpretation of time bank activities that starts to challenge the dominance of neoliberal values in public service provision.

Articulating non-market values

Chapter Three drew upon a broader theoretical analysis of time to illustrate a critique of the dominant notion of clock time in contemporary society and the way in which this generates a time-is-money narrative, dominant in social and economic relations. The 'utopian method' requires that we offer a critique of contemporary society, and for this to be achieved, the social theory of time has provided the critical lens to be applied. As such, the application of this framework has illustrated how time banking can be perceived as a measurement of duration that uses time as a means of exchange. Combined, this allows the use of time banking as an 'additive' to existing practice, rather than a transformation of service provision along non-market values (Glynos and Speed, 2012). Thus, in this section, the intention is to illustrate how time is a relevant concept for uncovering the non-market values of the core economy (Cahn, 2000) as the initial step of reframing time bank theory so that these alternative values are more clearly articulated and inform policy change.

Challenging time-is-money: credits

As previously discussed briefly in Chapter Four, money performs a number of functions in society. While for Simmel (1900), it is seen to engender a disengagement from reciprocal relations, for Zelizer (1994), money is embedded in psychological, social and cultural meanings. As noted, the sociological theory of money does not fully explore the diversification of money (Dodd, 2005; Zelizer, 2005), let alone paid informal activities (Williams, 2008; Williams and Windebank, 2001a, 2001b), which illustrate uses of money that do not fit with market practice. Here, we see the surface distinction between money and alternative currency becoming blurred. Members tend to see an intrinsic 'purchasing power' element to time credits, but often associated this with others' motivations for being involved in exchange:

> "The only way I can describe it is that I don't basically do it to get the time credits, I do it because I love doing what I do, love being out and love keeping this place ticking over. But with the time banking, for some people I suppose, it could be an incentive kind of thing: 'Come do an hour's work, get a time credit and save them up for a trip, especially for the kids'." (Pauline, P2A member)

Pauline offers a slightly blurred distinction between time credits and money. She is somewhat accepting of the similarity between the two (they both represent a form of purchasing power), yet she recognises that there are differences, although uncertainty existed in explaining these. Such uncertainty may reflect a challenge in promoting time bank activity as an alternative to the market. Articulating a distinction between time credits and money relies upon emphasising the restricted purchasing power of time banking in that members can access only what other time bank members offer and highlighting the purpose of credits as a recognition of the contribution people make, as Cahn (2000) has consistently argued. The data presented here offer some support for the perceived use value of time existing simultaneously with the treatment of time as a measure and means of monitoring activity. Members experience both. On the one hand, time acts as a 'gift' (Mauss, 1950) and fosters reciprocity, but, on the other, the use of credits establishes this within 'generalized exchange' (Alford, 2002); thus, the return of the 'gift' need not be to the gift giver, it can go to another member, the wider community or even be transferred to another, thus it does not work like monetary exchange. Additionally, members can gift credits to each other:

> "Well, I go on trips and I had enough last time to pay for my partner. I checked with [the time broker] first and she said that was fine." (Gwenda, P2A member)

> "And if one hasn't got credit, I have credit and I give some to my friend, I just say 'Have my credit', they can have my credit for that. We share, so to speak." (Poppy, P2P member)

This is an aspect of time bank practice that, due to the credit mechanism, reflects some of the characteristics of money to a lesser extent. Transfer is the focus here because it facilitates a move away from how time banking operates but may still reflect notions of gift giving more generally (Mauss, 1950). As such, it is not just the notion of co-production that might allow time banking to be co-opted (North, 2006a); as with other CCSs, there is sufficient similarity to how money is used for practices to be used to achieve other political goals.

These political goals have no association with money; rather, they illustrate the 'use value' of time credits. It is not what the credit can purchase that has the biggest effect on members' self-perceptions regarding their involvement; rather, it is how their use of time influences how they feel about themselves. Here, we draw extensively on a series of interview extracts to illustrate this point:

> **Pauline (P2A member):** "I've got to be honest, I take a lot of pride in some of the things I do, it makes me feel like I belong in the community then, that I have got a purpose here and, I mean, it has made a lot of difference to my life."

> *Interviewer:* "In what ways?"

> **Pauline (P2A member):** "A lot more confidence to do things. Sort of like a lot of the girls in the depression group now still ask others to do things because they are not confident, but I try and put it back on them so they get the confidence that is lacking....
> Between everything I do, I tend to, I think, now, I have a lot of pride in what I do and am proud of what I've achieved in the few years, and it's all down to Communities First."

"But it also makes you feel worthwhile because, again, when you retire, what's the question we ask each other 'What do you do for a living', when you're retired, you're nothing. That's the way I feel. I feel cheated, that I had to stop work so early, I feel cheated because of my illness, and I feel cheated that I'm no longer seen as a member of society, in my mind....

So we are all learning little things, and we are getting our pride back. We are doing something and being recognised, and you do feel a bit smug sometimes, you think 'Oh, that person thinks that what I did was rather nice'." (John, P2P member)

"Yeah, I think it kept me; it made me more confident ... in meeting people and more confident in my skills. It allowed me to develop my skills, any skills, even picking up the phone, or meeting people, or helping out. You're literally, not only do you have the impact of having whatever condition you have, but you also have the impact of low self-worth, so although the time bank is not like a voluntary job, you can still build that up, which is really important." (Meera, P2P member)

Interviewer: "So people can be recognised for their contribution?"

Euan (P2P member): "Yes, that's the whole point really isn't it? You've earned. You go home and think 'That was a good day today'."

While for Euan, there is a perception of 'having earned', this was associated with the recognition of contributing in some way to the community. In giving time to the community in this way, members experience a change in their sense of individual and collective achievement and realise that they have a purpose not associated with employment. Here, we find support for those who argue for the need to recognise the importance of time outside of work and the vital contributions that individuals can make to wider society. Time bank participation reflects a specific use of time and this has a greater impact on member participation and engagement than the 'exchange value' of credits. Members rarely spoke of how they use credits. Even when promoted, they would quickly deliver a list of activities they were involved in. However, ask them about how they earn credits and the reasons behind their participation and members enter into much more enthusiastic conversation about why they are involved and the range of activities they participate in. The argument suggests that time bank participation may provide renewed status, social purpose and self-confidence, diminishing member experiences of depression and isolation, and that this relates to an experience of time that does not fit into the time-is-money narrative. Rather, it is about how time is valued by members.

Time valued

Chapter Three illustrated how time is not just external duration, but also internal, qualitative experience (Leccardi, 1996; Gunning, 1997a; Zuccharmaglio and Talamo, 2000; Oechsle and Geissler, 2003; Brannen, 2005; Kremer-Sadlik and Paugh, 2007; Bouffartigue, 2010). Reflecting upon participants' activities and lives with a 'temporal lens' (Adam et al, 2008; McLeod and Thomson, 2009; Henwood and Coltart, 2012; Henwood and Shirani, 2012; Hughes and Emmel, 2012) allows us to explore the meaning and value of time within participants' time bank activity, exposing the multiple times they experience (Adam et al, 2008). Interviews exposed how time is perceived as both a measure and resource, but also lived experience, breaking down the dualistic thinking associated with time and illustrating how we can rarely hold on to both relative and absolute concepts of time simultaneously (Adam, 1990). The preceding discussion starts to explore how time bank members experience time use within exchanges and starts to make explicit some of the assumptions embedded in Cahn's (2000) core economy.

Thus, looking beneath the surface of time bank activity, beyond the measurement of time exchange, uncovers a view of time as holding meaning and significance beyond credit purchasing power, linking with the political goals of time banking:

> "The person. Time. It values the person's time. It's not about pound for pound, it's not about a person's experience or physical worth, it values their personal time. If someone gives you an hour of their time, which is a precious commodity, to their community, or someone in their community, there is a massive difference they can make. It values people's time commitment." (Gwenda, P2A member)

"It's the time the children actually spend volunteering in the community, I mean they get something back for what they do. It's not money or anything like that, but the amount of things they actually do, it means they can go and do what they want, whether its swimming or if one of the trips come up, so it values the time spent doing these things." (Mike, P2A member)

Through exchange and activity, time bank members realise that the credit recognises the contribution that they make, but also allows members to use this time, which has meaning to them. It is the use of time and the value attached to that use that remains the dominant focus of activity, not the 'monetary' value of the credit. This builds on Blanc's (2008: 8, cited in Zelizer, 2005: 558) suggestion that 'a deep, comprehensive analysis of money [requires] looking closely at what persons and organizations actually do with it: we must study money not simply as prescribed by law but as people live it'. Thus, understanding how people engage and use time credits is an essential prerequisite for exploring time bank activity and examining the perceived value of the credits by those who use them, for it is members' perceived valued of the credits that dictates how they are used. As we saw earlier, the focus of discussion tends to be dominated by an account of how members earn credits and the recognition they receive from this activity. This is important because North's (2006a) critique of time banking as being less radical can start to be refuted here. As one member stated in their interview, unprompted by the interviewer:

Harry (P2P member): "Well, with LETS, your contribution is weighted according to its worth, so it's less equal. Whereas with the time bank, it's not just on an hourly basis, but whatever contribution you make, which is more equal. So, some menial task is as equal as something much more intellectual."

Interviewer: "Because in LETS, activity can be determined in the same way as the market in terms of value?"

Harry (P2P member): "Yes. And I also see the time bank as giving protection against the money worlds and that's how I would justify it having employees. They are there to protect us from the money world. So, with [staff member], he's usually fund-raising, organising coaches and things like that where money has to be paid out. Whereas we don't have to get involved with all that."

Interviewer: "So you get to focus on the other side of things, I suppose?"

Harry (P2P member): "Yes. And, of course, the idea of people helping each other."

Harry distinguishes between LETS and time banking to illustrate how the latter offers a different basis for valuing activities. For him, time banking value relates to member contributions and the use value of the credits in facilitating member engagement in activities that would otherwise be denied to them (the focus on use value has been advocated in relation to CCSs by others; see Pacione, 1997; Bryson, 2007). This focus on people and their use of time reflects the preceding discussion of worth and can be seen in the following:

"It's the people. Put the people at the heart of things, and that's where it really changes, but that is also what makes it so hard as you're not just running, you know, a job club, a walking group, you are trying to find out what the people want, need and putting it on. That's the real art of making it work because sometimes what people want you can't afford, you can't arrange, you don't have the available time." (Richard, P2P member)

"Time bank wants everyone to be recognised for their own personal worth, and we have a code of conduct, everyone is equal.... They [credits] value our personal strengths, what we give each other, what we give to them." (Sara, P2P member)

"What it values is the capacity that people have to be active. It recognises that they have skills and knowledge and time. And, in fact, I think it values good will, but, generally speaking, if you have a warm environment where people are trusting and respected, they will give more. I think that it values that given the right conditions, you can do all sorts of stuff." (Lynne, P2P staff)

Lynne's interview extract broadens the discussion by calling attention to the specific qualities of people that are valued: skills, knowledge and time. This argument takes a different form for staff members in the person-to-agency time bank: "I think it's commitment and, ummm, yeah, benefits the community … benefit to the community basically. That's what it's all about; we're not doing it for anything else. We're benefiting the community but getting the reward to do it" (Bethan, P2A staff).

Consequently, two distinct narratives of value have been articulated here. The first, found predominately in the person-to-person time bank, places value on what individuals offer to each other, while the person-to-agency model draws attention to time given to the communities. Time remains at the core of both, and so while on the surface of activity, time is a commodity, the basis of exchange, it is not treated as such by those involved in the exchange. Earlier, a quote from Bethan discussing the monitoring and recording benefits of time banking stated that this was the 'other thing' that time banking does, suggesting that something else was the primary purpose of activity. Value is embedded in the task and activity itself, not in the mechanism of exchange. This starts to separate time within time banking from the time-is-money framework of the market economy.

Time as task and process

The fundamental core of time banking exchange is that an hour equals an hour. This is part of the radicalism of time banking that North (2006a) seems to have overlooked in his dismissal of the radicalism of time banking associated with co-production. Activity measured in this way breaks away from the link between speed, production and profit that underpins market economics. Combined with Cahn's (2000) core value of redefining work, creating a space for articulating non-employment-focused activity as a primary aspect of citizenship, a subtle shift towards 'task time' (Thompson, 1967) is present in time bank theory, although this is more difficult to clearly establish. To illustrate this, we can explore the activity of one member, Sara, as an example of the task orientation within time bank practice. Prior to the interview, the field notes record how Sara arrived at the office and struck up a conversation with a member of the time bank's Board of Trustees, who happened to be in the office. The Board Member complimented Sara on her hat, saying that she would like one for herself. Sara instantly offered to knit her one, adding that it would take a while. Later, during the interview, Sara explained:

> "Because I am knitting for them, I can do two or three hours a day because I've got nothing else to do. So when it comes to half past 10 and I have done a bit I can, and I am aching, so I need to sit and put my feet up, but I can't sit still. I have about six things on needles waiting to be done." (Sara, P2P member)

This illustrates how there is no urgency behind production; rather, the time taken must reflect a job well done – it will take as long as is required. This is the essence of 'task time' (Thompson, 1967; Southerton, 2003; Westenholz, 2006), where pre-capitalist production was linked to the time required to produce a high-quality product, rather than a high amount of profit. As Gregory (2014: 177) explains of Thompson's argument around task time:

> Different work situations have different notions of time and work-rhythms, so that time is task-orientated. Time to complete an activity is not fixed; it fluctuates depending on a range of different contextual circumstances. Further demonstrating the difference, Thompson lists three key points in relation to task time: 1) it is more humanly comprehensible than timed labour for the labourer works upon an observed necessity; 2) it shows least demarcation between 'work' and 'life': social intercourse and work are intermingled and so there is no conflict between labour and 'passing time'; 3) it appears wasteful to those accustomed to labour timed by the clock.

Sara is only able to knit for a few hours a day, and is working on several items at once. She was under no pressure to complete the knitting within a set time. Consequently, time bank activity exhibits a different connection between speed and production, illustrating how time is not used to increase the speed of production in order to generate profit. Rather, production is at a slower pace in order to fit with the wider contextual factors in which members exist and live their daily lives.

An alternative source of analysis can be drawn out of Davies's (1994) account of 'process time'. Task-oriented time retains a focus on the activity at hand, whereas the notion of process time illustrates that:

> [c]onsciousness and agency, on the part of the carer, are not primarily influenced by a 'technical-limited rationality' ... where instrumentality and economic motives are primary

determinants ... but rather by the capacity to take the needs and reality of the care-receiver into account. (Davies, 1994: 279)

When carrying out care activities, we cannot specify how much time is spent reflecting/considering/conducting care or when care work will be complete. Time is part of many abstract processes and so, as a concept, 'process time' must be embedded in the multiple times, timings and temporalities of the wider context of the carer and care-receiver. Additionally, and fitting into Cahn's (2000) narrative of 'love and caring', Davies (1994: 289) claims that:

> [g]iving love, security and satisfying emotional need ... are woven into the actual daily fabric of things. They are seldom separate, self-contained activities and with their linkage to process times, it can be hard to pinpoint exactly when they take place or see a direct result.

Thus, while it is difficult to measure the time demand of care activities, and, as such, it may not fit easily with the measured activity of time banking, both 'task time' and 'process time' require consideration of the broader contextual factors (and times) in which the task/care work take place. Multiple times are woven together and experienced simultaneously.

What this discussion illustrates is that not only does an account of time banking need to make explicit the different way in which members experience and perceive the value in comparison to time within the market economy, but it also brings to the forefront a different narrative of time and value. Noted, since Chapter Three, has been the dominance of the time–is–money calculation associated with the clock in contemporary society. In the market economy, time has an exchange value that reflects how X amount of A is equal to Y amount of B. On the surface of activity, time banking illustrates a similar form of exchange, but, here, each hour of A is equal to the same number of hours of B. This does not fit with the practices of the market economy. Underneath this, however, rests the use value of time, which refers to the benefits found in a commodity during its consumption. Here rests the essential value of time within time banking, for the credit by itself is of limited value. Rather, it is in (primarily) earning credits, but also their consumption, that members experience changing perceptions of self and recognise the contribution that others can make. This is underpinned by different experiences of time and production so that speed is not essential: there is no profit motive behind activities. Rather, activity advances the 'task' and 'process' concepts of time, which reflect non-market practices and explanations of human interaction. This is the foundation upon which an alternative narrative of time banking can be developed that seeks to challenge the dominance of neoliberal ideas within social organisation and social policy.

Repositioning time bank theory

As was discussed in Chapter Two, CCSs have formed part of a wider history of initiatives that offer alternative production and exchange practices to mainstream capitalism, but rarely have any had significant impact in challenging capitalism (Peacock, 2006; North, 2007). While likely to be tied to the resilience of local economies and communities (North, 2010b), they have been presented as part of a 'utopian' narrative of how to break away from neoliberal economics and the dominance of neoliberal ideas in contemporary society (Leyshon and Lee, 2003; Bryson, 2007; North, 2010a). Time banking has a place in this history and narrative. Furthermore, as the preceding discussion has indicated, the way in which time is treated as more than a medium of exchange and a measure of duration opens up 'radical' possibilities not offered by other CCSs that seek to match exchange mechanisms with those of the market. This is because time banking remains, predominately, a social rather than economic intervention. In fact, earlier discussions of community currencies have argued that value and exchange based on time foster self-determined activities by individuals (and communities) rather than an alternative to formal employment (Bowring, 1998). Subsequently, the challenge becomes one of articulating non-market values in a world dominated by the theories and practices of neoliberal economics.

This section seeks to move debate forward by starting to reposition time bank theory in order to make explicit the different value attached to time and to explore the ways in which this narrative around the 'use value' of time can be articulated. To guide this discussion, attention will again be drawn to the various stages of the 'utopian method'. An examination of the 'archaeological' will revisit the challenge posed by neoliberalism, but also the hindrances to the articulation of alternatives found in time bank practice. The discussion then moves on to explore the 'architectural' and 'ontological' – here, exploring existing political narratives that offer a means for rearticulating notions of 'self-help' in order to present time banking in a 'transformative' rather than 'additive' sense. Building on this, the final section explores some potential links between these alternative narratives, time and time bank member activity before returning to the concept of 'function' as a term to draw upon in articulating the discussion of alternative values of time in public discourse.

The archaeology – the neoliberal challenge

For time banking to promote core economy values and challenge the dominance of market values being applied to solutions to social problems, there is a need to forge links to existing efforts to articulate alternatives and examine the arguments for the need to challenge dominant neoliberal ideas. Essentially, there are three key challenges to reflect upon: first, the perceived relationship between the core and market economies, as outlined by Cahn (2000); second, the challenge posed by the concept of austerity in the wake of the 2008 financial crisis; and, finally, as Chapter Three illustrates, the dominance of clock time and the consequences that this has for social organisation.

The first challenge offered to the repositioning of time bank theory as a critique of the dominance of neoliberal ideas in society is found within the explanations of how time banking operates. The Cahn and Rowe (1992: 163) quote in Chapter One demonstrates the first challenge presented by time bank theorists themselves to the articulation of alternatives:

> The Time Dollar ... does not fit the standard groove. It has elements that appeal to the Right, elements that appeal to the Left; and overall, it's an idea that lies in a frontal zone that is unclaimed by either side.

Here, there is an explicit effort to present time banking as apolitical. It is not seeking to intercede in political divides and come down in favour of one ideology over another. Rather, it is seeking to appeal to all and, as such, potentially renders itself neutral within the broader debate about the consequences of neoliberal capitalism on society. Yet, Cahn's (2000) account of time banking is highly critical of the dominance of market values, for he sees these as damaging the core economy. In Cahn's (2000: 54) account, the core economy is the 'operating system' of society, but 'the present operating system – family, neighbourhood, community – is in bad shape'. Although he claims that there is no name for the 'virus' that has infected this system, others would quickly point to the dominant neoliberal ideas and practices that have filtered through social relations (Jordan, 2004). In fact, Cahn offers a rather conflicting account because he claims that the core economy must be of primary importance and is the source of change in society; he goes so far as to suggest that the core economy underpins the working of the market economy (Cahn, 2000: 39–58). Yet, his clear distinction between the two economies is presented with clear claims that the two are linked and complementary and is explicit in his suggestion that market values cannot be applied to the core economy – implicitly stating, therefore, that core economy values cannot be applied to the market. They may support each other, but the analytical boundaries Cahn develops provide no space for a narrative about which set of values should direct overall human endeavour. Rather, when discussing issues related to the family, community and democracy, the core economy values rule; for everything else, market values guide action. This seems a simplistic division to make, for despite his suggestion that actions in each market should be guided by the values of that market, he fails to fully comprehend the ways in which neoliberal values have permeated across a range of institutions and social relations (Clarke, 2004; Jordan, 2004, 2010a). Furthermore, this analytical distinction does not allow for non-market values to guide human endeavours in the same way as Tawney's (1921) concept of 'function'. As such, Cahn has positioned the core economy not as a challenge to neoliberal theory or as the primary source of value in society, but as the foundation of a functioning market. The implicit undertone here is that the market retains supremacy and the family, democracy and community should work in a way that supports market activity.

The second challenge rests within the notion of austerity. The financial crisis of 2008 has prompted government policy that seeks to cut back state provision while articulating a need for greater civil society engagement, which overlaps with a promotion of self-help schemes to reduce demands on public spending. Here, self-help is presented as a 'solution' (Burns and Taylor, 1998) for facilitating local resilience and coping because citizens engage with each other outside of the state to provide for their needs. This approach has been supported by efforts to pathologise social problems so that their cause is located within individual behaviours rather than broader, structural arrangements of society. Goodin (1985: 42) suggests that this:

> … does nothing to prevent vulnerability and dependency. Quite the contrary, it exacerbates the worst kind of dependency. Neither does this doctrine do anything to protect those who are vulnerable and dependent. Rather, it

insists that those most in need rely upon those who generally have fewest resources to help them.

Despite this, the increased influence of the ideas of risk and responsibilisation underpin government policy to promote active citizens, who take on a greater role in providing for their own needs. Wider analysis of the financial crisis, however, indicates that it is not the public sector that is at 'fault'; rather, this is how the crisis has been presented (Grimshaw and Rubery, 2012), consequently overlooking the faults with the financial system and transforming the narrative into a fiscal crisis (Gough, 2011). Furthermore, there is a growing critique of the dominance of productivist thinking and the dominance of capitalist over non-capitalist values, which has been revisited post-2008 to argue that the combined effects of an economic and environmental crisis suggest a need to rethink economic and social relations (Offe, 1992; Douthwaite, 1996; O'Connor, 1998; Dordoy and Mellor, 2000; New Economics Foundation, 2008d).

Despite sustained criticism, neoliberal hybrids have consistently argued for a rethinking of the state–citizen relationship so that citizens act more like consumers of services and, as such, take increased responsibility for satisfying their needs for solving the social problems that they experience. This narrative influences public attitudes towards welfare, mapped in the UK by changing welfare attitudes, which show: a decreasing percentage of the UK population supporting state spending on welfare for the unemployed; an increase in the view that less generous benefits will make individuals stand on their 'own two feet'; and an increase in the numbers who feel that benefits are too high. These changing attitudes reflect an increased belief that individuals are responsible for their lot in life, and for changing their situation. The neoliberal view of social problems and self-help have come to dominate and, as such, a challenge to these ideas needs to be presented in a language that not only provides a convincing argument to the public, but also cannot be co-opted into neoliberal practice. It is not clear that time banking can offer this narrative.

The third challenge posed by neoliberal thinking relates to time. As noted in Chapter Three, the dominance of clock time has been critiqued by a number of social theorists. Of relevance to the discussion here is the work of Bryson (2007: 2), who paid particular attention to inequalities in time, arguing that:

> [i]nequalities in the way that time is used and valued are therefore part of a vicious circle that leaves many women

economically dependent and vulnerable to exploitation and domestic abuse, whilst lack of free time makes it difficult for women to gain a political voice and express time-related expenses and needs.

Pascall (2012) offers a similar critique of the time demands on different genders. Here, specific attention is paid to the need to challenge the dominant time values in capitalist society and to critique the normative assumptions attached to citizenship that are generated by the motives of profit and accumulation. Bryson (2007) has suggested that time banking is an example of alternative practices that emphasise the importance of caring responsibilities over those of paid work – overlapping with Cahn's (2000) argument for redefining work. For Bryson, challenging this work-first attitude and the influence that this has on citizenship requires recognising the value of different activities, the time demands associated with these and the consequential need to challenge the inequalities in time use between genders.

As such, Bryson (2007) argues for a reordering of social structures though welfare state reforms ensuring that care activities are given greater prominence. Yet, as we saw in relation to the work of Gibson-Graham (1993, 1996), this hegemonic dominance is not easy to undermine, especially if, as argued earlier, time banking is open to co-option into neoliberal articulations of self-help. Seeking to promote the 'use value' of time will require drawing on wider debates regarding social policy and time (Fitzpatrick, 2004a, 2004b; Goodin, 2010). Isolated from this wider thinking, it is possible to suggest that Bryson overestimates the potential of time banking and LETS to offer alternative narratives to neoliberalism because they are hindered by co-option. As will be explored later, efforts to link her analysis with wider theories around relational time (Fitzpatrick, 2004b) may offer a broader narrative for articulating change. The development of such a narrative, and therefore the challenge to dominant neoliberal ideas, can be found in alternative definitions of self-help found outside of the neoliberal hybrids of New Labour and the Coalition government.

Architecture and ontology – alternative self-help narratives

Developing alternative narratives to inform the reconstruction of society through welfare reforms must be aware of the challenges outlined earlier. It is then possible to locate a source for articulating welfare reform, but this will need careful consideration. As will be shown in the discussion of the work of Ward (1996) and the ideas of 'Blue Labour', there is a need to separate out self-help from the state. Yet, the discussion of the devolved Labour government in Wales illustrates how the state may play a role in facilitating self-help initiatives. Consequently, there are a number of entangled issues here that cannot be easily separated out in the discussion that follows and will need careful thinking through in future. The aim here is to outline three potential sources within political discourse for articulating an alternative self-help narrative.

The first of these alternatives can be associated with a discussion of LETS within Ward's (1996: 17) suggestion of an anarchist response to social policy, critiquing the Fabian tradition:

> We stifled the localist and voluntarist approach in favour of conquest of the power of the state. We took the wrong road to welfare…. As the official welfare edifice, patiently built up by the Fabians and Beveridge, becomes merely the safety-net for the poor who can't afford anything better, the likeliest slow renewal of the self-help and mutual aid principle seems to me to emerge from the new so-called underclass of those people rejected by the economy in alliance with those déclassé people who just can't stomach current economic and social values. I am thinking of marginal activities like food co-ops, credit unions, tenant self-management, and LETS.

Here, Ward is offering a critique of state welfare to suggest that alternative forms of self-help may provide greater benefit to addressing social needs, but it requires accepting local variation: a break with universalism. This is a debate that has actually found its way into recent political debates about localism. Here, there are efforts to counter the criticism of local initiatives as generating a 'postcode lottery', traditionally seen as something to avoid in service provision, preferring instead to ensure that all citizens have equal access to services and equal outcomes. Rather, the developing argument is that localism requires postcode lotteries; this is something that politicians need to become accustomed to if the local variations result from decisions at the local level by empowered citizens.[3] However, there is some evidence which suggests that the public remain in favour of the equity argument over postcode lotteries.[4] Either way, the key point to highlight here is that there is a conceptualisation of self-help that does not fit within the neoliberal paradigm. As Ward (cited in Wilbert and White, 2011: 109) argued, 'whenever someone on a public platform eulogizes self-help and mutual aid, half the audience stop listening since they regard these words not merely as Conservative platitudes but as a smokescreen to conceal the abdication of governmental responsibilities'. For Ward, self-help and mutual activity was a dominant characteristic of working-class identity, which has been replaced in favour of central state policy. Consequently, self-help needs to be isolated from the state and seen as activity fostered at the local level, but, at the same time, distinguished from the neoliberal narrative of self-help that has become familiar within political discourse in the UK.

The second alternative narrative is related to devolution within the UK and the associated policy divergence that has resulted (Adams and Schmueker, 2005; Schmueker and Lodge, 2010). Taking the example of health, where time banking and co-production have frequently been suggested as a focus for service reform, illustrates some differences between two governments of the same political party and illustrates the alternative articulations of time banking. Greer (2005, 2010) claims that post-devolution Wales has developed a policy interest in local government and public health that places health policy (rather than health care) at the core of service provision. This emphasises localism, with a wider interest in the social determinants of health (Dahlgren and Whitehead, 1991) that exist beyond health systems. This approach to health has resulted from an ideological commitment to the values of 'old' social democracy (Sullivan and Drakeford, 2011) rather than the Third Way of New Labour. Consequently, Labour and Labour-led Welsh governments have not adopted New Labour's emphasis on citizen responsibilities, retaining a commitment to using the welfare state to achieve equality, social justice and social inclusion. Accordingly, Labour-led Welsh Assembly Governments have sought to emphasise collaboration, participation, communities and partnership in order to create 'citizen-centred' public services, and here a link to time banking has been encouraged.[5]

Creating 'citizen-centred' services has sought to establish a balance between consumer- and citizen-based approaches to public service delivery (Welsh Assembly Government, 2006; Martin and Webb, 2009). This results in a particular focus on citizen engagement and efforts to foster permeable organisation boundaries in order to help place citizens at the centre of local delivery. Transferring these ideas into health policy has taken a number of forms (Sullivan and Drakeford, 2011), although the interest in time banking and co-production overlaps with the paper *Designed to Add Value* (Welsh Assembly Government, 2008a), which provides an important foundation for a 'citizen-centred approach'. Suggesting that the third sector underpins a vibrant, independent and fulfilled life, community development efforts that engage volunteers are seen as central to public sector provision to support communities and residents to fulfil their potential. Linking volunteering, health and social care, the Welsh government seeks to bring citizens into the core of public service activities (Welsh Assembly Government, 2008b) in order to contribute to a healthy and active society. On the surface, there are clear overlaps with the active citizenship agenda found in New Labour thinking and the more recent narrative of the Big Society, but for the Welsh government, the focus can be seen to reflect the idea of efficacy co-production discussed in Chapter Two.

Unlike the New Labour and 'Big Society' articulations of self-help, this form is embedded within state-provided services and serves to act as a 'springboard' (Burns and Taylor, 1998) form of self-help, the aim of which is to use mutual support to integrate people into mainstream society and formal organisations. This requires a focus on efficacy co-production, building up citizen involvement and engagement and supporting them in developing new skills and confidence in order to achieve this. Thus, the use of time banking in this situation seeks to promote the participative 'good society' associated with 'old' social-democratic values (Drakeford, 2011) rather than a hybrid of social democracy and neoliberalism (see Chapter Two).

The final potential source of an alternative narrative can be detected in the UK Labour Party's ideological debates in the aftermath of the 2010 election defeat – although the extent of the rethink is debatable (Cruddas, 2010; Cruddas and Rutherford, 2010; Glasman, 2010, 2011; Purnell and Cooke, 2010; Glasman et al, 2011). Early debates gravitated around the idea of 'Blue Labour', with one proponent, Maurice Glasman, arguably shaping much of the debate. Glasman (2011) offered a historical analysis of the Labour Party, suggesting that the party had moved away from its own traditional values (reciprocity, association and organisation – that is, the focus on the power generated by local self-help and mutual activities) in favour of centralised responses to social problems. Subsequently, social democracy should return to its associational values in order to promote the 'good life' for citizens, which would require rebuilding 'relational power' (local/associational organising) to counterbalance the power of money. Here, two links can be made with time banking.

First, ideas of reciprocity and organising found within time bank practices are prominent in Blue Labour thinking, but also within the Big Society narrative, so it becomes important to pay attention to the differences in how localism is articulated by different ideological positions. Finlayson (2011) suggests that this organising is not seen as activity that challenges neoliberal capitalism *per se*; rather, it is resistance to the limited potential to develop mutual activities within capitalist frameworks. Consequently, this 'Blue Labour' organising could perpetuate the use of time banking as a tool for increasing active citizenship, engaging local people in resolving local problems and therefore changing the role of the state. However, this would continue to use time banking as it is currently being used in its 'co-opted' form (for a more detailed discussion, see Chapter Six). Second, unlike the 'Big Society', Blue Labour theory potentially allows for the use value of activities to be recognised because it accepts that value in human activity can be placed above the value of money (see Chapter Five). Generally, community currencies offer a different basis for production and consumption (North, 2011: 173–182). These currencies do not produce things in themselves, but recognise the production efforts that individuals contribute to communities, while facilitating the exchange of locally generated and produced goods and services. This reflects the type of mutualism supported by the Blue Labour thesis, allowing for the possibility of greater investment in community production, reciprocity and the fostering of social networks. This requires a need to draw upon the social theory of time to realise that time is not simply a medium for measurement and exchange; rather, it contains a number of qualitative experiences that help us to question the dominance of time-is-money and the associated employment-first notion of citizenship. Blue Labour theory and the ideas of Welsh Labour help promote a move away from the perception of employment as the first obligation. As such, Wilson and Bloomfield (2011: 24) have argued that:

> Time, too, is a critical issue at this intersection. 'New' Labour only valued paid work, and its support for childcare for lone parents came across as instrumental in this regard, rather than being motivated by concern for gender equality or child development.

While recent publications with regards to welfare reform indicate that the Labour Party is potentially refining its neoliberal hybrid rather than offering an alternative, the discussion of 'relational welfare' (Stears, 2011) may offer another alternative that links to the work of Fitzpatrick (2004a) and overlaps with the broader discussion of time. Relational welfare seeks to foster a critique of transactional relationships, which encourage people to see each other as tradable objects rather than as people with feelings, commitments, dependants and dependencies, and consequently to promote different values. These values are necessary to build new relationships that foster the mutual responsibility currently undermined by the transactional mindset. This has clear links with Cahn's (2000) argument about the core economy. Here, time becomes important, for it is required to develop effective relationships, which, by their nature, are slow and deliberate: there is a need to stop thinking about the quickest solution, which therefore contradicts the time-is-money logic of capitalism. Tied to a sense of place, relational welfare seeks to promote associational activity at the local level in order to foster a deliberative, everyday democracy that relocates power in society so that citizens have power to run their own lives or escape the overbearing dominance of others.

Challenging austerity – the starting point

Building on this link to relational welfare and notions of time, it is possible to draw upon Fitzpatrick's (2003) critique of New Social Democracy (essentially, New Labour). Here, he seeks to develop an alternative route for renewal within social-democratic theory – an alternative to the renewal of Labour into 'New Labour'. As discussed in Chapter Two in relation to active citizenship, Fitzpatrick (2003: 201) argues that New Labour shifted policy attention on to the individual rather than the social, and, in doing so, adopted the political rights narrative around the construction of social problems; as discussed in relation to welfare scandals in Chapter One, this reflects a 'shrinking of the social imagination around the extremist centre'. The consequence of this is the limitation it imposes on debating policy options outside of the dominant neoliberal hybrid. Consequently, at the core of his notion of social democracy, he presents three concepts that can help broaden policy debate, which also have relevance to the wider discussion of time: 'distributive justice', 'attention' and 'sustainability'.

Fitzpatrick (2003) pays particular attention to the idea of 'distributive justice': the philosophical aim to ensure that incidental inequalities are not generated by societies' structures and institutions. Here, Fitzpatrick seeks to create an argument for material equality as an essential foundation for reciprocity and responsibility. A focus on distributive justice requires consideration of the impact of today's action on future generations and illustrates a time-based element of the analysis. As seen in Chapter Three, Fitzpatrick's discussion of time is critical of the Rawlsian notion of justice for adopting the dominant neoliberal use of time as the framework in which justice is determined. The notion of distributive justice is relevant to time-based analysis because it relates to the relative time perspective in two ways. First, as Adam (1998: 26) notes in relation to environmental damage, 'the largest proportion of consequences, however, are invisible and, by the time they finally materialise as interconnected webs of symptoms, they will not be traceable with certainty to any particular causes'. This same argument can be applied to a range of social actions, which illustrates a need for rethinking how, in the present, we relate to the future generations of humans and the environment in which they will live. Second, Adam further argues that the dominant perception of time-is-money sees time as a resource. Within industrial societies, this alters the perception of present and future so that the latter belongs to the former. The development of technology and insurance to protect against spoiled futures has, Adam (1998: 57) suggests, established:

> ways of reaching into the immediate, near and distant future
> … based not on bargaining with ancestors and gods but on
> a techno-economic relationship to a resource that is to be
> used, predicted, allocated, managed, sold, colonised and
> controlled in the present.

This extension into the future consequently narrows the choices and life chances of beings in future generations far further into the future than we fully appreciate. Distributive justice, therefore, is not just about the allocation of goods and resources now, in the present; rather, it must not be estranged from intergenerational justice – time is therefore essential to developing this narrative. Time banking can offer very little here in terms of redistributing resources. It can, however, offer a practical means for people to start explicitly viewing time as something other than an external measure exchangeable with money.

The second concept offered by Fitzpatrick (2003) is the principle of 'attention'. Here, clear links can be established not only with the work of Bryson (2007), but also with a longer history of feminist analysis advocating the need to prioritise care work, both personal and familial (Sevenhuijsen, 1998; Lister, 2003). However, 'attention' is used more broadly to encompass both care and recognition. As Fitzpatrick (2003: 118) explains:

> Attention implies 'attending to', that is, we have a
> responsibility to recognise the diversity and difference out
> of which one's own identity is shaped; it also implies 'being
> attentive' or caring for the damage that is an ineluctable
> part of social and emotional relationships; finally, it also
> possesses a locutionary force (as in 'stand to attention!')

that implies a systematic approach to justice and care, which avoids treating all groups or all care claims as being of equal moral worth.

This has a clear link to time banking and the discussion of the use value of time and 'task time'. Engaging in time bank activity involves members in care work of various kinds, both with the community and with individuals. This contribution is recognised not only through a time credit, but also in the value that members give to their own and others' contributions. For Fitzpatrick, recognition is associated with notions of self-esteem and human dignity, which, as discussed earlier in the chapter, can be seen in relation to the feelings of pride and worth that members experience through engaging in time bank activity. Time banking is, essentially, a means by which this concept of attention can be practised.

The final term that Fitzpatrick (2003) suggests should form the core of social democracy is 'sustainability'; this overlaps with both CCSs broadly and with debates around the concept of time. Sustainability must be embraced as being critical to human well-being in both the present and the future. CCSs have long been promoted for this very reason: as an alternative form of production and exchange that avoids the environmental damage of capitalist practices (Lang, 1994; Fitzpatrick and Caldwell, 2001; Seyfang, 2006a; North, 2010b; Seyfang and Longhurst, 2013b). Here, there is a focus on community production and distribution in order to reduce global transportation and to respond to the peak oil crisis (North, 2010b), but also to reduce constant production by promoting the repair rather than replacement of goods alongside environmentally friendly purchasing (Lang, 1994: 36). From the temporal perspective, this overlaps with a broader concern over the imposition of clock time on social and economic relations and the discounting of multiple times within the environment, with the unknown damage that such an approach can generate (Adam, 1998; Kümmerer, 1996). Thus, for the New Economics Foundation, there is a need to rethink not only economics theory (Boyle and Simms, 2009), but also public service reform. For the latter, they promote co-production, of which time banking is one means of achieving this, as part of the model of zero-growth public services (New Economics Foundation, 2004a, 2008a, 2008c). Time banking, therefore, offers a means of promoting sustainability in terms of the environment and economics, but also socially, linking with the New Economics Foundation's 'triple crunch' (New Economics Foundation, 2008d) and an acceptance of the complexity and multiplicity of time.

Such public service reform to accomplish co-production must be part of a broader reorganisation in society which ensures that citizens have time to engage in the care activities of time banking. Here, the temporal analysis of Biesecker (1998) and Reisch (2001) offers essential elements of the developing narrative challenging neoliberal hybrids. The argument they offer is that time-is-money damages the social and environmental aspects of life and that a counter-narrative must develop around a 'wealth-of-time' perspective. Consequently, it becomes important to recognise that the contributions people can make to society other than paid employment are vital to the operation of society. This is clearly stated by Cahn (2000), in his argument for time banking, but, as noted earlier, he does not suggest that core economy values should be used as a guide for all human activity, just those located within the core economy. However, this does not fit with the wider theory of time critique of the dominance of clock time because this dominance has a range of damaging consequences to the environment and social worlds that we inhabit; therefore, the suggestion is that there is a need to challenge the dominance of clock time: time-based analysis provides a narrative for challenging the dominance of neoliberal values and ideas across a range of social, economic and political contexts. Drawing the new wealth-of-time narrative into the discussion of social-democratic thinking has been initiated in the earlier quote from Wilson and Bloomfield (2011), but it needs to become a more explicit consideration in social-democratic thinking.

Seeking reform requires that this complex debate about time be presented in a way that is acceptable to the broader public. Talking about multiplicities of time, while intuitively making sense, is a difficult policy narrative to create. The three principles offered by Fitzpatrick (2003) provide alternative concepts that help move economic and social policy away from the desire for productivity, affluence and growth within the values of emotional and ecological labour. However, essentially, these principles facilitate a consideration and critical review of the 'function' behind social and economic activity. It is this concept of 'function' – advanced by Tawney (1921) in order to challenge the 'acquisitive society' – which may provide a broader framework for advancing neoliberal critique and the promotion of alternative social and economic organisation. Furthermore, it offers a term that may help place core economy values as the primary source of value in human activity (this is a discussion returned to in Chapter Seven). By advancing this concept of 'function', and the embedded appreciation of multiple times that it can help to promote in policy discourse, it is possible to draw upon Fitzpatrick's (2003: 206) argument for 'participative equality'. The development of new forms of civic engagement in public spaces – subjecting public issues, debates and decisions to the 'democratic gaze' in order to bring the idea of function into public debate – requires that we devise new ways of engaging the public in political debate; no easy task when, in the UK, disillusion in politics is high. This is something that could possibly be developed through co-production, but there is a danger of such an approach perpetuating co-option if credits are used tokenistically to engage local people in policy decisions (Naughton-Doe, 2011b). Thus, the starting point must be efficacy co-production: allowing people to invest time in relations and communities, and to have contributions valued. As time banking develops the forms of co-production, relations will change and increase across a broader spectrum of possible co-production relationships, many of which give greater control to citizens (Gregory, 2009a, 2012b). However, this will need to develop alongside a broader range of changes, as indicated by the notion of 'distributive justice' and the 'wealth-of-time' perspective advocated earlier. Time banking, therefore, can offer something in relation to achieving these aims, but it must be part of a broader narrative of policy change built upon the foundation of an explicit engagement with multiple times. The development of the broader policy changes and the relevance of time to forming this agenda will be explored in Chapter Seven.

Conclusion

This chapter has explored data from research into time banking to illustrate the multiplicity of time involved in activities. It has been suggested that on the surface, time banking appears to be about measurement and monitoring, creating an alternative economic resource for members, and providing 'work experience' for citizens. Consequently, the use of time banking has been brought into narratives of self-help located within the neoliberal hybrids of New Labour and the Coalition governments. Yet, the discussion demonstrated that beneath the surface, time banking activity does not just reflect the notion of 'task time' and, to a certain extent, the concept of 'process time'; rather, for members, the measure of duration and exchange symbolised by the credit is of little worth in comparison to the feelings of pride and self-worth that they gain from time banking. This was then linked to alternative ideological positions that potentially offer an alternative narrative for time banking outside of the boundaries of neoliberal ideas. Pursuing this line of inquiry, some challenges to developing an alternative narrative were explored, and alternative conceptions of self-help that can draw upon the 'use value' of time and potentially build this into a broader narrative for reframing social-democratic thinking in a way that explicitly engages with temporality were examined. In Chapters Six and Seven, this repositioning of time banking theory and the challenges of co-production are considered in greater detail and further attention is given to the suggestion that, by itself, time banking cannot cause reform, but has to be part of a wider policy narrative. What time banking offers, however, can be summed up by two time bank members themselves, and they are given the final word in this chapter:

> "What it values is the capacity that people have to be active. It recognises that they have skills and knowledge and time." (Lynne, P2A staff member)

> "Yes. And I also see the time bank as giving protection against the money worlds and that's how I would justify it having employees. They are there to protect us from the money world." (Harry, P2A member)

Notes

[1] This refers to trips offered by the centre that members can access for credits, in particular, the term 'residential' is associated with activities across a weekend away from the estate for children/young people, often with parents using their credits in combination with their children's to pay for trips.

[2] See: http://www.guardian.co.uk/politics/2011/may/23/david-cameron-big-society-project and http://www.telegraph.co.uk/news/politics/david-cameron/8320702/Cameron-relaunches-Big-Society-with-moral-purpose.html

[3] For a Fabian Society piece on this debate, see: http://www.fabians.org.uk/social-justice-localism-and-the-postcode-opportunity/ as well as the argument of Nick Clegg, Deputy Prime Minister of the Coalition government in the UK, available at: http://www.libdems.org.uk/deputy_prime_minister_speech_to_demos_and_the_open_society_foundation

[4] See: http://www.nextleft.org/2009/08/you-cant-have-localism-without-postcode.html

[5] See the Public Services Management Wales paper on time banking, available at: http://www.justaddspice.org/images/stories/downloads/Evidence/timebanking_ss.pdf

SIX

Resistance or resilience?

> Resiliency is like a muscle ... that must be developed in advance and consistently exercised [to] be both strong enough to withstand severe challenges and flexible enough to handle a wide range of unpredictable forces.[1]

Chapter Five argued that time bank theory and practice needs to be more explicit about the value of time, the use value at the core of time bank practices. It further illustrated that time banking can be co-opted into government narratives because the surface value of time, as a measure of volunteering, offers a useful tool for monitoring active citizenship. Consequently, the potential of time banking to offer a more radical form of non-government self-help, as advocated by Ward (1996), and its potential to foster change in conceptualisations of citizenship (Bryson, 2007) are examined in this chapter within the broader policy context. The intention is to explore this debate within the concepts of 'resilience' and 'resistance'. The idea of resilience will be explored later, but, briefly, it refers to efforts to equip individuals and communities to cope with various types of shocks – from financial to environmental – so that individuals and community groups can better cope, and survive, in a turbulent neoliberal context. The term 'resistance', however, is used here to refer to efforts to challenge the dominant neoliberal political and economic ideas and practices: to question the structural causes of social problems and advocate change to this context, rather than making communities resilient and therefore uncritical of the circumstances in which they have to live.

The wider context in which this analysis of time within time banking, and its implications for social policy, must be considered has been illustrated in earlier chapters. It has been claimed that the concept of austerity is a means by which the Coalition government, specifically, the Conservative Party, has brought together neoliberal economic theory with the moral authoritarianism of the political Right, thus overcoming a tension noted with regards to the development of the New Right in the UK (Levitas, 1988; Gregory, 2014). Similarly, Harrison and Sanders (2014) suggest that the idea of the Big Society contrasts with a 'Big State', which squeezes out and over-regulates the private sector, thus fitting with neoliberal economic theory. This leads to the promotion of a reduced state and an expansion of citizen activities to secure their own (and their communities') welfare. Here, as will be discussed later, the ideas of self-help and resilience are essential to understanding policymaking in the current political climate. Furthermore, while the 'austerity programme' is set to continue until 2018,[2] there is also a growing call for 'permanent austerity' with regards to public spending.[3] Yet, it would be wrong to suggest that there has been no resistance to the imposition of 'austerity politics' and that efforts have not been made to challenge Coalition policy. For the following discussion, what needs to be established first is that restricted state finances, a reduction in public services and a renewed role for the state as an enabler of local community (and private) initiatives to secure welfare have become the dominant and accepted context. This relates to a global neoliberal order, presented as being beyond the control of the nation-state and, as such, something to be resilient against, rather than change.

'Resistance', on the other hand, is the term used here to bring together the arguments for change. As noted earlier, there have been efforts to challenge the Coalition government's agenda. Initially, in terms of protest, the 2010 development of the protest movement UK Uncut, which campaigned against tax avoidance, sought to raise awareness of the cuts to the public sector through direct action. Here, non-violent protests took place outside of companies accused of tax evasion in order to disrupt their business and discourage custom. While this activity led to the development of US Uncut across the Atlantic, the Occupy Wall Street movement transferred to the UK as the Occupy London activist group (supported by UK Uncut but also the London contingent of the Movimiento 15-M – a Spanish protest group). Alongside the formation of such groups, there have been a number of protest marches, such as the 2011 London anti-cuts protest, the March for the Alternative. Similar protest action has occurred across the globe in the US, Ireland and Europe (especially in Greece, which received particular media coverage due to the severity of 'austerity measures'). Additional 'resistance' has come in the form of legal cases against disability benefit decisions implemented by the Coalition government, although these have not been successful.[4] Thus, the protests and legal action that have sought to challenge the imposition of austerity throughout government policy illustrate that there is a political space in which alternatives are being articulated. What this and the final chapter of this text seek to do is offer a narrative for alternative political and economic options to be taken by policymakers. This chapter seeks to illustrate the current context and challenges before offering the source of resistance to be found within this context. Chapter Seven draws the book to a conclusion by offering a broader framework through which alternatives can be pursued.

Consequently, this chapter begins with an exploration of the concept of resilience and its relevance to the earlier discussions of neoliberalism and self-help. This is followed by an examination of how third sector organisations have changed in response to a focus on creating resistance within the context of austerity, and the drawing out of lessons for better understanding the consequences of co-option for time banking. Finally, the chapter examines the idea of resistance in order to draw together the arguments of the relevance of time as a concept for promoting alternative practices that do not fit within dominant neoliberal ideas, alongside the practices examined in relation to time banking as one potential model for promoting alternatives.

Resilience

Resilience is a concept appearing across a number of policy domains, but its pursuit by government has particular neoliberal undertones that seek to encourage citizen responsibility to survive within existing social structures, rather than state responsibility for addressing the harms caused by the various inequalities resulting from contemporary social organisation. Thus, to some extent, the concept varies across different policy domains, but, essentially, it refers to the ability of communities or individuals to survive crisis. This section examines how the concept can be found in use within discussions of responses to climate change, financial responsibility, health improvement and local economic and community development. Drawing upon these discussions illustrates how the concept is used to inform policymaking and provide insight into the broader argument developed across previous chapters: that the development of the neoliberal hybrids of the New Labour and Coalition governments facilitates the co-option of time banking. But through an analysis of time, it is possible to highlight contradictory practices and values that highlight the potential for offering an alternative to neoliberal politics and economics.

Resilience in policy

Efforts to introduce resilience into policymaking have cut across a number of policy domains, as well as a number of concepts. In exploring the term 'resilience', it will be necessary in this section to draw upon debates in health and environmental policy as illustrative examples of how resilience is defined, operationalised and pursued in policymaking. Consequently, after a brief discussion of the definition of resilience, these debates are drawn upon to illustrate the concept before exploring its association with self-help and time banking.

One key area in which the concept has gained relevance is in relation to environmental concerns. In particular, the Joseph Rowntree Foundation (JRF) has considered community-based resilience in relation to the financial crisis (Flint, 2010), which contributes to an understanding of the concept of resilience in policymaking and practice. Cinderby et al (2014: 4), in their research into community action for developing resilience funded by the JRF, suggest that at the community level, resilience 'involves improving the capacity of neighbourhoods to recover from crises (typically environmental, such as flooding) or respond and adapt to ongoing changes (economic, environmental and social)'. This overlaps with the use of the concept in relation to socio-environmental concerns, where, for example, the term has been used by Holling (1973: 14) to mean 'a measure of the persistence of systems and of their ability to absorb change and disturbance and still maintain the same relationships between populations or state variables'. The following discussion, however, adopts Folke's (2006: 253) more critical definition of resilience, which illustrates how:

> A lot of work on resilience has focused on the capacity to absorb shocks and still maintain function. But, there is also another aspect of resilience that concerns the capacity for renewal, re-organization and development, which has been less in focus but is essential for the sustainability discourse.

While resilience is used in this chapter to refer to the 'absorption' requirement of policy efforts, the term 'resistance' is utilised to refer to the latter part of the quote, the need to reorganise. Similar ideas present resilience as a positive adaption within a context of significant diversity (Luthar et al, 2000; Ungar, 2004), focused on an ability to remain strong and survive various difficulties, especially relevant for excluded individuals (Mohaupt, 2009), and for facilitating well-being in particular socio-economic groups and individuals (Edwards, 2007), as well as the survival of organisations in changing political contexts (Milbourne, 2013). Overlapping with the concept of social capital, resilience is often related to social and economic resources that facilitate stability – although, as Milbourne points out, these resources can themselves be destabilised. Regardless, resilience is presented as a positive outcome, 'highlighting individual and group resourcefulness and achievements in overcoming misfortune' (Milbourne, 2013: 157). Presenting resilience in this way establishes clear links to themes discussed in Chapter Two: active citizenship, responsibilisation and community participation. Individual and community, not state, action to protect oneself from external harms becomes the primary policy focus – not the questioning of how such harms are generated.

Thus, the focus on ecological resilience has grown alongside a focus on 'community resilience' and the role of the welfare state and social work professionals in promoting resilience (Pierson, 2002; Taylor-Gooby, 2002; Bonanno, 2008; Norris et al, 2008, 2009; Canvin et al, 2009). While there have been critiques that such a narrative presents responses to social (and environmental) problems within individualistic terms, thus limiting wider, structural reforms and the misapplication of resilience in its ecological sense to social relations (Gregory, 2012a, 2013a, 2014; MacKinnon and Derickson, 2013), the concept of resilience is continuing to gain wider application. A number of academics have located these practices within green/environmental ideologies (Lang, 1994; Fitzpatrick and Caldwell, 2001; North, 2007), offering alternative production and exchange systems to those found in the market. Contemporary accounts make links between currencies and the 'Transition Town' movement (North, 2010b), emphasising community resilience to fluctuations in capitalist economic systems. This section explores these arguments in relation to time banking. Such approaches retain the association between resilience and social capital that facilitates the use of these self-help initiatives within neoliberal paradigms.

Recent work has sought to add theoretical depth to the concept of resilience: its foundation as a concept in policymaking is rooted in an association with environmental issues exploring the relationship between ecological and human resilience, as well as environmental management (Adger, 2000; Hughes et al, 2003; Adger et al, 2005; see also, generally, the journal *Ecology & Society*). The focus on resilience in relation to policy and practice has gained increasing attention, especially in the wake of the 2008 financial crisis (Hancock et al, 2012; Stafford, 2012). Such accounts of resilience pay particular attention to the adaptability of individuals and communities reliant upon the ability to act collectively. Consequently, resilience relies upon user participation, a body of literature that has long been established within the social sciences (Arnstein, 1969; Beresford, 2002a; Henn et al, 2007; Parker, 2007b; Henn and Foard, 2012). Concepts such as resilience and participation are therefore used as a panacea to social problems, much in the same way as time banking has been developed to address the problems of the core economy. This analysis serves as a reminder of the relationship that cuts across a number of policy areas to create a 'wicked issue'[5] (Blackman et al, 2006; Adamson, 2008), bringing together the environmental and community development literature, as well as a focus on the associations between health, poverty and resilience (Batty and Flint, 2010; Elliott et al, 2010; Flint, 2010; Cattell, 2011). Here, social capital is seen as an essential element in efforts to promote resilience (Adger, 2003); as Cinderby et al (2014: 44) suggest in relation to their participants' views of social capital, it was regarded as in need of being 'strengthened, with a recognition that working co-operatively for a collective future is necessary at a local level in order to tackle global problems'. The use of social capital within policy usually relates to the definition presented by Putnam (2001: 18–19):

> the core idea of social capital theory is that social networks have value ... social contacts affect the productivity of individuals and groups ... social capital refers to connections among individuals – social networks and the norms of reciprocity and trustworthiness that arise from them.

Social capital focuses upon three types of networks: bonding and bridging (Putnam, 2001) and linking (Szreter and Woolcock, 2004). Bonding capital refers to close ties between individuals, such as family, while bridging capital refers to looser connections that can be fostered between individuals, for example, within a shared geographical location. Linking capital refers to vertical ties between individuals and people in positions of power. There is a range of research that advocates the need for strong networks and calls for policy that seeks to foster network formation (Berkman and Syme, 1979; Cattell, 2001; Powell and Dalton, 2003; Chiu and West, 2007). This has become of particular relevance in the community development and health literatures, where the concept of resilience is reliant upon the formation of social networks. Consequently, Gamarnikow and Green (2000) suggest that links are forged between social capital and community resilience that establish normative and non-contentious assumptions about local action as the basis of local resilience (rather than other contributing factors) and thus generate support for bridging and linking social capital – deficit in either indicates a need for resilience.

Resilience and social capital

The focus on resilience and community-based initiatives to address social problems has been renewed in the wake of the economic crisis of 2008 and the austerity politics that followed (Day, 2009; Athwal et al, 2011; Hudson et al, 2011; Ariizumi and Schirle, 2012), and the need to create resilient communities. Where resilience is concerned, social networks and social capital offer a means of helping communities to survive and cope with shocks and strains (Norris et al, 2008; Hawkins and Maurer, 2010; Castleden et al, 2011), but have been presented within a neoliberal framework that shapes the intent and purpose of community initiatives. Developing social networks can facilitate local community coping strategies and help individuals and/or communities to maintain healthy, 'symptom-free' functioning (Bonanno, 2008; Davydov et al, 2010). However, the use of social capital is limited to government-prescribed uses of the term in practice (see later), which present policy initiatives as an addition to existing services, rather than a transformation of service provision in line with non-neoliberal values (Glynos and Speed, 2012).

To illustrate this, it is possible to look at how the term 'social capital' has been drawn into debates about health inequalities and health improvement – essentially, enhancing citizen resilience. Here, under the previous Labour government and the Coalition government post-2010, policy has placed emphasis upon participatory and social capital approaches to tackling these challenges (Curtis and Rees Jones, 1998; O'Neill and Williams, 2004). Such approaches emphasise the psychosocial aspects of health and Wilkinson's (1996: esp ch 10) argument for the potential benefits of social capital. The essential argument here is that health inequalities result in psychosocial harm due to the stress and anxiety that is placed on individuals as a result of wider structural inequalities (Wilkinson, 1997; Charlesworth et al, 2004). This has led to the promotion of social capital in tackling ill-health and promoting resilience to ill-health within citizens. Community resilience to ill-health thus seeks to develop community practices that develop social capital as a means of generating resilience and therefore improving health outcomes, and this overlaps with an interest in the use of time banking and co-production within health services (Simon, 2003; Hyde and Davies, 2004; Glasby, 2008; Dunston et al, 2009). Focusing upon community resilience more broadly, Morris and Gilchrist (no date) place such approaches at the core of welfare reform under their discussion of the 'Big Society' and their Connected Communities project,[6] going as far as to suggest that social networks can have health benefits. However, they do not make clear how this is brought about through engagement in what they term 'community hubs'. What this illustrates is the continued importance of the concepts of resilience and community participation to health in policymaking (Zakus and Lysack, 1998; Wallerstein and Duran, 2006; Letcher and Perlow, 2009; Poortinga, 2012).

The argument of the psychosocial approaches relate to the epidemiological transition, and the focus on chronic conditions (Omran, 1971).[7] Policy responses to chronic conditions have focused on the interconnections between sufferers and the networks that they rely on to cope with their conditions (Anderson and Bury, 1998; Chiarella et al, 2010), as well as mental health (Kawachi and Berkman, 2001; McKenzie et al, 2002). This relates to concern with social capital as a means of improving psychosocial health, as advocated by Wilkinson and Pickett (2007), as well as issues of status anxiety (Sennett and Cobb, 1993). In fact, this literature on health inequalities, while highlighting the psychosocial dimension, argues that it is structural inequality in society that is causing these ill-health outcomes, and it is this broader issue of inequality that needs to be addressed (Wilkinson, 1996; Wilkinson and Pickett, 2007). However, this is often overlooked in policymaking (Smith, 2010) in favour of attention to the social capital and community dimensions that fit with individualised/behaviourist explanations of social problems. Thus, the concept of resilience is given centre stage in policymaking in relation to health, but there is no comment about what it is that communities are to be resilient against. This lack of questioning embedded in the concept of resilience promotes the status quo rather than challenges dominant power relations, separating communities from the structural and social causes of social problems, despite efforts to locate these problems within the wider context (Bauman, 2001). A similar argument can be developed in relation to community initiatives, resilience and environmental crises.

Consequentially, a debate has developed between which factors are important to determining health and which should inform policy responses. Neoliberal hybrids have pointed towards social capital and individualised explanations and have selectively drawn on research evidence to support these interpretations – thus advocating for community self-help initiatives.

Social capital, resilience and neoliberal self-help

The New Labour government (1997–2010) and the Coalition government (post-2010) advocated a need for increased resilience within communities, which relies on the development of social capital. The positive overtones of such policy discussion are underpinned by the reworking of citizenship discussed in Chapter Two in order to enhance individual culpability for the disadvantage and social problems experienced. Active, responsible citizens can avoid social harm through their own (and their communities') efforts to foster their own resilience to negative externalities. Within the neoliberal hybrids, each citizen's duty is to protect themselves from the harsh reality of global capitalism, against which states are relatively powerless. Rather, as prime ministers, both Tony Blair and David Cameron have argued that the UK needs to compete in a competitive global marketplace, implying that these economic demands are paramount and should direct policy endeavours. For the 'Third Way' ideology, this required investment in the human and social capital of citizens (Giddens, 2003), leading some, such as Jenson (2012), to suggest that New Labour's response to global pressures – the development of a social investment welfare state – sought to break away from neoliberalism. However, as discussed in Chapter Two, the changes in welfare provision over New Labour's time in office promoted the claim that their ideology formed a neoliberal hybrid.

This hybrid contained a concern for communitarian policy as part of the then government's efforts to invest in individuals and communities, keen to spend public resources on 'good' welfare provision (Powell, 1999a), such as education and early years provision. However, how such welfare was provided fundamentally altered the mixed economy of welfare provision in the UK and changed the role of the state, which instead sought to foster partnerships with private and voluntary/community organisations. With the latter, this overlapped with the communitarian theme in New Labour ideology (see the discussion in Chapter Two with regards to citizenship); however, this approach was often critiqued for its top-down conceptualisations of community, empowerment and social capital (Dinham, 2005; Fremeaux, 2005 Mowbray, 2005 Mooney and Fyfe, 2006). This generated a policy space with favourable conditions for developing time banking, leading Seyfang and Smith (2002: 52) to suggest that time banking 'is an idea whose time has come'. However, as discussed later, this opportunity for time bank development has been shaped by a particular intention in developing such initiatives – community resilience – which reduces the role of the state in providing welfare.

Similar uses of the concepts of resilience and social capital are found within the 'Big Society' agenda. This agenda built upon the individualised discourse of problems in the Centre for Social Justice's argument of 'Broken Britain' and continued a focus on individuals and communities found under New Labour, but it also re-established links to the earlier Thatcher and Major governments (1979–97), with a focus on 'underclass' and culture of poverty narratives. In particular, Davies and Pill (2012) suggest that the 'Big Society' is a return to such narratives without the use of the moralistic underpinnings of the earlier underclass thesis. Illustrating this approach, the government and media attention on 'troubled families' in the aftermath of the 2011 England riots facilitated policy development around intense work with identified families and not the broader socio-economic contexts within which these families live (Levitas, 2012a, 2012c; Morris, 2013a). Hawkins and Maurer's (2010: 1789) suggestion that social workers can help clients 'connect to and use their positive social capital as a survival mechanism, as a strength builder and as a resource for rebuilding' local communities illustrates how the state can alter its method of providing welfare services to promote individual resilience through forms of self-help that create individuals and communities that are less dependent on external help in times of disaster (Castleden et al, 2011).

Overlapping with the discussion in previous chapters, Norris et al (2008: 146) suggest that from this use of community resilience and self-help within the 'Big Society', '[i]t would not be too difficult for the concept of resilience to erode into one more way of stigmatizing suffering individuals and communities'. The exploration of time banking, the promotion of alternative values and the co-option of time banking support this assertion. Efforts to foster resilience through reinforcing social capital via non-state, self-help activities can result in this outcome because the 'Big Society' is only concerned with individuals coping, thus it denies the possibility of addressing the structural explanations of social harms. Such concerns could be reflected in the growing critique of how resilience is framed in governmental terms (Gregory, 2012a, 2013a, 2014; MacKinnon and Derickson, 2013). Consequently, as discussed earlier in relation to health inequalities, a focus on social capital and individual/community capability detracts attention from broader, structural determinants. Here, the connections between time banking, self-help and resilience may serve to promote this continued, localised focus in policy responses.

Third sector organisation, co-option and resilience

Much of the discussion in this text has drawn upon time banking as an illustrative example of three broad themes: 1) the relevance of time theory to policy analysis; 2) the effects of self-help and resistance; and 3) the co-option of local community/voluntary organisations into neoliberal definitions of self-help. To illustrate the relevance of this initiative to the broader argument, this section places time bank practice into the wider discussion of the changes occurring in voluntary sector organisations (VSOs) in the UK. There is, as always, a definitional debate between the 'third sector' and the 'voluntary sector', but this is overlooked here as it would detract from the main focus of the discussion (but see Kendall and Knapp, 1995). Consequently the following discussion explores the changing context of the voluntary sector in the UK, paying attention to the New Labour and Coalition governments so as to match up with the previous discussion. It then examines how these broader themes and debates relate to time banking before turning to a discussion of the role of VSOs in resisting co-option, which leads on to the final discussion of this chapter around the idea of resistance.

Changing context – political intentions?

It needs to be noted that in choosing to overview government attention to the voluntary sector since 1997, this does not imply that changes to the context did not pre-date this. In fact, Milbourne (2013) claims that there have been four broad historical stages of the state–voluntary sector relationship: the enormous charity organisations of the first half of the 20th century; the consolidation of distinct/complementary roles; mainstreaming from 1997; and the retreat of the state from service delivery, the shift towards the corporate market and the growing emphasis on localism and voluntarism. Generally, there is an argument of decline in forms of mutual aid, cooperatives, philanthropy and other forms of voluntary activity with the rise of centralised welfare provision. Hilton and McKay (2011) argue that such an analysis is not accurate and it would be more appropriate to claim that not only has there been changing political interest in VSOs across different UK governments, but VSOs have also adapted and changed in response to these political pressures: they have not diminished, but changed.

Significant attention has been given to the role of VSOs in delivering welfare services through the concept of partnerships under the previous New Labour governments (Lewis, 2005) as part of a 'mainstreaming' agenda (Kendall, 2003). Here, a number of policy initiatives were designed to increase the role of VSOs in the delivery of welfare. For Kendall, these policies positioned the voluntary sector as having greater financial dependence on both central and local governments, creating reliance on government funds over other sources (a new relationship for the UK but not necessarily in other countries). This formed part of the wider changes to the mixed economy of welfare so that the state acts as a financer of services that are delivered by other sectors (see Chapter Two); thus, VSOs are positioned as service delivery organisations, which may not fit neatly with the wider independence of the sector (discussed later). New Labour policy facilitated a move towards the increased use of VSOs, but also social enterprises, mutuals and cooperatives, as partners in service delivery, which contributes to the view that the public realm has dissolved under the onslaught of the Third Way neoliberal hybrid (Clarke, 2004), creating a welfare system that supports the renewed concept of citizens as welfare consumers (Needham, 2003; Clarke et al, 2007).

As discussed briefly earlier, the efforts to promote these developments have relied on the use of community-based initiatives, which facilitates a changing definition of citizenship. Consequently, the idea of social capital as a form of investment to promote resilience filtered into government activity around VSOs and positioned these initiatives as complementary solutions to state action, which allowed the state to roll back its own direct delivery and potentially reduce financial costs (Burns and Taylor, 1998). Initiatives such as Sure Start not only sought to use and promote self-help initiatives as part of an early years investment strategy, but drew upon the concept of co-production to promote active citizen engagement in this investment – although this was done very much on the government's terms (Pemberton and Mason, 2008). Kendall (2003) suggests that the use of VSOs has resulted in both positive and negative outcomes in terms of service delivery, from wider public engagement to a narrow focus on performance measures. Yet, others have critiqued the top-down approach of these initiatives as betraying the rhetoric around community involvement, with 'inappropriate' forms of social capital being developed at the local level (Mooney and Fyfe, 2006) or local decision-making mechanisms being designed to ensure that government aims are achieved (Fussey, 2004).

New Labour efforts to integrate the voluntary sector into service delivery within centrally defined/controlled frameworks was part of a modernisation approach that drew VSOs into formal welfare systems and, therefore, extended dominant arrangements and eroded the potential alternative values and practices offered by VSOs and the use of self-help as an alternative to welfare provided by the state (Ward, 1996; Burns and Taylor, 1998). Similar criticisms have gained prominence in relation to the 'Big Society' agenda of the Coalition government.

A detailed discussion of the 'Big Society' can be found earlier (see Chapter Two). Here, the intention is to examine the consequences of this policy initative in relation to VSOs and the consequences of both this and the previous New Labour agenda. Milbourne (2013: 17) argues that the aim of the 'Big Society' is to create better, more responsive local services, but she questions this claim, suggesting that the market-driven arrangements and large contracts that form service tenders may not achieve such outcomes, but create a 'shadow state' 'divested of its normal welfare accountabilities'. Furthermore, Hilton and McKay (2011: 25) suggest that the purpose of the voluntary sector within the 'Big Society' narrative is limited to one role associated with socially conservative Anglicanism, which places the Church's engagement with social issues at the core of community initiatives. Consequently, the 'Big Society' presents an image of a particular type of voluntary imitative to be supported while overlooking alternative forms of activity that disrupt this cosy image (Hilton and McKay, 2011).

Macmillan (2013) argues that while the 'Big Society' has always been larger than the voluntary sector, it has generated significant interest in VSOs in relation to service delivery. Yet, those who work within this sector have been unwilling to buy into the policy due to their distrust and hostility towards the 'Big Society' concept. Alcock (2012) earlier noted how Prime Minister Cameron reportedly banned the use of the term 'third sector' and government documents frequently refer to charities, social enterprises and VSOs – indicating a potentially broader view of the voluntary sector that allows the inclusion of faith-based organisations (Torry, 2012) and private companies (Boffey, 2012). For Alcock, this broader focus is potentially embodied in the rebranding of New Labour's 'Office of the Third Sector' as the 'Office for Civil Society'. However, civil society has been established as a space for independent action (Deakin, 2001), and while this may reflect neoliberal interest in non-state activity, it also represents a space for alternative political constructions potentially against the dominant ideas embedded within neoliberal theory (Annestts et al, 2009; Ayres, 2004; Cox and Gunvald Nilsen, 2014).

The 'Big Society' has continued the development of a changing political context within which VSOs must survive. Yet, Milbourne (2013) suggests that this has promoted an entrepreneurial environment that not only changes the organisational structure, practices and activities of VSOs and their staff (see also Bennett, 2013), but also transfers responsibility for service provision concerned with addressing people's need from the state to organisations whose primary motivation is profit. Often, VSOs cannot successfully bid for service tenders, but are subcontracted by private organisations to deliver on the front line, making the voluntary sector a tool in dismantling the welfare state. As such, Milbourne (2013: 96) explains:

> At the time when resources are scarce, the unplanned outcomes from powerful market bidders competing for service funding are likely to be exacerbated, and the re-engineering of public and community-based services accelerated. Marketisation ... can be happenstance and provide unintended casualties among providers and service users; unexpected resistances; and an unjust reshaping of provision across different services.

While the rhetoric has focused on the voluntary sector, policy development has promoted private sector and social enterprises, linking with the ideas of 'TESCO-isation' (Macmillan, 2010), as fewer, larger organisations secure resources and the private sector becomes increasingly involved in service delivery (eg the development of Virgin Care[8]). In its effort to respond to 'Broken Britain' (see Chapter Two), the Coalition government has adopted a policy strategy that removes the state from responding to crisis in favour of the ad hoc advance of VSOs, of which there is little support for the suggestion that this creates space for the voluntary sector to 'flood in' (Alcock, 2010). Rather, this seems to be privatisation through other means as VSOs shift their forms of operation and practice to replicate the practices of private companies in order to secure new contracts based upon payment by results (Ryan, 2014).

Consequently, as Milbourne (2013) explores, there has been a range of isomorphic pressures exerted on the voluntary sector since 1997 that has radically changed the operation and practices of VSOs to fit centrally determined political agendas. Such agendas place market ideas of efficiency and delivery at the forefront of practice as neoliberal political and economic thinking dominates the halls of power. Kendall (2003) suggests that this pressure fosters homogeneity across the sector, subsequently obscuring the original values and aims of VSOs. Although Shapely (2011) argues that VSOs can be a vehicle for change and funnel citizen frustrations into action for change, and Berridge and Mold (2011) suggest that VSOs present a mix of countercultures within pressure group/service provider activities, the argument of isomorphic pressures seem to illustrate how neoliberal hybrids integrate these alternatives into one perceived form of practice – as suggested by Kendal (2003) earlier. Growing concern over the independence of the sector is being articulated by some elements of the voluntary sector (see, eg, the publications of the National Coalition for Independent Action). Although such arguments rest on the claim that the two sectors (state and voluntary) are separate and not 'mutually co-constructive' (Harris, 2003), the perceived association between the two is one of dependency within the 'Big Society' narrative – and VSOs must become free of their state dependency.

Time banking and the voluntary sector context

The New Labour and Coalition government policy initiatives have sought to draw upon the effectiveness and responsiveness of organisations to deliver services and social change while also addressing concerns with active citizenship. Voluntary organisations have welcomed such developments as they offer new opportunities (Milbourne, 2013), and this has been true of time banking. Early time banking activity promoted the use of the exchange mechanism within health and social inclusion initiatives (Callison, 2003; Seyfang, 2003b, 2004c; Harding et al, 2006; Naughton-Doe, 2011a, 2011b; Gregory, 2012c; Madaleno, 2012). However, as Harris and Young (2010) highlight, this expansion has also been matched by a limitation for grassroots organisations to extend their roles without loss of autonomy – a theme noted in recent time bank research (Glynos and Speed, 2012; Gregory, 2012a).

What the previous section illustrated is that VSOs have adapted and shifted to changing political contexts in an effort to survive and continue to provide services. This repurposing of their activities potentially changes their service delivery motives away from citizen needs and towards other agendas, one of which is potentially profit as private sector interests creep into the delivery mix. For those outside of the private sector, entanglement within New Public Management practices, outcome targets and other neoliberal economic tools has shifted practice to facilitate the government steering of service delivery activities without direct state involvement. Earlier, it was noted that this may not only prompt fears of 'co-option' into government agendas, but also separate VSOs from their ability to create alternatives to mainstream government provision – a potential separation of VSOs and 'civil society' that can only briefly be alluded to here. Such pressures have also been brought to bear on time banking, but it would be inaccurate to claim that this was the only isomorphic pressure; rather, there are two entwined issues to outline.

The first relates to the isomorphic pressures suggested by Milbourne (2013). As noted in Chapter Five, on the surface, time banking can relate to issues of the measurement of volunteer action, of citizen activity. This produces numerical data that, as was shown, can be beneficial in writing funding bids. However, for VSOs, such numerical data fulfil government target monitoring criteria with greater ease, and the development of such numerical systems has been linked to the suppression or steering of voluntary sector activity to fit dominant cultures (Rose, 1999). This potentially leads to a more tokenistic use of time credits (Naughton-Doe, 2011b) that moves practice away from some of the broader political agendas associated with time banking (such as those outlined in Chapter Three). Additionally, government interest in developing time banking as part of the 'Big Society' has resulted in new funding being provided for 'start-up' initiatives (NESTA, 2012), while longer-established time banks struggle for the continuation of funding – both being located within the same geographical area.

Furthermore, there has been growing interest in social enterprises use of time-based exchanges and the term 'time banking'. For example, Slivers of Time is a social enterprise that offers an online resource for different sectors (corporate, National Health Service, housing agencies, local authorities, etc) in order to 'create a talent pool of local people' – essentially, matching workers/volunteers with the needs of the different sectors. This system aims to join up potential employees and volunteers with opportunities, although their website is unclear as to how this fully works. Thus, the video demonstrating the 'Breakaway for Carers' scheme offers many ideas and practices similar to time banking practice, for example, the online booking of local people to provide services, in this case, to take over care work in order to allow the main carer to have some respite. However, there is no indication of what the volunteer receives in this exchange. As such, it achieves the aim of allowing people to volunteer odd hours of time, but it is unclear what the motives and aims of the organisation are in promoting these interactions. While not intending to critique the initiative, this discussion illustrates how time as a mechanism of exchange, and its prominence in current non-state activities, complicates the promotion of time banking because similar activities become associated with other aims and ambitions as organisations are shaped by political support for time-based exchange (Cabinet Office, 2011).

Further 'muddying the waters' is the Department of Health's use of time banking as an example of social care reforms (Department of Health, 2010), drawing upon the Japanese use of time banking for elder care (BBC News, 2010). Yet, analysis of this model indicates that the state has had to step in with social care provision as the amount of demand and need for services was greater than the provision available under the time bank system (Hayashi, 2012). This claim for policy innovation, which does not match the research evidence, demonstrates the reverse of the 'Big Society' aim. Rather than reduce the Big State, here is an example where the use of a VSO indicates that there is a need for state intervention. Thus, as Hilton and McKay (2011: 25) claim:

> It might be possible in certain areas of the social services for example that the voluntary sector can take over from the state, but in other areas, it is just as likely that a revitalised voluntarism will acknowledge its own limits and make claims upon the state for further intervention, increased spending and in effect, an expansion of Big Government.

Isomorphic pressures on time banking have, therefore, resulted in two changes: first, an increased use in time exchange by other actors in the non-state sectors that may draw attention, and finance, away from existing time bank initiatives; and, second, the highlighting of the need for state provision. However, an associated argument to consider in relation to co-option is the role and history of time banking itself: including its earlier incarnation as 'service credits' and the association with co-production (Cahn, 1986, 2000) which present time banking as a tool for welfare provision to be used by the state (discussed in Chapter Four). Part of the challenge here, however, and underpinning the co-option analysis, is that this limits the 'transformative' potential of time banking (Glynos and Speed, 2012), potentially using the tool to nudge citizens into a specific form of activity (Gregory, 2012a), thus validating North's (2006a) critique of its less radical potential.

Neoliberal self-help, dividing delivery and alternative political formations

The essence of this section is that the political actors committed to various neoliberal hybrids have co-opted the self-help initiatives of the voluntary sector into their own political aims and ambitions. Such a shift has resulted from three broad features identified by Milbourne (2013) as:

1. an ideological commitment to the superiority of the market as a model of efficiency and effectiveness to be emulated by other sectors;
2. the development of New Public Management, centralised government objectives and the devolution of services and responsibilities through outsourcing efforts; and
3. new governance models based around partnership working.

These form key elements of the isomorphic pressures that have shifted the sector through a combined interest in perceived economic advantages, social improvement and budget restraint enacted through 'austerity politics'. Time banking has been subjected to the same pressures, alongside efforts to integrate practice into mainstream welfare provision, which has consequently undermined its alternative narrative around value (associated with time use). The focus on delivery has sidelined the 'civil society' focus on creating alternative political articulations and collective spaces for promoting non-market activities and values. This development reflects Rees's (2014) division between 'delivery third sector organisations' (DTSOs) and civil society. The former have moved into service provider roles following the isomorphic pressures of professionalisation, commercialisation and TESCO-isation to separate out from the wider sector (civil society). For Rees, this distinguishes DTSOs from civil society, and, as such, they have lost 'authenticity'. This form of organisation, however, is the only supported and accepted form within the 'Big Society' narrative. As Milbourne (2013) suggests, the 'Big Society' is only interested in the 'entrepreneurial' ideology of the voluntary sector – accepting market ideas – and has no interest in the community orientation or democratic renewal ideologies. Thus, the 'Big Society' extends the state into civil society and curbs its autonomy (linking to concerns about co-option outlined earlier). Such a view could be extended to explain time bank development in the UK, where its efforts to grow saw it push itself increasingly into all sectors of service provision, rather than putting similar effort into promoting the alternative values associated with those practices and the implications that they have for policy and welfare more broadly.

Consequently, time banking experiences the same pressures as other VSOs to become tools of the state – reflecting Morgan's (1988) suggestion that mutual aid and voluntary organisations eventually relinquish social values in favour of growth and expansion. Positioned as DTSOs, the ability of time banks to offer alternative service models and create approaches to transform those same services is replaced by the use of time banking as an addition to existing services in order to help monitor service user engagement and promote self-help so that the state can withdraw and allow citizens to develop their own resilience to social problems. This, of course, is a commentary specific to the UK development of time banking and may not be the same globally. Nevertheless, it demonstrates how time banking has been established upon the conceptualisation of citizenship within neoliberal hybrids (see Chapter Two) that promotes its use in service provision. Yet, as Milbourne (2013: 183–184) adds, citizen participation can be found within three forms: 1) advocacy to access rights; 2) political concerns addressing the democratic deficit within existing social structures; and 3) participation as community action for change. It may be possible that time bank practice can draw upon these other forms of practice and offer alternatives to this use of the initiative in order to foster resilience and engage instead the alternative values promoted and experienced in practice.

Resilience and social change

Both New Labour and Coalition governments have each created an influential neoliberal hybrid within the UK that, through the prominence given to market ideas, a redefinition of citizenship and a reduced role of the state, has positioned self-help activities within a particular perspective that facilitates the use of collective activity towards the achievement of neoliberal ends. Yet, this co-option need not be an automatic and unchallenged response to neoliberal dominance. Milbourne (2013), for example, does provide some discussion of resistance (although she frames this VSO resistance as a form of resilience, whereas, in this discussion, the two terms are distinguished from each other). From her case study research, she demonstrates how organisations may adopt or resist the isomorphic pressures generated by government policy and that either strategy can have different outcomes in terms of survival: some 'adopters' still fail, while 'resisters' prosper. Retaining a strong identity at the grassroots level may ensure the survival of VSOs, although this may be dependent upon the field of activity in which they work. However, Milbourne does not reflect more broadly on how robust organisations may comply with or challenge the government's wider neoliberal ideology and so does not engage in a discussion of how resistance may, or may not, provide alternative narratives and goals.

Positioning time banking as resistance

The discussion of time banking thus far indicates that it can, and has, been co-opted in the sense that its social change agenda has been overlooked in favour of the potential benefits that it offers to forms of service delivery that rely more on the state control of citizens. Potentially, time banking is a method for 'nudging' citizens to act in a specific way and to engage in building the forms of social capital that governments support as sources of resilience. Yet, the discussion of resilience as a longer-term transformational change is a way of framing efforts to critique and challenge neoliberal hybrids, which overlaps with the discussion of the utopian method (Levitas, 2005). Such analysis can be found within the wider community currency literature, which promotes alternative production and exchange mechanisms as a specific response to an anti-capitalist critique of contemporary economic and social policy (Lang, 1994; Williams, 1996; Croall, 1997; Bowring, 1998; Fitzpatrick and Caldwell, 2001; Seyfang, 2001a, 2004a; Seyfang and Longhurst, 2013b). The most recent innovation in this area in the UK is focused around Transition Towns and the development of the Bristol and Brixton pounds (Hickman, 2009; North, 2010b; Whitehead, 2010a, 2010b; Rodgers, 2013), which argue for the need for communities to be resilient, but are actually advocating practical ways of fostering collective, community action to develop alternative ways of living outside of the dominant values of the market – scarcity, acquisition and profit.

Time banking potentially forms part of this wider practical approach to changing local practices in order to fit into wider environmental agendas (Fitzpatrick, 2011: 150–152). Yet, the 'Big Society' presents time banking as a tool for 'efficiency co-production' (Gregory, 2012a) in order to promote community resilience, which does not question why there is a need to be resilient – a questioning of the social structures and the harms that they generate. The case studies of the research drawn upon in Chapter Five (Gregory, 2012a) did provide some limited evidence as to time bank members having a more questioning attitude about the imposition of 'austerity'. Thus, within the person-to-person time bank, three members demonstrated wider community involvement than just engagement in order to exchange services. One member, Richard, was actively involved in setting up a number of other local time banks in an effort to promote larger-scale local change in the community. However, for members Beth and Poppy, they drew upon their bridging and linking social capital to foster connections between wider service providers and campaign groups within the community: putting the tools of resilience to use in resisting dominant neoliberal ideas. For Beth, joining the time bank allowed her to build up self-confidence in order to become actively involved in a number of community campaigns against public sector cuts and pension reforms. While for Poppy, this wider activity developed in the opposite direction as she was already involved in a range of community organisations and groups prior to her time bank participation and continues to be involved in a number of activities, including community education. Time banking also promotes, in practice, the use value of time, which offers a different value base upon which to build human activity and can be drawn upon to question dominant neoliberal ideas and concepts. Promoting use value alongside evidence, albeit small, of time banking members engaging in wider campaigns to challenge structural inequalities offers a possibility for community mobilisation and turning resilience into resistance. What remains unclear is both the willingness and capability of communities to organise and campaign for such change.

As Taylor (2011: 293) has argued, communities are associated with the 'ideas of empowerment, participation and partnership, with communities expected to take their place in radically new forms of service delivery and governance'. However, Taylor notes, there is a need for a more realistic view of the possibilities of locally organised challenges to international capital. Communities, Taylor suggests, must engage in 'popular spaces', where citizens are able to define themselves and create their local solidarity, from which change may occur, in order to allow them to build up confidence and voice, before they engage in 'invited spaces' . A similar discussion of 'invited' and 'created' spaces in relation to time banking has previously suggested that time banking works in the reverse to this: offering members a chance to build up confidence and skills prior to taking more active, community change roles (Gregory, 2009a). The potential 'danger' here is that the use of invited spaces draws citizens into predefined forms of participation and, as such, facilitates the co-option of citizens into neoliberal agendas. Created spaces allow citizens to develop their own agendas and forms of participation, to which the state must then respond. This issue of invited and created spaces will need further investigation, especially in relation to the previous discussion about DTSOs.

Such discussion overlaps with renewed interest in community organising since the election of Barack Obama (Schutz and Sandy, 2011; Teater and Baldwin, 2012). Such approaches seek to promote more radical, active, campaigning communities, which may facilitate debate and engagement with the political goals of time banking that this research has outlined. Attached to this broader focus, time banking and co-production may go further than promoting resilience in order to build up member confidence and skills and promote social change more broadly and realise Gibson-Graham's (2006: 196) suggestion 'that changing the self is a path towards changing the world, and that transforming one's environment is a mode of transforming the self'. Time banking can be conceptualised within the theoretical framework presented in earlier chapters in order to challenge and change neoliberal ideas and practices rather than become a tool for furthering them. However, the challenge is now promoting this possibility with a re-articulation of time bank values while not relying on time banking to be the only mechanism for promoting change.

Initial considerations for repositioning time banking

Neoliberal hybrids promote forms of self-help that embrace specific forms of social capital and initiatives in order to engage citizens so as to foster individual and community resilience, alongside increasing the responsibilities of citizens for themselves. Different forms of social capital can be employed within policy to ensure that citizens act in an expected way, from nudges to more overt discipline (Harrison and Sanders, 2014), creating a context in which the promotion of alternatives is challenging. Enhancing the challenge, as has been argued, is the integration of alternative ideas and practices into neoliberal praxis. Despite claims of diminished radicalism (North, 2006a), time banks offer an example of practices and living different temporal values that alter the 'worth' of an activity – breaking away from the primary outcome of citizen activities being income and profit.

Offering a potential starting block for repositioning time banking as a tool of resistance, the argument thus far has sought to establish an analytical framework and argument for change. Time banking activity within community development illustrates how members' collective efforts can alter their localities and enhance their members' capabilities (Gregory, 2012a). However, the value attached to these activities is not based on the time-is-money motive of the market economy; rather, the use value of time dominates and, consequently, there is no profit motive. In the case studies discussed in Chapter Five, the members and staff of time banks illustrated that the benefits of participation were similar to those of 'volunteering', making the credit earned a recognition of effort and equal worth to others in the community, but not the purpose of participation. Credit earning was done not in order to use credits to access goods and services, but to be involved in voluntary activity. The same cannot be said for money, thus illustrating a need to consider 'time' in exploring community-based policy as an illustrative example of temporality and its relevance to human well-being (Lee and Piachaud, 1992; Dey, 1999; Fitzpatrick, 2004a, 2004b; Goodin et al, 2004; Burchardt, 2010). In doing so, it becomes possible to explore ties between different policy initiatives through the temporal lens and to develop a broader narrative of resistance. Time banking puts into practice essential theoretical ideas necessary to achieving broader political and structural change.

However, the co-option of practice into neoliberal thinking limits these possibilities through the promotion of technical over political goals in order to fit dominant political ideas. Resistance to this requires repositioning Cahn's (2000) theory around time banking and co-production to make its political goals (different time value, community empowerment for social change and efficacy co-production, which foster the development of citizen-created participatory spaces) explicit and capable of shaping practice. The danger in doing so is that such a narrative becomes the desires of 'middle-class radicals' (Hilton and McKay, 2011) and anti-capitalists, formulating a blueprint to be imposed (Chatterton and Pickerill, 2010) rather than fostering debate about the purpose of citizen activities and the social structure that supports this. In response to this, it can be argued that in focusing upon 'time', it is possible to appreciate Fitzpatrick's (2004a) discussion around the promotion of created spaces to argue for deliberative space within public contexts for citizens to engage and debate the form of society and lives they wish to lead. As such, in seeking to reposition time banking and to develop a critique of neoliberal society, the aim is not to impose an alternative, but to create space in which that alternative can be formed. This is important because rethinking citizenship and reordering social institutions and collective resources to support this reworking must be guided by other, non-neoliberal ideas, and, here, time as a concept in analysis helps to articulate values and practices outside of neoliberal orthodoxy.

Attempts to promote this alternative must address two challenges offered by the development of the neoliberal hybrids. First, the 'Big Society' is not interested in forms of self-help beyond its narrow interest in developing resilience to global economic turbulence. Advocates of the 'Big Society' desire individual community members to have the capabilities and confidence that time banking can generate but prohibit a questioning of broader social determinants of social harm that would disrupt the individualised and privatised view of social problems (Drakeford, 2000. Second, the language of the social theory of time does not easily translate into public discourse, and, as such, it may be necessary to find alternative concepts within which to encompass the debates offered in this analysis – here, as Chapter Seven explores, the idea of function may be relevant.

Conclusion

There is a need to realign time bank theory and practice to promote resistance to neoliberalism. This should be pursued not in order to impose an alternative social order, but, rather, to create the social structures and definitions of citizenship that allow people to engage the local community in action and debates about the lives they wish to lead. Importantly, this challenges many current assumptions about the duties of citizens and the working of social institutions, and so, by its very nature, while arguing for citizens to be able to engage, it must also create the context in which such engagement is possible. Separating self-help activities from neoliberal conceptualisations is a vital step in this process as it facilitates the realisation of non-market values, which exist in their multitude across our social lives (Gibson-Graham, 2006). To achieve this, it has been necessary to engage with the philosophical debates around time, which have, in turn, highlighted two important analytical points that may help to generate resistance, and that form the focus of Chapter Seven:

1. Through the multiple values of time, it is possible to reinvigorate a notion of 'function' to foster public debate regarding key terms such as 'citizenship', 'responsibilities', 'need', 'equality' and 'exclusion' and how the state engages with these terms (explored further in Chapter Seven).
2. Alternative values of time provide a critique of the existing social order, while recognising that time-use and time-value are politically constructed and thus need to be reconstructed through broader deliberative activities focused on exploring how citizens wish to live their lives and the forms of social arrangements necessary to support this.

Essentially, the analysis of time banking, the priority given to temporality, opens up a discursive space for developing a broader agenda for change and resistance to neoliberal praxis. This is the focus of Chapter Seven.

Notes

[1] Quote from: http://www.cultivate.ie/community-resilience/1195-what-is-community-resilience52

[2] See: http://www.telegraph.co.uk/news/politics/georgeosborne/10552454/George-Osborne-to-cut-taxes-by-extending-austerity-and-creating-smaller-state.html

[3] See: http://www.theguardian.com/politics/2013/nov/11/david-cameron-policy-shift-leaner-efficient-state

[4] See: http://www.disabilityrightsuk.org/news/2014/february/benefits-cap-case-fails-court-appeal

[5] Wicked issues are problems that can be difficult to solve due to their incomplete, contradictory and changing nature; consequently, they are resistant to resolution.

[6] This is project run by the Royal Society for the Arts, seeking to develop action research projects to learn from community development practice in order to find new ways of generating participation in public services. This should not be confused with the Arts and Humanities Research Council (AHRC) project of the same name.

[7] Omran suggests that there are three stages of this transition: the age of pestilence and famine; the age of receding pandemics; and the age of degenerative and man-made diseases.

[8] See: http://www.virgin.com/company/virgin-care

SEVEN

Conclusion

> Mainstream economics is deeply embedded in modernity's vision of material progress and growth. If 'time' is considered at all, it is perceived as an 'input factor' or as a constraint – but not as having an intrinsic value per se or as a genuine aspect of personal well-being or national welfare.… The goal of 'having enough time at the right time and feeling comfortable with one's time frames and institutions' – which is the basic idea of 'wealth in time' … is thus an alien concept. (Reisch, 2001: 369–370)

A number of theoretical ideas and arguments have been introduced and drawn together across the chapters of this book, and while they have been presented in a way that highlights overlapping and interlinking chains of thought, this has very much remained at the broader theoretical level. In doing so, a framework of analysis has been presented around the concept of time, which was then applied to a discussion of time banking in order to demonstrate the relevance of temporality to understanding how time can have relevance to policy analysis – and the broader subject of social policy. In this chapter, the intention is to reiterate the key elements of this framework and discuss how it can be drawn upon to develop a broader political narrative (beyond time banking) for debates about how to enhance human welfare (the claimed aim of social policy; see Dean, 2012), before some concluding reflections upon the relevance of time for social policy as a subject and academic pursuit are considered. Before starting this discussion, however, there are a few things that should be made clear from the outset.

What follows is not the definitive or final claim as to the relevance of time as a concept in policy analysis; rather, it is a starting point. Additionally, the following argument is not a finalised idea outlining a policy prescription to be pursued, but the bringing together of several debates to illustrate how time is essential to policy discussion. Following this, it is important to stress that the ideas of a broader 'policy coalition' associated with time will be critiqued and resisted by many (that is an argument that forms part of this analysis), and while I am personally sympathetic to the various arguments presented (and supportive of their use of time in analysis), as with the framework itself, this is an early indication of the type of debate and argument possible when drawing on the theory of time – it is not the intention here to put forward an argument for welfare reform (that can be saved for later work).

As noted at the end of Chapter Six, there is a potential critique of what follows that it is an imposition of a middle-class, radical politics, developed within academic ivory towers and devoid of engagement with people's daily lives. Yet, here is the advantage of the argument presented. While it has engaged with the theoretical level, it has built this understanding upon the example of time banking, which required direct research into people's involvement and experience of the use of time banking in order to achieve a number of policy ends (Collom, 2008; New Economics Foundation, 2008c; Naughton-Doe, 2011b; Glynos and Speed, 2012; Gregory, 2012b; Hayashi, 2012). The use of time banking as an illustrative example of the debates in the previous chapters seeks to ensure that the discussion remains tied to lived experience while drawing upon appropriate theory. Additionally, as noted earlier, the aim is to adopt Bryson's (2007) suggestion that the 'blueprint' is not a finalised plan to be imposed, but the start of the debate.

The analytical framework: time

The focus of this book has been the use of the social theory of time within policy analysis. This has been presented as a concept for informing our understanding of society and the policies developed to sustain and enhance welfare. As Chapter Three illustrated, time offers a critique of contemporary Western society for the pervasive influence of the clock (Glennie and Thrift, 1996; Bauman, 2000; Adam, 2004), which disrupts our appreciation of alternative values associated with time. Thus, time offers both a critique of existing social relations and guidance for rethinking and redesigning social institutions and our lives. To help provide a framework for understanding this analysis, the discussion drew upon Levitas's (2005) 'utopian method' because this allows for an imaginary rethinking of how to organise society in order to facilitate debate about the future direction and development of our individual and collective lives. In this section, the stages of the 'utopian method' are drawn upon to frame the discussion across the initial chapters in order to provide the wider framework in a clear, summarised form.

The archaeological mode: investigating contemporary society

The 'archaeological' requires that an account of contemporary society is provided and critiqued, highlighting deficiencies that are to be corrected by the reimagining of society (Levitas, 2005). In Chapter Two, this account was initiated through a discussion of the financial crisis and the politics of austerity linked to the development of neoliberalisms within the Western world (focusing specifically on the UK as an illustrative example). This focus on hybrid forms of neoliberalism was essential for a number of reasons. Initially, it exposed the construction of citizenship, a core concept in policymaking and analysis, as being influenced by political, social and economic pressures. In particular, the discussion illustrated how under New Labour and the Coalition government, the normative assumptions of citizenship have changed. Shifting away from the 'traditional welfare' concept of citizenship influenced by Marshall, the modern (UK) construction draws together a communitarian concern with citizen participation, market influences of service consumers and increasing personal responsibilities for addressing social problems (similar constructions of active citizenship have developed in the US and across Europe; see Jansen et al, 2006; Nie et al, 1996). This was initially attached to New Labour's 'rights and responsibilities' agenda, continued under the Coalition government (Lister, 2011), but needs to be considered within the broader realisation that this is not just about creeping conditionality (Dwyer, 2004), but also a more subtle promotion of responsibility for personal finances, savings (Langley, 2004, 2006) and addressing community problems (Adamson, 2006; Cattell, 2011). Essentially, it seeks new forms of social control (Harrison and Sanders, 2014) and the embedding of neoliberal explanations of social problems deep within social welfare policy.

The construction of citizenship is important for two reasons. First, it illustrates dominant neoliberal views of how citizens should behave. Facilitating this change requires a rearranging of social, economic and welfare systems to support *individuals* to act in ways expected of them within neoliberal thinking. Clarke (2004) has illustrated how the public sector has changed in the UK – running parallel to similar debates across social policy since the 1980s – it has undergone a series of changes that have diminished the state's role and promoted non-state actors, predominately the private sector (Le Grand and Robinson, 1984; Drakeford, 2000; Kramer, 2000; Powell and Miller, 2014). The mixed economy of welfare has been altered so as to support dominant political and economic theories – which, at the time of writing, are neoliberal. The second important issue emanating from this discussion for citizenship it that it is a concept, like many others, open to debate and change. The Marshall model may have been critiqued from feminist perspectives for its male bias (Lister, 1997) but it is the shift to active citizenship that illustrates the impact that powerful discourses can have on the shape of key concepts in social policy. Both of these points are important because they demonstrate that it is possible to change these key concepts again with an alternative power-political discourse and to pursue policy reforms that create institutions that both facilitate and support the changes in how concepts are defined and enacted by individuals and communities. The initial aspect of the 'archaeological' investigation shows that concepts have changed; this changes how citizens are expected, and encouraged, to act and this, in turn, fosters changes in welfare systems.

While the construction of citizenship and the changes to the mixed economy of welfare are essential elements for understanding contemporary society, this discussion was linked to the analysis of self-help initiatives in order to demonstrate how, despite a wide range of purposes behind self-help, neoliberal hybrids promote particular forms that can be integrated into the narrative of social problems and solutions that find favour in this ideological position. The most recent incarnation of this co-option, the 'Big Society', was explored as part of the wider discussion of austerity – a fusing together of neoliberal concern with a small state and conservative moral authoritarian concern with moral and social order (Gregory, 2014). Combined with the changed conception of citizenship, this creates a powerful political discourse to explain how social life and the associated social problems we experience can, and should, be understood. The politicisation of concepts such as need has promoted individualised conceptualisations of social problems, which have been combined with cycles of deprivation explanations of poverty and understandings of health inequalities as matters of social capital to reaffirm that the cause and solution of social harms is outside the remit of the state and in the hands of the individual. Consequently, in the UK, the Social Attitudes Survey has mapped over 30 years of changing attitudes towards welfare provision, with the most recent survey indicating: a lessening of collectivist values in the UK despite continuing support for welfare provision to 'vulnerable' groups; a hardening of attitudes towards 'disadvantaged' groups; and the possibility that austerity may be changing public attitudes, causing them to be more supportive of assistance to impoverished groups. Essentially, in the UK, these changing attitudes have been attributed to changing explanations of the causes of problems, such as poverty, which are predominately defined within the government's terms (Clery et al, 2013). The influence of political discourse in explaining social problems is made apparent in research that illustrates how different articulations of the involvement of the state, individuals and other institutions in explaining social problems influence welfare provision (Blekesaune and Quadagno, 2003). Neoliberal hybrids, it could be argued for the UK, have successfully embedded their conception of citizenship and the required working of welfare and other systems and institutions in contemporary society to support this. However, this can be changed through the successful promotion of alternative conceptions of citizenship and explanations of social problems.

The archaeological mode: the critique

Understanding the existing social structures and institutional arrangements is the first part of the archaeological mode – which, in this discussion, has explored the influence of neoliberal theory on the provision of welfare. A critical appraisal is also necessary, and this was the function of Chapter Three and the core aspect of this analysis: time. Drawing the social theory of time into a discussion of neoliberal hybrids first required outlining how time can be defined and how this, in turn, influences social organisation. The discussion outlined 'absolute' and 'relative' time (Adam, 1990) to argue that the former, associated with 'clock time', dominates in contemporary Western society, embedding the idea that 'time is money' into economic and social interactions. Influential in the development of industrialisation and therefore the establishment of neoliberal capitalism, this clock-time perspective colonises social life as it permeates not only economic relations, but also our social interactions – to the extent that 'quality time' itself becomes a measured segment of time, experiencing the same temporal pressures as other 'times' in our lives (Kremer-Sadlik and Paugh, 2007).

'Relative time', however, offers a different understanding of how time is experienced and interwoven throughout social life. While a range of different 'times' have consequently been put forward, the analysis in Chapter Three paid particular attention to 'task time' and 'process time' as useful concepts for examining different social activities (Thompson, 1967; Davies, 1994). Embedded within these debates exists a critique of clock time, an exploration of the dangers of its dominance in Western society and, subsequently, a critique of a key tenet of neoliberal economic theory. To this, it is possible to add a number of other critiques of the damaging consequences of unbridled neoliberalism: from environmental damage (Bullard and Johnson, 2000; Bell, 2011; Walker and Burningham, 2011), which overlaps with a temporal critique of Western society (Kümmerer, 1996; Adam, 1998), to wealth and health inequalities (Marmot, 2010; Mackenbach, 2011; Katikireddi et al, 2013), poverty, disadvantage and exclusion (Hussain et al, 2011; Bennett, 2014; Gordon, 2014), and cycles of 'low-pay, no-pay' (Shildrick et al, 2012). While an analysis around time can offer a critique, as illustrated in Chapter Three, it also contains the potential to go beyond critique to suggest alternative values, informing different conceptions of citizenship and the institutional arrangements needed to support these. It can provide a framework for social action and renewed political endeavour.

Poverty, for example, can be, and is, highlighted as a persistent problem in contemporary society. However, a range of solutions to this issue exist. Some of these solutions can be found within neoliberal theory and so the solution suggested is a restriction on welfare provision (or its outright removal) in order to enhance worker discipline and encourage individuals to return to employment and get themselves out of poverty (Mead, 1986; Murray, 1990). At the same time, social-democratic explanations have focused on the structural causes of poverty and argued for state intervention to create jobs and provide unemployment support in times of needs (see Barber, 2009)[1]. Both positions offer different explanations for poverty and different solutions, but essentially speak the same language of industrialisation – spending *time* in employment produces income and profits – thus both accept the dominance of clock time. The introduction of relative time as an explicit concept to account for social and economic activities questions this shared language by offering a counter-narrative to the dominance of the clock. As such, time offers the opportunity for a much broader rethinking of how we, as citizens, should live our lives (the 'ontological mode') while developing new social institutions and interactions to support this revised idea of the 'good life' (the 'architectural mode'). This is essentially the core of the Reisch (2001) quote at the opening of this chapter: money as wealth dominates our social organisation and political debate to the extent that time is considered only as an input and constraint – its intrinsic value is dismissed – thus diminishing the potential for a time-as-wealth perspective.

Consequently, Chapter Three suggested that the concept of 'time wealth' offered by Reisch (2001) overlaps with other attempts to develop alternative narratives of time in relation to contemporary society. In particular, attention was drawn to Biesecker's (1998) argument for a 'new economy of time', which allows citizens to engage in public debate about the policies that impact upon their lives. For Fitzpatrick (2004b), Chapter Three demonstrated how this was dependent upon a more equal distribution of time, which shares some similar ideas to the argument of Goodin and colleagues around the idea of temporal well-being and the ways in which state provision influences the amount of free time that citizens have outside of necessary paid labour, personal and caring time (Goodin, 2010; Goodin et al, 2004, 2008). A critique of contemporary welfare provision through the social theory of time, therefore, requires that we rethink social relations – and this will be the focus of the following sections.

Archaeological mode: co-option

Part of this exploration of contemporary society and the analysis of time, however, highlighted the potential of co-option. It was suggested that capitalism deploys a number of techniques that seek to incorporate alternative forms of production into its dominant framework for understanding social activity. This drew upon the work of Gibson-Graham (1996, 2006) and made links with analysis of community currency systems (CCSs) in relation to their work (Leyshon and Lee, 2003; Williams et al, 2003) and more broadly (Pacione, 1997; Peacock, 2006). To help explore this potential co-option, Chapter Four outlined the history, theory and development of time banking, looking specifically at the UK context but with commentary on global developments as well. This paid particular attention to the relevance of the concept of co-production to time banking, the initiatives associated with self-help and thus its relevance as an illustrative example of how self-help initiatives can be positioned as alternatives to and co-conspirators of neoliberal practices .

The key issues drawn out here included the critique presented by North that 'time money' is less radical than other forms of CCSs and, as such, does not offer the same potential to challenge dominant neoliberal ideas. Rather, the association with co-production limits the radical potential. While some sympathy for this argument can be found in the distinction between the 'additive' and 'transformational' uses of co-production explored in Chapter Four (Glynos and Speed, 2012), it has been suggested that such a view overlooks the alternative values promoted and explicitly recognised through an engagement with relative definitions of time. Particularly important here is that time banking exchange may implicitly contain an acknowledgement of these alternative values, but that these are not overtly recognised in time bank theory. Here, the distinction between the political and technical goals of time banking (Gregory, 2009a) offered a means of making these differences explicit, alongside Cahn's use of the core and market economy dualism. The real limitations to the promotion of alternatives, however, was located with the presentation of time banking by Cahn (2000) as a form of service delivery reform that seeks to be politically neutral (Cahn and Rowe, 1992).

Chapter Five examined the tension between co-option and the promotion of alternatives. This drew upon the concept of time suggested by Adam (1998) in her development of a 'timescape' – the development of an understanding of the multiple times within society or a social institution. In a small way, but not in the full sense in which Adam has sought to do, Chapter Five offers an overview of time banking, dividing the discussion into an account of the surface level of time banking (the measurement) and an account of how time is experienced and lived underneath that surface – linking to the discussion of 'task time' and 'process time'. The argument here was that time banking shows that we cannot accept just one expression of time when discussing social interaction, but must appreciate the multiple times that will be involved in time bank activities. The challenge, however, relates to the co-option argument broadly. The dominance of the measurement of time that time banking facilitates not only provides a useful auditing tool for monitoring active citizenship, but also helps to bring the initiative into neoliberal hybrid conceptions of both citizenship and self-help. Time treated as a resource can easily be attached to the time-is-money mantra dominant in contemporary Western society.

However, Chapter Five also illustrated that there are alternative values to time that are the primary drivers of time bank activity for time bank staff and members. This account of interaction and engagement, therefore, does not easily fit into the dominant perspective of time banking as a form of 'Big Society' self-help because it requires that individuals have the time free from employment and personal/family care to invest in their communities. It opens up space for starting to question the dominant conception of 'active citizens' whose primary duty is employment in order to maintain economic growth, accumulation and profit creation. However, as has been noted, time banking alone is not capable of achieving the broader critique necessary to promote change – this is discussed in more detail later.

Essentially, the co-option focus of the 'archaeological' analysis is presented to demonstrate the challenges to be overcome if alternatives are to be promoted. In particular, Chapter Six offers an account of how this co-option may be occurring with reference to the wider voluntary sector in the UK. Much in the same way as how citizenship has been redefined and the mixed economy of welfare altered to support this alternative conception, powerful, political discourses have influenced how voluntary organisations seek to maintain their daily activities and services. Attention was given to isomorphic pressures, which have shifted and changed the voluntary sector and associated it with the concept of resilience. Resilience itself is presented in a positive way, and, as such, is difficult to critique. However, the argument in Chapter Six is that the concept of resilience seeks to position self-help as a form of community engagement which ensures that communities can survive turbulent global economic changes that impact upon the local, but does not encourage a questioning of the need for resilience or what communities need to be resilient against. To do so would expose the dominant neoliberal ideology in the UK (and beyond) to criticism, for which it may have few, if any, answers. Rather, the alternative idea of 'resistance' was offered to provide a space for articulating the alternative values of time found in the earlier discussions and position collective action as against dominant neoliberal ideas. The suggestion here, as noted earlier, is that this questioning should not lead to the imposition of another powerful, political set of ideas and practices, but, rather, create space in which the purpose of citizens and collective life are debated and decided, with economic, political and social institutions designed to best support this process and, eventually, the outcome of those deliberations. The analysis of policy embedded in the theory of time illustrates the limitations on social action and the potential damage and harm caused by contemporary social arrangements, and offers a language for creating the discursive spaces and forms of citizenship necessary for creating alternatives.

Developing alternative policies

In drawing the social theory of time into an analysis of society and welfare policy, the aim is not only to provide a critique of contemporary society, but to offer up alternative social organisations and definitions of key welfare concepts that can be explored and advocated in the pursuit of greater human well-being within a sustainable environmental and economic context. It is not the intention here to provide a full account of this; to do so would require an in-depth engagement with a range of different concepts and welfare practices, which is not the intention behind this book. Rather, here, the discussion will explore the need to articulate alternatives, how this can be done and, by drawing on the concept of time, how it is possible to draw together a range of policy ideas to start to present a coherent alternative. As noted earlier, this is an example of what can be done, which needs to be further explored and developed in later work. Subsequently, this is the initial stage of a wider body of work, which sets out key areas for consideration within a discussion of the need to promote alternatives. In what follows, therefore, the discussion returns to the idea of 'function' highlighted in Chapter Three, delves a bit deeper into the idea of 'time-wealth' and outlines a potential policy coalition based upon temporal analysis. The final section of this chapter concludes with some reflections on the relevance of time for social policy as a study and academic pursuit. Thus, drawing upon the 'utopian method' (Levitas, 2005), this discussion establishes the foundation for the 'architectural' and 'ontological' modes – thinking about how we can *be* differently and the social institutions that can help support this alternative.

Function and time

It has been argued that time banking exhibits the dominance of the use value of time rather than its exchange value and that this illustrates how alternative values exist in time bank practice, as embedded within Cahn's (2000) concept of a 'core economy'. However, Cahn argued that the core and market economy are complementary, each with their own set of values to guide the activities that are carried out within each. While we should therefore not impose the values of one onto the other, there is growing critique that neoliberal values have pervaded across a range of social institutions and interactions, including the welfare state, which pushes to one side non-market values (Jordan, 2010a, 2010b). While Jordan, for example, is critical of this development, Chapter Three illustrates how, from the perspective of time, there are a number of critiques that can be levelled at this development. When considering the common purpose of society, this leads to a debate about whether we can suggest that particular sets of values should remain embedded within their own 'domain' or whether there should be some broader values that direct human activity. From the perspective of social policy, there must be support for the latter position, concepts such as need, equality, citizenship and inclusion cut across social institutions and actions, but these are informed by different political and philosophical traditions. The current dominant articulations are heavily influenced by neoliberal thinking, but, as noted earlier, this comes with a number of social harms that diminish citizen well-being. Where you live, your parents' employment and your access to wealth or even transport can still impact upon how long you live, your educational opportunities, your inclusion and your participation in mainstream society. Neoliberal dominance is having severe negative impacts that need to be continually questioned and alternatives need to be promoted.

Tawney's (1921: 1–2) introduction to *The Acquisitive Society* is relevant here as he suggests that:

> Most generations, it might be said, walk in a path which they neither make, nor discover, but accept; the main thing is that they should march. The blinkers worn by Englishmen enable them to trot all the more steadily along the beaten road, without being disturbed by curiosity as to their destination.

The argument here is that people follow the apparent set path for society unquestioningly, without consideration of the destination or the consequences that this path may have. Such an argument overlaps with Cahn's (2000: 201) suggestion that:

> [t]he challenge our species now faces is to create a healthy ecological niche: communities that nurture, space that is non-toxic, exchanges that do not deplete, relationships based on love and caring, transactions powered by the renewable energy of compassion and empathy and reciprocity.

Yet, he does not provide an argument for the promotion of non-market values over those of the market to help meet this challenge. Tawney requires that we question the path upon which society travels in order to expose the potential and actual damage caused by this blinkered march and to search for alternatives. The critique based on the dominance of the clock and its colonising effects blinds us to an overt and explicit appreciation of non-clock time and how this is lived and experienced and enriches our daily lives. Essential to any efforts to promote alternatives is the need to find the appropriate language to articulate them. Here, Tawney's (1921: 8) notion of 'function', which as discussed in Chapter Three, is defined as:

> an activity which embodies and expresses the idea of social purpose. The essence of it is that the agent does not perform it merely for personal gain or to gratify himself, but recognizes that he is responsible for its discharge to some higher authority.

Function requires us to rethink what social activities should be valued and pursued in the achievement of society's common purpose and collective well-being. Here, we need to move away from the acquisitiveness and profit-seeking activities of contemporary society, which contain environmentally destructive and individualising consequences, and pursue and prioritise acts which enhances human well-being. The intention behind the concept of function is to break away from private profit-making and acquisitiveness in order to ask what the underpinning social purpose is behind certain activities and practices and to ensure that only activities that enhance collective human well-being, not individual profit, are pursued. This debate is not easy to settle, as current debates of what is 'just' and 'fair' demonstrate – ideas of meritocracy remain prominent in the public conscious. However, as Inequality Briefing[2] has demonstrated in relation to wealth distribution, the current spread of wealth does not match up with the public perception of what that distribution should be. Thus, in this example, acquisitiveness has priority over function in contemporary society. This generates inequalities and disadvantages and excludes many from society and the range of opportunities that wealth can provide; however, within the dominant neoliberal language of politics, this is an acceptable state of affairs – although the public disagree .

Thus, the use of concepts such as function provides us with a language that can help to question current social relations in a way that is accessible to the wider public. Where time is relevant to this discussion is that it provides us with a broader narrative to underpin and help define what we mean by function. As illustrated in Chapter Three, time has been considered in relation to: time use and ensuring that citizens have discretionary time (Goodin, 2010); the environmental consequences of neoliberal capitalism (Kümmerer, 1996); community and family life (Kenyon, 2000); as well as our work lives (Oechsle and Geissler, 2003) . Many of these are critiques of clock-time dominance that seek to promote alternative times and our explicit recognition of their importance, and to encourage us to think about alternative social arrangements that allow us to live our lives in very different ways from how they currently are. In essence, time provides a thread that brings together a range of social concerns and policy domains, offering both a critique and suggestions of alternatives. This helps us to consider Tawney's (1921: 2–3) suggestion that society has a choice: 'to move with the energetic futility of a squirrel in a revolving cage … [or seize the moment with] a clear apprehension both of the deficiency of what is, and of the character of what ought to be'. Function, underpinned by an explicit understanding of the multiplicity of time, offers an opportunity to grasp the deficiency of what is and what ought to be and requires that we start to think about a new 'wealth-of-time'.

Wealth-of-time

A running theme in the discussion across the previous chapters is that there is a need to ensure that citizens have the time to engage in a range of deliberative activities and community 'care work' in order to secure democratic participation in decisions around policy development, the articulation of a common purpose and the definition of citizenship. This, in turn, requires the reform of social institutions, in particular, welfare services, in order to support a different conception of citizenship and the rights and duties demanded of this new definition. For Bryson (2007), it was shown that such duties need to involve care work as being the primary duty of citizens – individual care, family care and community care. For Fitzpatrick (2004b), this required a critique of Rawls's notion of justice and the embedded acceptance of normative expectations of industrial societies as the baseline of citizen activities. For others, such as Jordan (2004), there is a need to pursue forms of collective action and social provision that allow individuals and communities to engage in a range of social activities and associations outside of the market and employment in order to foster local attachment, community cohesion and new sources of well-being. Such views overlap with calls for new forms of leisure time consumption that do not require purchases within the market, thus fuelling continual growth and profit seeking (Soper, 2008), and organisations promoting life outside of employment (such as the Idle Foundation[3] and the Unemployment Movement[4]).

The achievement of these alternatives requires that a clear, well-articulated alternative to neoliberal theory is presented. One starting point for this is the promotion of multiple economics in order to illustrate the work that occurs outside of the marketplace (Gibson-Graham et al, 2013) and to recognise the numerous forms of non-market activity and the contribution that they make to communal and individual life (Williams and Windebank, 2001a, 2001b). Such a development must be underpinned by the appreciation of multiple times and the critique of the dominance of the clock, as outlined in Chapter Three, potentially guided by the arguments of Biesecker (1998) and Reisch (2001).

Biesecker (1998) argues that the association of time with either money or as a resource maintains the constant acceleration of market activity in Western societies, which has negative consequences for social life and the natural environment – as noted by others in Chapter Three. This economic rationality must be questioned if we are to ensure sustainable living and maintain human life and well-being (an overlapping theme in environmentalist critiques of current economic practices; see Boyle and Simms, 2009; Bell, 2011). Biesecker (1998: 86) therefore argues for a new economy of time, which 'entails the liberation of the social life-world from time structures governed by the economy and the imperative of acceleration'. Not only will individuals and groups across society live and experience different temporal rhythms (Kenyon, 2000), but there is also a need to safeguard times outside of employment and to liberate these times from the directives of consumerism. Such arguments overlap with the New Economics Foundation's suggestion of shorter working weeks (see later), although, for Biesecker (1998: 87), this is tied to basic incomes as the:

> liberation from work time can only be accomplished with a reduction in affluence. However, it may be that the wealth of having time limits the need for money. However, a certain amount of financial security is necessary to enjoy the increase in time.

Biesecker is arguing for a complete reform of economic practices along the lines of non-economic principles, putting non-market values at the forefront of the functions of different activities to achieve human well-being, as such, there in an overlap with Reisch's (2001) wealth-of-time perspective.

Reisch (2001) seeks to redefine wealth, starting with a similar critique of the dominant economic model. She suggests that:

> Beyond a certain income level, the marginal utility of more available time is higher than the marginal utility of more available income. Yet, economists usually do not recognize any value creation in those activities performed outside formal work.... Personal pursuits, networks of reciprocity, and public associations do not enter the welfare function and thus leave material consumption in the limelight. (Reisch, 2001: 377)

She suggests that a basic income can help secure people's income so that they are able to take time away from employment to engage in other, non-work activities essential to human well-being (similar to the suggestions found in Jordan, 2004). Thus, the creation of a new wealth-of-time model in society must encompass five key aspects: a *chronometric* dimension, having the necessary time to carry out different activities; a *chronologic* dimension, having time at the right time for natural and social rhythms (such as festivities); *personal time autonomy/ sovereignty* in setting the pace of our work and its content; *synchronisation* with the time constraints of others (families and friends); and a *plurality of 'timescapes'*, essentially, the establishment of public offices to coordinate institutions in order to diminish the disruptions caused by the multiplicity of times that will flourish. Reisch realises that the promotion of rearranging time use within society will be challenging, not only for the disruption to the current order and pattern of time use that we already appreciate and experience, but because it will require breaking away from forms of consumption and living with which we are comfortable, but that are socially and environmentally damaging.

Once again, it is possible to argue for the concept of function based on these ideas. Function allows us to question and uncover the purpose behind our social actions and economic organisation to achieve human well-being. We can ask these questions in the broader sense of questioning the social and environmental consequences of the dominance of the market logic and the promotion of market consumption as the main source of leisure, enjoyment and well-being. Through this narrative, we can start to question the dominant perception of time as a means of exchange and as a resource, and realise that the use value of time offers new insights into achieving human well-being, potentially, in environmentally sustainable ways, which seek to challenge and roll back the dominance of the market over social life. Embedded in these debates are a number of policy suggestions, which will briefly be explored before some general conclusions are made.

Policy coalition for alternatives

In exploring the potential of time as a concept in policy analysis for promoting non-market values and offering alternatives to the neoliberal hybrids dominant in political and economic thought, the example of time banking as a CCS has been examined. The suggestion was that despite an appearance of this initiative as being suitable to neoliberal forms of self-help, its practices exhibit an engagement with and experience of non-market values. For CCSs, this has been a key argument for the promotion of sustainable, non-market practices that develop local economies and social relations outside of capitalist values (Williams, 1996; Seyfang and Pearson, 2000; North, 2006b; Seyfang and Longhurst, 2013a). This has been the basis of the 'Transition Town' movement, which has sought to promote CCSs as an initial stage in changing economic practices in order to create environmentally sustainable forms of production and exchange. This has been built upon the alternative economic writings of authors such as Ruskin (1862) and Schumacher (1974), which have also informed the work of the New Economics Foundation (2008d, 2009) in their broader analysis of the social, environmental and economic crisis, as well as in its support for the use of co-production and CCSs. Time has relevance here for a number of reasons.

First, as was shown in Chapter Five, the multiplicity of times within time bank activity demonstrates that time offers a means by which the alternative values of CCS exchange can be understood. Beyond this, however, the use of time to analyse time bank activities demonstrates that different temporal rhythms, related to the ideas of task time and process time, guide activity. Similar consideration has been given to Local Exchange Trading Systems (LETS) in order to demonstrate how time-based exchange and different temporal practices are embedded in the core of CCS activity and how these may conflict with dominant perceptions of clock time (Bowring, 1998; Cooper, 2013). For such activities to flourish, however, there is a need to recognise that 'work' not only refers to employment, but also to a wider range of activities. This is part of the core values established by Cahn (2000) and is represented in discussions of alternative forms of production and exchange (Williams and Windebank, 2001a, 2001b; Leyshon and Lee, 2003; Williams et al, 2003; Gibson-Graham et al, 2013) and local circuits of value (discussed in Chapter Three; see also Lee et al, 2004; Lee, 2006). Second, it demonstrates the different temporalities that people live within one community, let alone within and across nations (Kenyon, 2000). Third, the promotion of these alternative forms of work overlaps with the feminist critique about the role of women as primary carers and a need for a notion of citizenship that creates greater equality across genders in this care activity (Jenson and Sineau, 2001). This has clear links with Bryson (2007), who has built her time-based analysis upon this relationship between care and citizenship and drawn CCSs into her account as a practical example of how alternative values associated with time use are practised in contemporary settings.

This care work is essential to the 'core economy' promoted by Cahn (2000) and can relate to care activities for the self, for family and for the wider community. The ability to engage in these care activities requires that citizens not only recognise the importance of these activities, but are also able to have the time to engage within this activity. Goodin et al (2004) have demonstrated how the welfare state can subtly influence how much 'discretionary time' individuals have; thus, there needs to be an explicit account of time within welfare provision to better understand its relevance to human well-being. One often repeated recommendation is the development of a basic income as a means of providing financial security to all citizens so that they have greater temporal autonomy. Fitzpatrick, Reisch and Biesecker have all suggested that a basic income is a vital tool in creating temporal autonomy, allowing citizens to engage in increased leisure and associational activity, but also to become involved in deliberative processes around policymaking and implementation and the formation of a collective purpose. For Fitzpatrick, this is an essential element of his concept of 'relational time', which may foster links with debates in favour of 'associational democracy' (Hirst, 1994). In fact, the discussions of citizen-centred welfare and 'relational welfare' discussed in Chapter Five require that citizens have time outside of employment to engage in the public sector in various ways.

Whether we wish to pursue these reforms, and how well they relate to each other, is open to debate. What has briefly been attempted here is a demonstration that through an understanding of time, it is possible to offer a particular critique of contemporary society and welfare provision. Questioning the impact dominant values have on social life, as well as the environmental consequences of the ways of life these values generate, have been brought together here by a critique of the dominance of clock time as the driving force behind social and economic life based. This opens up a discussion of multiple times that not only offers a new perspective to consider in relation to well-being, but suggests the need for urgent changes to how society operates in order to ensure that social and environmental life are sustainable, and offers some insight into the need for different economic theories and practices to support these changes (a recent collection of essays on time offers many insights into these topics; see Coote and Franklin, 2013). The multiplicity of time is embedded within all of our social interactions and institutions. What this argument has tried to offer is an explanation as to how an explicit recognition of this not only offers a new critique of society, but also creates new insight into the possible alternatives and how these can be achieved in order to provide all citizens with the opportunity to have greater time sovereignty in achieving their individual, as well as collective, welfare.

Conclusion

There remain challenges to the promotion of a renewed social purpose, a re-conceptualisation of citizenship and the development of welfare institutions that support the alternatives suggested by a temporal analysis. Some of these have been explored earlier in relation to the idea of co-option. However, the first major challenge is to find the right language for promoting these alternatives, and the suggestion has been that the concept of 'function' is relevant here, for it offers an understandable way of expressing in public the key questions: 1) 'How does this activity improve collective well-being?'; 2) 'What environmental impact does this activity have?'; and 3) 'Does this activity contribute to our collective purpose and the "good society"?'. Yet, as the imposition of 'austerity politics' resulting from the economic crisis of 2008 unleashes neoliberal theory and practice on to welfare policy with renewed zeal, it is important to recall Pierson's (2006: 233) view: 'within the envisageable future, the "real" issue is not going to be whether we have a welfare state ... but what sort of welfare state regime it will be'.

Chapter Six explored some early efforts to resist 'austerity' in the UK (and beyond), indicating a disenfranchisement with government agendas to cut welfare provision. Rarely, however, do these movements offer a clear alternative other than to maintain traditional forms of welfare provision supported by the increased taxation of corporations. While this in and of itself is not necessarily a bad thing, the real challenge rests in finding convincing alternatives to the logic of neoliberalism that not only provide a clear critique of its practices, but can also foster the development of a series of welfare reforms targeted an enhancing human welfare, securing environmental sustainability and renewing key concepts in policymaking, such as citizenship. Such a challenge must be able to remain coherent under the discursive onslaught of neoliberal arguments that locate social problems with individuals, but it must also be able to reverse the current situation in welfare provision, as outlined by Hayward (2012):

> Market fundamentalism results in market failure and state defeatism. When the inequalities and instabilities of the deregulated market system cannot be justified, their excesses are presented as unavoidable. The secure do not need state support, so the most devoted patriots are the poor and insecure because they know they have little else to depend upon than their compatriots' solidarity. Their only hope is

that once again, the squalid consequences of liberty without
solidarity will lead to a reassertion of statecraft as a corrective
to self-serving acquisitiveness.

Critical theory offers one potential option for critiquing current social
arrangements and finding the alternative pathway demanded of us
by Tawney. Drawing upon the 'utopian method' outlined by Levitas
(2005) as a guide, this text has combined the ideas of Gibson-Graham
(1993, 1996) with the social theory of time to offer an account of
how social policy can engage in the search for alternative non-market
values, examine their development within welfare provision and
draw upon them, potentially, within the wider narrative of 'function'
(Tawney, 1921), in order to articulate alternative welfare arrangements.
To promote such alternatives will require a greater understanding
of the interrelationship between time and social welfare, which the
discussion in Chapter Three demonstrated as already being underway.
Furthermore, a form of social policy must be accepted that is willing to
be overt in its critique and suggested alternatives – a more prescriptive
than descriptive study of welfare provision.

The development of neoliberal hybrids and their co-opting discursive
practices pre-date the economic challenges of the 2008 financial crisis.
Yet, this crisis has created an opportunity to seek alternatives (Do we
really wish to build social life on an economic system prone to crash?)
and to start to question the relationship between the state, market,
citizen, community and environment in order to find new forms of
sustainable living that enhance the well-being of all. A number of
different 'varieties of crises' (Farnsworth and Irving, 2011) exist due
to the global nature of the economic crash, and different national
contexts will underpin different national responses. However, the
global dominance of neoliberal economics means that there is potential
for the discussion in this book to cut across national boundaries.
Tawney (1921) suggested that there was a need to find alternative
paths to secure human well-being and bring to an end the destructive
consequences of acquisitiveness. The economic crisis and its impact
on unemployment, continuing health and educational inequalities,
the environmental damage of economic activity, the crisis in housing
provision and homelessness, and a range of other issues all remind us
that neoliberalism is not working. Yet, it persists as the dominant means
of understanding human interaction and for framing human activities.
However, alternatives exist.

Contemporary efforts to promote alternatives can be found within
the New Economics Foundation's suggestion of operating welfare

provision based on zero-growth economics, co-production and shorter working hours (Boyle and Simms, 2009; Coote and Franklin, 2010, 2013). Such arguments continue a tradition of anti-productivist[5] approaches to organising society (Offe, 1992; Douthwaite, 1996; O'Connor, 1998; Dordoy and Mellor, 2000) and recent accounts on the promotion of sustainable ways of delivering social policy and social work (Jordan and Drakeford, 2012). Alternatives are abound; the concept of time, however, can help to draw these alternatives together into a coherent narrative based around the function of different activities – their intentions, benefits and (economic, environmental and social) costs.

Essentially, these critiques seek to find ways of breaking with the drive for production and profitability in order to allow for a wider consideration of how we define, measure and provide welfare and well-being to encompass social and environmental concerns. What is essential to promoting and bringing these ideas together is an appreciation of the use value of time. C. Wright Mills (1959) offered a sociological analysis that focused upon the connection between the micro- and macro-levels of society in order to highlight how personal troubles relate to public issues of social structure. Cattell (2011) builds on this in her work on poverty, health and community in order to integrate Engels's view of 'social murder', where structural arrangements of society are to blame for ill-health and early deaths (a theme revised in the idea of social harm, see Pemberton, 2015). She argues that cuts in public services, the rolling back of the state and the promotion of the 'Big Society', on top of existing inequalities, will not only fail, but also potentially further damage the lives of the poorest. In doing so, she reflects the recent focus on Titmuss's suggestion that policies should be judged by how they impact on the worst off in society – and that failure to make a positive impact is the mark of an irresponsible society (Sinfield, 2011). In a similar way, the intention here has been to draw on Tawney's (1921) argument that it is necessary to know both the destination of society's path and the consequences of following that path. In knowing the destination, it may be necessary to search out alternatives. When the multiplicity of time and its relevance to social policy and human welfare –promoting alternative forms of economic activity and protecting the environment – is understood, it is possible to start to question wider social structures, dominant political discourses and the social and environmental harms that they cause, and to start the search for alternatives. Time, therefore, is at the core of a raft of potential reforms that can help to resist the dominance of neoliberal logic in social and economic organisation.

Notes

1 See: https://www.tuc.org.uk/international-issues/globalisation/international-development/global-economic-justice-campaigns

2 See: http://inequalitybriefing.org/brief/wealth-video

3 See: http://idlefoundation.org/

4 See: https://twitter.com/unemploymentmov

Anti-productivism is an approach to addressing environmental concerns by breaking with the productivist paradigm in which material well-being is equated with exponential production, stimulated by the pursuit of profit. Instead, it seeks sustainable ways of ensuring well-being outside of a drive for productivity and profitability.

References

Adam, B. (1990) *Time and Social Theory*, Cambridge: Polity Press.

Adam, B. (1994/95) Time for Feminist Approaches to Technology, 'Nature' and Work. *Arena journal* 4: 91–104.

Adam, B. (1996) Beyond the Present. *Time & Society* 5: 319–338.

Adam, B. (1998) *Timescapes of Modernity: The Environment and Invisible Hazards*, London: Routledge.

Adam, B. (2001) When Time is Money: Contested Rationalities of Time and Challenges to the Theory and Practice of Work. *Working Paper 16*. Published by Cardiff School of Social Sciences, Cardiff University, Cardiff. Available at: http://www.cf.ac.uk/socsi/research/publications/workingpapers/index.html

Adam, B. (2004) *Time*, Cambridge: Polity Press.

Adam, B. and Groves, C. (2007) *Future Matters: Action, Knowledge, Ethics*, Leiden and Boston, MA: Brill.

Adam, B., Hockey, J. and Thompson, P. (2008) WP1 – Researching Lives Through Time. Available at: http://www.timescapes.leeds.ac.uk/assets/files/timescapes/WP1-Researching-Lives-Through-Time-June-2008.pdf

Adams, J. and Schmueker, K. (2005) *Devolution in Practice 2006: Public Policy Differences Within the UK*, London: IPPR.

Adamson, D. (2006) Community Regeneration Policy, the State and Civil Society. In: G. Day, D. Dunkerley and A. Thompson (eds) *Civil Society in Wales: Policy, Politics and People*, Cardiff: University of Wales Press, pp 271–293.

Adamson, D. (2008) Still Living on the Edge? *Contemporary Wales* 21: 47–66.

Adger, W.N. (2000) Social and Ecological Resilience: Are They Related? *Progress in Human Geography* 24: 347–364.

Adger, W.N. (2003) Social Capital, Collective Action, and Adaptation to Climate Change. *Economic Geography* 79: 387–404.

Adger, W.N., Hughes, T.P., Folke, C., Carpenter, S.R. and Rockström, J. (2005) Social-Ecological Resilience to Coastal Disasters. *Science* 309: 1036–1039.

Ahuja, A. (2009) Estonia's Bank of Happiness: Trading Good Deeds. Available at: http://www.thetimes.co.uk/tto/life/article1855495.ece

Ainsworth, D. (2009) Third Sector Should Be Called 'First Sector', Cameron Says. Available at: http://www.thirdsector.co.uk/third-sector-called-first-sector-cameron-says/policy-and-politics/article/917732

Alcock, P. (2004) Participation or Pathology: Contradictory Tensions in Area-Based Policy. *Social Policy and Society* 3: 87–96.

Alcock, P. (2010) Building the Big Society: A New Policy Environment for the Third Sector in England. *Voluntary Sector Review* 1: 379–389.

Alcock, P. (2012) The Big Society: A New Policy Environment for the Third Sector? Available at: http://www.birmingham.ac.uk/generic/tsrc/documents/tsrc/working-papers/working-paper-82.pdf

Alford, J. (1998) A Public Management Road Less Travelled: Clients as Co-producers of Public Services. *Australian Journal of Public Administration* 57: 128–137.

Alford, J. (2002) Defining the Client in the Public Sector: A Social-Exchange Perspective. *Public Administration Review* 62: 337–346.

Anderson, R. and Bury, M. (1998) *Living with Chronic Illness: The Experience of Patients and Their Families*, London: Unwin Hyman Ltd.

Annetts, J., Law, A., McNeish, W. and Mooney, G. (2009) *Understanding Social Welfare Movements*, Bristol: The Policy Press.

Ariizumi, H. and Schirle, T. (2012) Are Recessions Really Good for Your Health? Evidence from Canada. *Social Science & Medicine* 74: 1224–1231.

Arnstein, S.R. (1969) A Ladder of Citizen Participation. *Journal of the American Institute of Planners* 35: 216–224.

Arvidson, M., Lyon, F., McKay, S. and Moro, D. (2013) Valuing the Social? The Nature and Controversies of Measuring Social Return on Investment (SROI). *Voluntary Sector Review* 4: 3–18.

Athwal, B., Brill, L., Chesters, G. and Quiggin, M. (2011) *Recession, Poverty and Sustainable Livelihoods in Bradford*, York: JRF.

Ayres, J.M. (2004) Framing Collective Action Against Neoliberalism: The Case of the "Anti-Globalization" Movement. *Journal of World-Systems Research* X: 11–34.

Bagguley, P. and Mann, K. (1992) Idle Thieving Bastards: Scholarly Representations of the Underclass. *Work, Employment and Society* 6: 113–126.

Bandura, A. (1977) *Social Learning Theory*, Englewood Cliffs, NJ: Prentice Hall.

Bandura, A. (1994) Self-Efficacy. In: V.S. Ramachandran (ed) *Encyclopaedia of Human Behaviour*, San Diego, CA: Academic Press, pp 71–81.

Batty, E. and Flint, J. (2010) *Self-Esteem, Comparative Poverty and Neighbourhoods*. Research Paper No. 7, Living Through Change in Challenging Neighbourhoods: A Research Project funded by the Joseph Rowntree Foundation, York: JRF.

Bauman, Z. (2000) Time and Space Reunited. *Time & Society* 9: 171–185.

Bauman, Z. (2001) *Community: Seeking Safety in an Insecure World*, Cambridge: Polity.

Bauman, Z. (2009) The Absence of Society. In: D. Utting (ed) *Contemporary Social Evils*, Bristol: The Policy Press, pp 147–157.

BBC News (2010) Minister Hails Japan Care Scheme. Available at: http://www.bbc.co.uk/news/uk-11657006

BBC News (2012) Germany's Merkel Urges Greek Commitment to Austerity. Available at: http://www.bbc.co.uk/news/world-europe-18474437

Bean, P., Ferris, J. and Whynes, D. (1985) *In Defence of Welfare*. London: Tavistock Publications

Beck, U. (1992) *Risk Society*, London: Sage.

Becker, S. (1997) *Responding to Poverty: The Politics of Cash and Care*, Essex: Longman Press Limited.

Beckett, A. (2013) What is the 'global race'. *The Guardian* http://www.theguardian.com/politics/2013/sep/22/what-is-global-race-conservatives-ed-miliband

Befu, H. (1977) Social Exchange. *Annual Review of Anthropology* 6: 255–281.

Bell, K. (2011) Environmental Justice in Cuba. *Critical Social Policy* 31: 241–265.

Ben-Ami, D. (2012) *Ferraris for All: In Defence of Economic Progress*, Bristol: The Policy Press.

Bennett, F. (2014) The 'Living Wage', Low Pay and in Work Poverty: Rethinking the Relationships. *Critical Social Policy* 34: 46–65.

Bennett, H. (2013) Squeezed in the Middle? A Case Study of Organisational Change in "the Wise Group" 1998–2010. TSRC Birmingham Seminar Series, Birmingham.

Beresford, P. (2001) Service Users, Social Policy and the Future of Welfare. *Critical Social Policy* 21 498–512.

Beresford, P. (2002a) Participation and Social Policy: Transformation, Liberation or Regulation? In: R. Sykes, C. Bochel and N. Ellison (eds) *Social Policy Review 14: Developments and Debates: 2001–2002*, Bristol: The Policy Press.

Beresford, P. (2002b) Thinking About 'Mental Health': Towards a Social Model. *Journal of Mental Health* 11: 581–584.

Beresford, P. (2010) Service Users and Social Policy: Developing Different Discussions, Challenging Dominant Discourses. In: I. Greener, C. Holden and M. Kilkey (eds) *Social Policy Review 22: Analysis and Debate in Social Policy, 2010*, Bristol: The Policy Press.

Beresford, P. and Croft, S. (1993) *Citizen Involvement: A Practical Guide for Change*, Hampshire: The Macmillan Press Ltd.

Berkman, L.F. and Syme, L. (1979) Social Networks, Host Resistance and Mortality: A Nine-Year Follow-up Study of Alameda County Residents. *American Journal of Epidemiology* 109: 186–204.

Berridge, V. and Mold, A. (2011) Professionalisation, New Social Movements and Voluntary Action in the 1960s and 1970s. In: M. Hilton and J. McKay (eds) *The Ages of Voluntarism: How We Got to the Big Society*, Oxford: Oxford University Press, pp 114–134.

Biesecker, A. (1998) Economic Rationales and a Wealth of Time. *Time & Society* 7: 75–91.

Birchall, J. (2001) *The New Mutualism in Public Policy*, London: Routledge.

Blackman, T., Greene, A., Hunter, D.J., McKee, L., Elliott, E., Harrington, B., Marks, L. and Williams, G. (2006) Performance Assessment and Wicked Problems: The Case of Health Inequalities. *Public Policy and Administration* 21: 66–80.

Blair, T. (1995) 'The 1995 Mais Lecture', reprinted as 'Blair Sets Out Framework to Cure Economic Ills: Mais Lecture'. *Financial Times* 23 May

Blair, T. (1996) *New Britain: My Vision of a Young Country*, London: Fourth Estate Limited.

Blekesaune, M. and Quadagno, J. (2003) Public Attitudes toward Welfare State Policies: A Comparative Analysis of 24 Nations. *European Sociological Review* 19: 415–427.

Blond, P. (2008a) David Cameron Needs a Fourth Way. Available at: http://www.theweek.co.uk/27069/david-cameron-needs-fourth-way

Blond, P. (2008b) A Deeper Shade of Blue. Available at: http://www.guardian.co.uk/commentisfree/2008/aug/21/conservatives.economy

Blond, P. (2008c) On the Right Road. Available at: http://www.guardian.co.uk/commentisfree/2008/oct/06/conservatives.labour

Blond, P. (2008d) Thatcher Is Back. Available at: http://www.guardian.co.uk/commentisfree/2008/nov/20/comment-thatcher-economics-conservatives-spending

Blond, P. (2008e) What Would the Tories Do? Available at: http://www.guardian.co.uk/commentisfree/2008/sep/19/economics.marketturmoil

Blond, P. (2009a) Allow Me to Suggest, George. Available at: http://www.guardian.co.uk/commentisfree/2008/sep/27/conservatives.toryconference

Blond, P. (2009b) Let's Get Local. Available at: http://www.guardian.co.uk/commentisfree/belief/2009/jan/30/davos-religion

Blond, P. (2009c) Philip Blond: The Tories Must Take on the Private Cartels That Dominate Economy. Available at: http://www.independent.co.uk/opinion/commentators/philip-blond-the-tories-must-take-on-the-private-cartels-that-dominate-economy-1515763.html

Blond, P. (2010) *Red Tory: How Left and Right Have Broken Britain and How We Can Fix It*, London: Faber and Faber Limited.

Bochel, H. (2011) Conservative Social Policy: From Conviction to Coalition. In: C. Holden, M. Kilkey and M. Ramia (eds) *Social Policy Review 23: Analysis and Debate in Social Policy, 2011*, Bristol: The Policy Press, pp 7–24.

Boffey, D. (2012) Serco Set to Take Charge of 'Big Society' Initiative. Available at: http://www.theguardian.com/society/2012/aug/05/serco-bid-national-citizen-service

Bonanno, G.A. (2008) Loss, Trauma, and Human Resilience: Have We Underestimated the Human Capacity to Thrive after Extremely Aversive Events? *Psychological Trauma: Theory, Research, Practice, and Policy* S: 101–113.

Bouffartigue, P. (2010) The Gender Division of Paid and Domestic Work. *Time & Society* 19: 220–238.

Bowring, F. (1998) LETS: An Eco-Socialist Alternative? *New Left Review* November – December: 91–111.

Boyle, D. (2000) *Funny Money: In Search of Alternative Cash*, London: HaperCollins Publishers.

Boyle, D. and Bird, S. (2014) *Give and Take: How timebanking is transforming healthcare*. Stroud, Gloucester: TimeBanking UK

Boyle, D. and Harris, M. (2009) *The Challenge of Co-production*, London: New Economics Foundation/NESTA.

Boyle, D. and Simms, A. (2009) *The New Economics: A Bigger Picture*, London: Earthscan.

Boyle, D., Clarke, S. and Burns, S. (2006) *Hidden Work: Co-Production by People Outside Paid Employment*, York: JRF.

Boyle, D., Coote, A., Sherwood, C. and Slay, J. (2010a) *Right Here, Right Now*, London: NEF/NESTA.

Boyle, D., Slay, J. and Stephens, L. (2010b) *Public Services Inside Out*, London: New Economics Foundation.

Boyle, N. (1988) Thatcher's Dead Souls. *New Statesman and Society* 14: 27–30.

Brandsen, T. and Pestoff, V. (2006) Co-Production, the Third Sector and the Delivery of Public Services. *Public Management Review* 8: 493–501.

Brannan, T., John, P. and Stoker, G. (2006) Active Citizenship and Effective Public Services and Programmes: How Can We Know What Really Works? *Urban Studies* 43: 993–1008.

Brannen, J. (2005) Time and the Negotiation of Work–Family Boundaries. *Time & Society* 14: 113–131.

Brudney, J.L. (1984) Local Coproduction of Services and the Analysis of Municipal Productivity. *Urban Affairs Quarterly* 19: 465–484.

Bryson, V. (2007) *Gender and the Politics of Time: Feminist Theory and Contemporary Debates*, Bristol: The Policy Press.

Bullard, R.D. and Johnson, G.S. (2000) Environmentalism and Public Policy: Environmental Justice: Grassroots Activism and Its Impact on Public Policy Decision Making. *Journal of Social Issues* 56: 555–578.

Burawoy, M. (1991a) The Extended Case Method. In: M. Burawoy, A. Burton, A. Arnett Ferguson K.J. Fox, J. Gamson, N. Gartrell, L. Hurst, C. Kurzman, L. Salzinger, J. Schiffman and S. Ui (eds) *Ethnography Unbound: Power and Resistance in the Modern Metropolis*, Berkeley, CA, and Oxford: University of California Press, pp 271–290.

Burawoy, M. (1991b) Reconstrusting Social Theory. In: M. Burawoy, A. Burton, A. Arnett Ferguson K.J. Fox, J. Gamson, N. Gartrell, L. Hurst, C. Kurzman, L. Salzinger, J. Schiffman and S. Ui (eds) *Ethnography Unbound: Power and Resistance in the Modern Metropolis*, Berkeley, CA, and Oxford: University of California Press, pp 8–27.

Burawoy, M., Burton, A., Arnett Ferguson, A. Fox, K.J., Gamson, J., Gartrell, N., Hurst, L., Kurzman, C., Salzinger, L., Schiffman, J. and Ui, S. (1991) *Ethnography Unbound: Power and Resistance in the Modern Metropolis*, Berkeley, CA, and Oxford: University of California Press.

Burchardt, T. (2010) Time, Income and Substantive Freedom: A Capability Approach. *Time & Society* 19: 318–344.

Burns, D. and Taylor, M. (1998) *Mutual Aid and Self-Help*, Bristol: The Policy Press.

Bussey, M. (2007) The Public Clock: Temporal Ordering and Policy. *Futures* 39: 53–64.

Butler, I. and Drakeford, M. (2005) *Scandal, Social Policy and Social Welfare*, Bristol: The Policy Press.

Cabinet Office (2010) Applying Behavioural Insight to Health. Available at: http://www.cabinetoffice.gov.uk/sites/default/files/resources/403936_BehaviouralInsight_acc.pdf

Cabinet Office (2011) *Giving White Paper*, London: The Stationery Office Limited.

Cahn, E. (1986) *Service Credits: A New Currency for the Welfare State*, London: London School of Economics and Political Science.

Cahn, E. (2000) *No More Throw-Away People: The Co-Production Imperative*, Washington, DC: Essential Books.

Cahn, E. (2001) On LETS and Time Dollars. *International Journal of Community Currency Research* 5.

Cahn, E. and Rowe, J. (1992) *Time Dollars: The New Currency That Enables Americans to Turn Their Hidden Resource-Time into Personal Security & Community Renewal,* Chicago, IL: Family Resource Coalition of America

Callison, S. (2003) 'All You Need is Love'? Assessing Time Banks as a Tool for Sustainable Economic Development. *Local Economy* 18: 264–267.

Cameron, D. (2009) The Big Society. Available at: http://www.conservatives.com/News/Speeches/2009/11/David_Cameron_The_Big_Society.aspx

Cameron, J. (1996) Throwing a Dishcloth into the Works: Troubling Theories of Domestic Labor. *Rethinking Marxism* 9: 24–44.

Canvin, K., Marttila, A., Burstrom, B. and Whitehead, M.(2009) Tales of the Unexpected? Hidden Resilience in Poor Households in Britain. *Social Science and Medicine* 69: 238–245.

Carruthers, B.G. and Espeland, W.N. (1998) Money, Meaning, and Morality. *The American Behavioural Scientist* 41: 1384–1408.

Castleden, M., McKee, M., Murray, V. and Leonardi, G. (2011) Resilience Thinking in Health Protection. *Journal of Public Health* 33: 369–377.

Cattell, V. (2001) Poor People, Poor Places, and Poor Health: The Mediating Role of Social Networks and Social Capital. *Social Sciences and Medicine* 52: 1501– 1516.

Cattell, V. (2011) *Poverty, Community and Health: Co-operation and the Good Society*, Hampshire: Palgrave Macmillan.

Centre for Social Justice (2006a) *Breakdown Britain*, London: Centre for Social Justice.

Centre for Social Justice (2006b) Breakdown Britain Executive Summary. Available at: http://www.centreforsocialjustice.org.uk/publications/breakdown-britain-executive-summary

Charlesworth, S.J., Gilfillan, P. and Wilkinson, R. (2004) Living Inferiority. *British Medical Bulletin* 69: 49–60.

Chatterton, P. and Pickerill, J. (2010) Everyday Activism and Transitions Towards Post-Capitalist Worlds. *Transactions of the Institute of British Geographers* 35: 475–490.

Chiarella, M., Salvage, J. and McInnes, E. (2010) Celebrating Connecting with Communities: Coproduction in Global Primary Health Care. *Primary Health Care Research & Development* 11: 108–122.

Chiu, L.F. and West, R.M. (2007) Health Intervention in Social Context: Understanding Social Networks and Neighbourhood. *Social Science and Medicine* 65: 1915–1927.

Cinderby, S., Haq, G., Cambridge, H. and Lock, K. (2014) Practical Action to Build Community Resilience: The Good Life Initiatives in New Earswick. Available at: http://www.jrf.org.uk/sites/files/jrf/community-sustainability-environment-full.pdf

Clarke, J. (2004) Dissolving the Public Realm? The Logics and Limits of Neo-Liberalism. *Journal of Social Policy* 33: 27–48.

Clarke, J. and Newman, J. (2012) The Alchemy of Austerity. *Critical Social Policy* 32: 299–319.

Clarke, J., Newman, J., Smith, N., Vidler, E. and Westmarland, L. (2007) *Creating Citizen-Consumers: Changing Publics & Changing Public Services*, London: Sage.

Clery, E., Lee, L. and Kunz, S. (2013) Public Attitudes to Poverty and Welfare, 1983–2011. Available at: http://www.natcen.ac.uk/media/137637/poverty-and-welfare.pdf

Coffey, A. (2004) *Reconceptualising Social Policy*, Maidenhead: Open University Press.

Collom, E. (2008) Engagement of the Elderly in Time Banking: The Potential for Social Capital Generation in an Aging Society. *Journal of Aging & Social Policy* 20: 414–436.

Cooper, D. (2013) Time Against Time: Normative Temporalities and the Failure of Community Labour in Local Exchange Trading Schemes. *Time & Society* 22: 31–54.

Coote, A. and Franklin, A. (2010) Transforming Welfare: New Economics, New Labour and the New Tories. *Soundings: A Journal of Politics and Culture* 44: 47–56.

Coote, A. and Franklin, J. (2013) *Time on Our Side: Why We All Need a Shorter Working Week*, London: New Economics Foundation.

Cornwall, A. (2008) Unpacking 'Participation': Models, Meanings and Practices. *Community Development Journal* 43: 269–283.

Cox, L. and Gunvald Nilsen, A. (2014) Viewpoint: Social Movements and Neoliberalism. *Discover Society* 11

Croall, J. (1997) *LETS Act Locally: The Growth of Local Exchange Trading Systems*, London: Calouste Gulbenkian Foundation.

Cruddas, J. (2010) The Future of Social Democracy. Compass. Available at: www.compass.org.uk

Cruddas, J. and Rutherford, J. (2010) Ethical Socialism. *Soundings: A Journal of Politics and Culture* 44: 10–21.

Curtis, S. and Rees Jones, I. (1998) Is There a Place for Geography in the Analysis of Health Inequality? *Sociology of Health & Illness* 20: 645–672.

Dahlgren, G. and Whitehead, M. (1991) *Policies and Strategies to Promote Social Equity in Health*, Stockholm: Institute of Futures Studies.

Darier, É. (1998) Time to be Lazy. *Time & Society* 7: 193–208.

David, M. (2000) New Labour's Post-Thatcherite Modernisation Project: A Third Way? *Journal of Social Policy* 29: 143–146.

Davies, J.S. and Pill, M. (2012) Empowerment or Abandonment? Prospects for Neighbourhood Revitalization Under the Big Society. *Public Money and Management* 32: 193–200.

Davies, K. (1990) *Women, Time and the Weaving of the Standards of Everyday Life*, Aldershot: Avebury.

Davies, K. (1994) The Tensions between Process Time and Clock Time in Care-Work. *Time & Society* 3: 277–303.

Davydov, D.M., Stewart, R., Ritchie, K. and Chaudieu, I. (2010) Resilience and Mental Health. *Clinical Psychology Review* 30: 479–495.

Day, K. (2009) *Communities in Recession. The Reality in Four Neighbourhoods*, York: JRF.

Deakin, N. (2001) *In Search of Civil Society*, Basingstoke: Palgrave Macmillan.

Dean, H. (2010) *Understanding Human Need*, Bristol: The Policy Press.

Dean, H. (2012) *Social Policy*, Cambridge: Polity Press.

Deeds Ermarth, E. (2011) *History in the Discursive Condition: Reconsidering the Tools of Thought*, Oxon: Routledge.

Department of Health (2010) *A Vision for Adult Social Care: Capable Communities and Active Citizens*, London: Department of Health.

Dey, I. (1999) Parental Support for Young Adults. *Time & Society* 8: 231–247.

Dinham A. (2005) Empowered or over-powered? The real experiences of local participation in the UK's New Deal for Communities. *Community Development Journal* 40: 301-312.

Dodd, N. (2005) Reinventing Monies in Europe. *Economy and Society* 34: 558–583.

Dordoy, A. and Mellor, M. (2000) Ecosocialism and Feminism: Deep Materialism and the Contradictions of Capitalism. *Capitalism Nature Socialism* 11: 41–61.

Douglas, C.H. (1920) *Economic Democracy*, London: C. Palmer.

Douglas, C.H. (1921) *Credit-Power and Democracy: With a Draft Scheme for the Mining Industry*, London: C. Palmer.

Douthwaite, R. (1996) *The Growth Illusion: How Economic Growth Has Enriched the Few, Impoverished the Many and Endangered the Planet*, Tontes: Green Books Ltd.

Drakeford, M. (1997) *Social Movements and their Supporters*, Hampshire and London: Macmillan Press Ltd.

Drakeford, M. (2000) *Privatisation and Social Policy*, Essex: Pearson Education Limited.

Drakeford, M. (2011) Strengths, Weaknesses, Opportunities and Threats. In: J. Osmond (ed) *Growing Wales' Civil Society*, Cardiff: Institute of Welsh Affairs, pp 68–74.

Drakeford, M. and Butler, I. (2007) Everyday Tragedies: Justice, Scandal and Young People in Contemporary Britain. *Howard Journal* 46: 219–235.

Drakeford, M. and Gregory, L. (2010a) Asset-Based Welfare and Youth Justice: Making It Local. In: J. Brayford, F. Crowe and J. Deering (eds) *What Else Works? Creative Work with Offenders*, Devon: Willan Publishing, pp 155–168.

Drakeford, M. and Gregory, L. (2010b) Transforming Time: A New Tool for Youth Justice. *Youth Justice* 10: 143–156.

Dunston, R., Lee, A., Boud, D., Brodie, P. and Chiarella, M. (2009) Co-Production and Health System Reform – From Re-Imagining to Re-Making. *The Australian Journal of Public Administration* 68: 39–52.

Dwyer, P. (2002) Making Sense of Social Citizenship. *Critical Social Policy* 22: 273–299.

Dwyer, P. (2004) Creeping Conditionality in the UK: From Welfare Rights to Conditional Entitlements? *The Canadian Journal of Sociology* 29: 265–287.

Edwards, A. (2007) Working Collaboratively to Build Resilience: A CHAT Approach. *Social Policy and Society* 6: 255–264.

Elliott, E., Harrop, E., Rothwell, H.M., Shepherd, M. and Williams, G. (2010) The Impact of the Economic Downturn on Health in Wales: A Review and Case Study. Working Paper 134, published by Cardiff School of Social Sciences, Cardiff University, Cardiff.

Elliott, L. (2010) Co-operatives Offer Template for David Cameron's Big Society. *The Guardian* 1st August 2010

Ellison, N. (2011) The Conservative Party and the 'Big Society'. In: C. Holden, M. Kilkey and M. Ramia (eds) *Social Policy Review 23: Analysis and Debate in Social Policy, 2011*, Bristol: The Policy Press, pp 45–62.

Elsrud, T. (1998) Time Creation in Travelling: The Taking and Making of Time Among Women Backpackers. *Time & Society* 7: 309–334.

Evans, D. (2011) The Big Society Needs Robust Public Health Evaluation. *Journal of Public Health* 33: 11–12.

Farnsworth, K. (2011) From Economic Crisis to a New Age of Austerity: The UK. In: K. Farnsworth and Z. Irving (eds) *Social Policy in Challenging Times: Economic Crisis and Welfare Systems*, Bristol: The Policy Press, pp 251–270.

Farnsworth, K. and Irving, Z. (2011) Varieties of Crisis. In: K. Farnsworth and Z. Irving (eds) *Social Policy in Challenging Times: Economic Crisis and Welfare Systems*, Bristol: The Policy Press, pp 1–30.

Finlay, J. (1972) *Social Credit: The English Origins*, London: McGill-Queen University Press.

Finlayson, A. (2011) Should the Left Go Blue? Available at: http://www.compassonline.org.uk/news/item.asp?n=12862

Fitzpatrick, T. (1999) *Freedom and Security: An Introduction to the Basic Income Debate*, Hampshire: Macmillan Press Ltd.

Fitzpatrick, T. (2000) LETS and Benefit Claiming in the UK: Results of a Pilot Project. *International Journal of Community Currency Research* 4.

Fitzpatrick, T. (2003) *After the New Social Democracy: Social Welfare for the Twenty-First Century*, Manchester: Manchester University Press.

Fitzpatrick, T. (2004a) Social Policy and Time. *Time and Society* 13: 197–219.

Fitzpatrick, T. (2004b) Time, Social Justice and UK Welfare Reform. *Economy and Society* 33: 335–358.

Fitzpatrick, T. (2011) Environmental Justice: Philosophies and Practices. In: T. Fitzpatrick (ed) *Understanding the Environment and Social Policy*, Bristol: The Policy Press, pp 131–153.

Fitzpatrick, T. and Caldwell, C. (2001) Towards a Theory of Ecosocial Welfare: Radical Reformism and Local Exchanges and Trading Systems (LETS). *Environmental Politics* 10: 43–67.

Flint, J. (2010) Coping Strategies? Agencies, Budgeting and Self Esteem Amongst Low-Income Households. Living Through Change in Challenging Neighbourhoods: A research project by the Joseph Rowntree Foundation, York: JRF.

Foley, P. and Martin, S. (2000) A New Deal for the Community? Public Participation in Regeneration and Local Service Delivery. *Policy and Politics* 28: 479–492.

Folke C. (2006) Resilience: The emergence of a perspective for social–ecological systems analyses. *Global Environmental Change* 16: 253-267.

Frayne, D. (2011) Critical Social Theory and the Will to Happiness: A Study of Anti-Work Subjectivities. PhD Thesis, Cardiff University. Available at: http://orca.cf.ac.uk/18497/

Fremeaux I. (2005) New Labour's appropriation of the concept of community: a critique. *Community Development Journal* 40: 265-274.

Freedland, J. (2010) There's a Good Idea in Cameron's 'Big Society' Screaming to Get Out. Available at: http://www.guardian.co.uk/commentisfree/2010/jul/20/good-idea-camerons-big-society-screaming-get-out

Freeman, R. (1992) The Idea of Prevention: A Critical Review. In: S. Scott, G. Williams, S. Platt and H. Thomas (eds) *Private Risks and Public Dangers*, Aldershot: Avebury.

Fussey, P. (2004) New Labour and New Surveillance: Theoretical and Political Ramifications of CCTV Implementation in the UK. *Surveillance & Society* 2: 251–269.

Galbraith, J.K. (1958) *The Affluent Society*, London: Penguin Books.

Gamarnikow, E. and Green, A. (2000) Citizenship, Education and Social Capital. In: J. Cairns and R. Gardner (eds) *Education for Citizenship*, London: Continuum.

Gamson, J. (1991) Silence, Death and the Invisible Enemy: AIDS Activism and Social Movement 'Newness'. In: M. Burawoy, A. Burton, A. Arnett Ferguson K.J. Fox, J. Gamson, N. Gartrell, L. Hurst, C. Kurzman, L. Salzinger, J. Schiffman and S. Ui (eds) *Ethnography Unbound: Power and Resistance in the Modern Metropolis*, Berkeley, CA, and Oxford: University of California Press, pp 35–57.

Gannon, Z. and Lawson, N. (2008) *Co-Production: The Modernisation of Public Services by Staff and Users*, London: Compass.

Garland, D. (2001) *The Culture of Control*, Oxford: Oxford University Press.

Gesell, S. (1918) The Natural Economic Order. Available at: http://www.geokey.de/literatur/doc/neo.pdf

Gibson-Graham, J.K. (1993) Waiting for the Revolution, or How to Smash Capitalism while Working at Home in Your Spare Time. *Rethinking Marxism* 6: 10–24.

Gibson-Graham, J.K. (1996) *The End of Capitalism (As We Knew It): A Feminist Critique of Political Economy*, Minneapolis, MN: University of Minnesota Press.

Gibson-Graham, J.K. (2006) *Postcapitalist Politics*, Minneapolis, MN: University of Minnesota Press.

Gibson-Graham, J.K., Cameron, J. and Healty, S. (2013) *Take Back the Economy: An Ethical Guide for Transforming Our Communities*, Minneapolis, MN: The University of Minnesota Press.

Giddens, A. (2002) *Runaway World: How Globalisation is Reshaping Our Lives*, London: Profile Books Ltd.

Giddens, A. (2003) *The Third Way*, Cambridge: Cambridge University Press.

Giddens, A. (2004) *The Third Way and its Critics*, Cambridge: Polity Press.

Gilbert, J. (2004) The Second Wave: The Specificity of New Labour Neo-Liberalism. *Soundings: A Journal of Politics and Culture* 26: 25–45.

Glasby, J. (2008) Co-Production and Personalisation in Social Care: Changing Relationships in the Provision of Social Care. *Health & Social Care in the Community* 16: 559–559.

Glasman, M. (2010) Society not State: The Challenge of the Big Society. *Public Policy Research* 17: 59–63.

Glasman, M. (2011) Labour as a Radical Tradition. In: M. Glasman, J. Rutherford, M. Stears and S. White (eds) *The Labour Tradition and the Politics of Paradox*, London: Soundings.

Glasman, M., Rutherford, J., Stears, M. and White, S. (2011) *The Labour Tradition and the Politics of Paradox*, London: Soundings.

Glennie, P. and Thrift, N. (1996) Reworking E. P. Thompson's 'Time, Work-Discipline and Industrial Capitalism'. *Time & Society* 5: 275–299.

Glynos, J. and Speed, E. (2012) Varieties of Co-Production in Public Services: Time Banks in a UK Health Policy Context. *Critical Policy Studies* 6: 402–433.

Goodin, R.E. (1985) Self-Reliance versus the Welfare State. *Journal of Social Policy* 14: 25–47.

Goodin, R.E. (2010) Temporal Justice. *Journal of Social Policy* 39: 1–16.

Goodin, R.E., Parpo, A. and Kangas, O. (2004) The Temporal Welfare State: The Case of Finland. *Journal of Social Policy* 33: 531–552.

Goodin, R.E., Rice, J.M., Parpo, A. and Eriksson, L (2008) *Discretionary Time: A New Measure of Freedom*, Cambridge: Cambridge University Press.

Gordon, D. (2014) 3rd Peter Townsend Memorial Conference. Available at: http://www.poverty.ac.uk/take–part/events/final-conference

Gorz, A. (1999) *Reclaiming Work: Beyond the Wage-Based Society*, Cambridge: Polity Press.

Gough, I. (2011) From Financial Crisis to Fiscal Crisis. In: K. Farnsworth and Z. Irving (eds) *Social Policy in Challenging Times: Economic Crisis and Welfare Systems*, Bristol: The Policy Press, pp 49–64.

Gouldner, A.W. (1956) Explorations in Applied Social Science. *Social Problems* 3: 169 – 181.

Great Britain (2011) *Localism Act: Elizabeth II*, London: The Stationary Office.

Greer, S. (2005) The Politics of Health-Policy Divergence. In: J. Adams and K. Schmueker (eds) *Devolution in Practice 2006: Public Policy Differences Within the UK*, London: IPPR.

Greer, S. (2010) Devolution and Health: Structure, Process and Outcomes Since 1998. In: G. Lodge and K. Schmuecker (eds) *Devolution in Practice 2010*, London: IPPR.

Gregory, C.A. (1982) *Gifts and Commodities*, London: Academic Press Inc.

Gregory, L. (2009a) Change Takes Time: Exploring Structural and Development Issues of Time Banking. *International Journal of Community Currency Research* 13: 13–36.

Gregory, L. (2009b) Spending Time Locally: The Benefits of Time Banks for Local Economies. *Local Economy* 24: 323–333.

Gregory, L. (2012a) Improving Health Through Participation: Time Banks as a Site for Co-Production. PhD Thesis, Cardiff University. Available at: http://orca.cf.ac.uk/46310/

Gregory, L. (2012b) Local People Rebuilding Their Communities: An Exploration of Welsh Time Banking. *Contemporary Wales* 25: 40–57.

Gregory, L. (2012c) Time and Punishment: A Comparison of UK and US Time Bank Use in Criminal Justice Systems. *Journal of Comparative Social Welfare* 28: 195–208.

Gregory, L. (2013a) Co-option, Resilience or Resistance? Lessons for Community Currency Systems from the UK Development of Time Banking. Second International Conference on Community Currency Systems, International Institute of Social Studies, The Hague.

Gregory, L. (2013b) Time Banking and the Dangers of Ideological Elasticity. Social Policy Association Conference, Sheffield University.

Gregory, L. (2014) Resilience or Resistance? Time Banking in the Age of Austerity. *Journal of Contemporary European Studies* 22 (2): 171-183 .

Grice, A. (2009) 'Big Society' Is the Solution to Poverty, Declares Cameron. Available at: http://www.independent.co.uk/news/uk/politics/big-society-is-the-solution-to-poverty-declares-cameron-1818209.html

Grimshaw, D. and Rubery, J. (2012) The End of the UK's Liberal Collectivist Social Model? The Implications of the Coalition Government's Policy During the Austerity Crisis. *Cambridge Journal of Economics* 36: 105–126.

Gunning, M. (1997a) Gender and the Use of Time: An International Forum: Gendered Time in Law: Towards a New Concept of the Caring Citizen. *Time and Society* 6: 323–336.

Gunning, M. (1997b) Gendered Time in Law: Towards a New Concept of the Caring Citizen. *Time & Society* 6: 323–336.

Hall, K., Alcock, P. and Millar, R. (2012) Start Up and Sustainability: Marketisation and the Social Enterprise Investment Fund in England. *Journal of Social Policy* 41: 733–749.

Hall, S. (1988) *The Hard Road to Renewal*, London: Verso.

Hall, S. (2005) New Labour's Double-Shuffle. *Review of Education, Pedagogy, and Cultural Studies* 27: 319–335.

Hall, T., Williamson, H. and Coffey, A. (2000) Young People, Citizenship and the Third Way: A Role for the Youth Service. *Journal of Youth Studies* 3: 461–472.

Hancock, L., Mooney, G. and Neal, S. (2012) Crisis Social Policy and the Resilience of the Concept of Community. *Critical Social Policy* 32: 343–364.

Harding, M., James, S., Thomas, M. and Warden, M. (2006) *Evaluation of the Timebank Projects in Rhondda Cynon Taf for Rhondda Cynon Taf – Community Regeneration Fund*, Swansea WICC.

Harris, J. (2003) Introduction; Civil Society in British History: Paradigm or Peculiarity? In: J. Harris (ed) *Civil Society in British History: Ideas, Identities, Institutions*, Oxford: Oxford University Press, pp 1–12.

Harris, M. and Young, P. (2010) Building Bridges: The Third Sector Responding Locally to Diversity. *Voluntary Sector Review* 1: 41–58.

Harrison, M. and Sanders, T. (2014) Introduction. In: M. Harrison and T. Sanders *Social Policies and Social Control: New Perspectives on the 'Not-So-Big Society'*, Bristol: The Policy Press.

Harrison, M. and Singer, M. (2007) The Timesqueeze Generation: What the Public Are Doing with Their Spare Time. In: S. Creasy (ed) *Participation Nation: Reconnecting Citizens to the Public Realm*, London: Involve, pp 49–61.

Hawkins, R.L. and Maurer, K. (2010) Bonding, Bridging and Linking: How Social Capital Operated in New Orleans Following Hurricane Katrina. *British Journal of Social Work* 40: 1777–1793.

Hayashi, M. (2012) Japan's Fureai Kippu Time-Banking in Elderly Care: Origins, Development, Challenges and Impact. *International Journal of Community Currency Research* 16: 30–44.

Hayward, J. (2012) From Citizen Solidarity to Self-Serving Inequality: Social Solidarity, Market Economy and Welfare Statecraft. In: J. Connelly and J. Hayward (eds) *The Withering of the Welfare State: Regression*, Hampshire: Palgrave Macmillan, pp 1–18.

Henn, M. and Foard, N. (2012) Young People, Political Participation and Trust in Britain. *Parliamentary Affairs* 65: 47–67.

Henn, M., Weinstein, M. and Hodgkinson, S. (2007) Social Capital and Political Participation: Understanding the Dynamics of Young People's Political Disengagement in Contemporary Britain. *Social Policy and Society* 6: 467–479.

Henwood, K. and Coltart, C. (2012) Researching Lives Through Time: Analytics, Narratives & the Psychosocial. Available at: http://www.timescapes.leeds.ac.uk/resources/publications

Henwood, K. and Shirani, F. (2012) Extending Temporal Horizons. Available at: http://www.timescapes.leeds.ac.uk/resources/publications

Herrmann, G.M. (2006) Special Money: Ithaca Hours and Garage Sales. *Ethnology* 45: 125–141.

Hickman, L. (2009) Will the Brixton Pound Buy a Brighter Future? Available at: http://www.guardian.co.uk/environment/2009/sep/16/will-brixton-pound-work

Hill, M. (2011) The Economic Crisis and Paradigm Change. In: Farnsworth K and Irving Z (eds) *Social Policy in Challenging Times: Economic Crisis and Welfare Systems*, Bristol: The Policy Press, pp 31–48.

Hilton, M. and McKay, J. (2011) *The Ages of Voluntarism: How We Got to the Big Society*, Oxford: Oxford University Press.

Hirst, P. (1994) *Associative Democracy: New Forms of Economic and Social Governance*, Cambridge: Polity Press.

Hiskett, W.R. (1935) *Social Credits or Socialism*, London: Victor Gollancz Ltd.

Hodkinson, S. and Robbins, G. (2013) The Return of Class War Conservatism? Housing Under the UK Coalition Government. *Critical Social Policy* 33: 57–77.

Holling, C.S. (1973) Resilience and Stability of Ecological Systems. *Annual Review of Ecology and Systematics* 4: 1–23.

Horne, M. and Shirley, T. (2009) *Co-Production in Public Services: A New Partnership with Citizens*, London: Cabinet Office, The Strategy Unit.

Hudson, M., Davidson, R., Durante, L., Grieve, J. and Kazmi, A. (2011) Recession and Cohesion in Bradford. JRF. Available at: www.jrf.org.uk

Hughes K, and Emmel N.D. (2012) *Analysing Time: Times and Timing in the Lives of Low-Income Grandparents*, Timescapes Methods Guides Series, Guide No. 9

Hughes, T.P., Baird, A.H., Bellwood, D.R., Card, M., Connolly, S. R., Folke, C., Grosberg, R., Hoegh-Guldberg, O., Jackson, J. B. C., Kleypas, J., Lough, J. M., Marshall, P., Nyström, M., Palumbi, S. R., Pandolfi, J. M., Rosen, B. and Roughgarden, J. (2003) Climate Change, Human Impacts, and the Resilience of Coral Reefs. *Science* 301: 929–933.

Hunter, D.J. (2009) The Case Against Choice and Competition. *Health Economics, Policy and Law* 4: 489–501.

Hussain, N., Byrne, B., Campbell, A., Harrison, E., McKinley, B. and Shah, P. (2011) *How People in Poverty Experienced Recent Global Economic Crises*, York: JRF.

Hyde, P. and Davies, H.T.O. (2004) Service Design, Culture and Performance: Collusion and Co-Production in Health Care. *Human Relations* 57: 1407–1426.

Ingham, G. (1999) Capitalism, Money and Banking: A Critique of Recent Historical Sociology. *British Journal of Sociology* 50: 76–96.

Ingham, G. (2000) Class Inequality and the Social Production of Money. In: R. Crompton, F. Devine, M. Savageand J. Scott (eds) *Renewing Class Analysis*, Oxford: Blackwell, pp 66–86.

James, S. (2005) *The Impact of Co-Production on People Outside of Paid Work*, Rhondda: Wales Institute for Community Currency.

Jansen, T., Chioncel, N. and Dekkers, H. (2006) Social Cohesion and Integration: Learning Active Citizenship. *British Journal of Sociology of Education* 27: 189–205.

Janz, N.K. and Becker, M.H. (1984) The Health Belief Model: A Decade Later. *Health Education & Behavior* 11: 1–47.

Jenson, J. (2012) Redesigning Citizenship Regimes after Neoliberalism: Moving Towards Social Investment. In: N. Norel, B. Oalier and J. Palme (eds) *2012*, Bristol: The Policy Press, pp 61–87.

Jenson J. and Sineau M. (2001) Who Care? Women's work, Childcare and Welfare State Design. Toronto; Canada: University of Toronto Press Incorporated.

Jessop, B. (2004) Comments on 'New Labour's Double-Shuffle'. Available at: eprints.lancs.ac.uk/236/01/E-2004e_Hall-Shuffle.doc

Jochum, V., Patten, B. and Wilding, K. (2005) *Civil Renewal and Active Citizenship: A Guide to the Debate*, London: NCVO.

Johnson, N. (1990) *Reconstructing the Welfare State: A Decade of Change*, Hertfordshire: Harvester Wheatsheaf.

Jordan, B. (2004) *Sex, Money and Power: The Transformation of Collective Life*, Cambridge: Polity Press.

Jordan, B. (2010a) *What's Wrong with Social Policy and How to Fix It*, Cambridge: Polity Press.

Jordan, B. (2010b) *Why the Third Way Failed: Economics, Morality and the Origins of the 'Big Society'*, Bristol: The Policy Press.

Jordan, B. (2012) The Low Road to Basic Income? Tax–Benefit Integration in the UK. *Journal of Social Policy* 41: 1–17.

Jordan, B. and Drakeford, M. (2012) *Social Work and Social Policy under Austerity*, Hampshire: Palgrave Macmillan.

Jowell, T. (2009) Why Mutualism Is the Way Forward for Public Services. *The Guardian* 14th December 2009.

Katikireddi, S.V., Higgins, M., Smith, K.E. and Williams, G. (2013) Health Inequalities: The Need to Move Beyond Bad Behaviours. *Journal of Epidemiology and Community Health* 67: 715–716.

Kawachi, I. and Berkman, L. (2001) Social Ties and Mental Health. *Journal of Urban Health* 78: 458–467.

Kellner, P. (1998) *New Mutualism: The Third Way*, London: The Co-operative Party.

Kemshall, H. (2002) *Risk, Social Policy and Welfare*, Buckingham: Open University Press.

Kendall, J. (2003) *The Voluntary Sector*, London: Routledge.

Kendall J and Knapp M. (1994) A loose and baggy monster: boundaries, definitions and typologies. In: Davis Smith J., Rochester C. and Hedley R. (eds) *An introduction to the voluntary sector.* London: Routledge, 66-95.

Kenyon, E. (2000) Time, Temporality and the Dynamics of Community. *Time & Society* 9: 21–41.

Keynes, J.M. (1936) *The General Theory of Employment, Interest and Money.* London: MacMillan

King, N. (2014) Making the Case for Sport and Recreation Services: The Utility of Social Return on Investment (SROI) Analysis. *International Journal of Public Sector Management* 27 152–164.

Kingfisher, C. (2002) *Western Welfare in Decline: Globalization and Women's Poverty*, Philadelphia, PA: University of Pennsylvania Press.

Kiser, L. (1984) Toward an Institutional Theory of Citizen Coproduction. *Urban Affairs Quarterly* 19: 485–510.

Kiser, L. and Percy, S.L. (1980) *The Concept of Coproduction and Its Implications for Public Service Delivery*, Bloomington, IN: Indiana University.

Knapp, M., Bauer, A., Perkins, M. and Snell, T.(2010) Building Community Capacity: Making an Economic Case. Personal Social Services Research Unit. Available at: www.pssru.ac.uk/pdf/dp2772.pdf

Kotz, D.M. (2009) The Financial and Economic Crisis of 2008: A Systemic Crisis of Neoliberal Capitalism. *Review of Radical Political Economics* 41: 305–317.

Kramer, R.M. (2000) A Third Sector in the Third Millennium? *Voluntas: International Journal of Voluntary and Nonprofit Organizations* 11: 1–23.

Kremer-Sadlik, T. and Paugh, A.L. (2007) Everyday Moments. *Time & Society* 16: 287–308.

Kümmerer, K. (1996) The Ecological Impact of Time. *Time & Society* 5: 209–235.

Lam, W.F. (1997) Institutional Design of Public Agencies and Coproduction: A Study of Irrigation Associations in Taiwan. In: P. Evans (ed) *State–Society Synergy: Government and Social Capital in Development*. University of California International and Area Studies Digital Collection, Edited Volume #94, pp 11–47, California, CA: University of California Press. Available at: http://repositories.cdlib.org/uciaspubs/research/94/3

Lang, P. (1994) *LETS Work; Rebuilding the Local Economy*, Bristol: Grover Books.

Langan, M. (1998) The Contested Concept of Need. In: M. Langan (ed) *Welfare: Needs, Rights and Risks*, London: Routledge, pp 3–34.

Langley, P. (2004) In the Eye of the 'Perfect Storm': The Final Salary Pensions Crisis and Financialisation of Anglo-American Capitalism. *New Political Economy* 9: 539–558.

Langley, P. (2006) The Making of Investor Subjects in Anglo-American Pensions. *Environment and Planning D: Society and Space* 24: 919–934.

Langley, P. (2008) Financialization and the Consumer Credit Boom. *Competition & Change* 12: 133–147.

Larner, W. (2000) Neo-Liberalism: Policy, Ideology, Governmentality. *Studies in Political Economy* 63: 5–25.

Larner, W. (2003) Neoliberalism? *Environment and Planning D: Society and Space* 21: 509–512.

Larner, W. (2005) Neoliberalism in (Regional) Theory and Practice: The Stronger Communities Action Fund in New Zealand. *Geographical Research* 43: 9–18.

Lawler, E.J. (2001) An Affect Theory of Social Exchange. *American Journal of Sociology* 107: 321–352.

Lawson, H. (2001) Active Citizenship in Schools and the Community. *Curriculum Journal* 12: 163–178.

Leadbeater, C. and Christie, I. (1999) *To Our Mutual Advantage*, London: Demos.

Leccardi, C. (1996) Rethinking Social Time: Feminist Perspectives. *Time & Society* 5: 169–186.

Lee, R. (1996) Moral Money? LETS and the Social Construction of Local Economic Geographies in Southeast England. *Environment and Planning A* 28: 1377–1394.

Lee, R. (2006) The Ordinary Economy: Tangled Up in Values and Geography. *Transactions of the Institute of British Geographers* 31: 413–432.

Lee, R., Leyshon, A., Aldridge, T., Williams, C.C. and Thrift, N. (2004) Making Geographies and Histories? Constructing Local Circuits of Value. *Environment and Planning D: Society and Space* 22: 595–617.

Lee, T. and Piachaud, D. (1992) The Time-Consequences of Social Services. *Time & Society* 1: 65–80.

Le Grand, J. (1991) Quasi-Markets and Social Policy. *The Economic Journal* 101: 1256–1267.

Le Grand, J. and Robinson, R. (1984) *Privatisation and the Welfare State*, London: Unwin Hyman.

Letcher, A.S. and Perlow, K.M. (2009) Community-Based Participatory Research Shows How a Community Initiative Creates Networks to Improve Well-Being. *American Journal of Preventive Medicine* S292–S299.

Levitas, R. (1988) Competition and Compliance: The Utopias of the New Right. In: R. Levitas (ed) *The Ideology of the New Right*, Cambridge: Polity Press.

Levitas, R. (2005) The Imaginary Reconstitution of Society: Or Why Sociologists and Others Should Take Utopia More Seriously. Available at: http://www.bris.ac.uk/spais/files/inaugural.pdf

Levitas, R. (2012a) The Government Has Misrepresented Research Findings on 'Troubled Families', Blaming the Poor, Not Coalition Policies, for Rising Poverty Levels. *British Politics and Policy*, LSE.

Levitas, R. (2012b) The Just's Umbrella: Austerity and the Big Society in Coalition poLicy and Beyond. *Critical Social Policy* 32: 320–342.

Levitas, R. (2012c) There May Be 'Trouble' Ahead: What We Know About Those 120,000 'Troubled' Families. Available at: http://www.poverty.ac.uk/policy-response-working-papers-families-social-policy-life-chances-children-parenting-uk-government

Lewis, J. (2005) New Labour's Approach to the Voluntary Sector: Independence and the Meaning of Partnership. *Social Policy and Society* 4: 121–131.

Leyshon, A. and Lee, R. (2003) Introduction: Alternative Economic Geographies. In: A. Leyshon, R. Lee and C.C. Williams (eds) *Alternative Economic Spaces*, London: Sage, pp 1–26.

Lister, R. (1997) Citizenship: Towards a Feminist Synthesis. *Feminist Review* 57 28–48.

Lister, R. (2003) *Citizenship: Feminist Perspectives*, Hampshire: Palgrave Macmillan.

Lister, R. (2011) The Age of Responsibility: Social Policy and Citizenship in the Early 21st Century. In: C. Holden, M. Kilkey and M. Ramia (eds) *Social Policy Review 23: Analysis and Debate in Social Policy, 2011*, Bristol: The Policy Press, pp 63–84.

Lovelock, C.H. and Young, R.F. (1979) Look to Consumers to Increase Productivity. *Harvard Business Review* May–June: 168–178.

Luthar, S., Cichetti, D. and Becker, B. (2000) The Construct of Resilience: A Critical Evaluation. *Child Development* 71: 543–562.

Mackenbach, J.P. (2011) Can We Reduce Health Inequalities? An Analysis of the English Strategy (1997–2010). *Journal of Epidemiology and Community Health* 65: 568–575.

MacKinnon, D. and Derickson, K.D. (2013) From Resilience to Resourcefulness: A Critique of Resilience Policy and Activism. *Progress in Human Geography* 37: 253–270.

Macmillan, R. (2010) The Third Sector Delivering Public Services: An Evidence Review. Available at: http://www.birmingham.ac.uk/generic/tsrc/documents/tsrc/working-papers/working-paper-20.pdf

Macmillan, R. (2013) Making Sense of the Big Society: Perspectives from the Third Sector. Available at: http://www.birmingham.ac.uk/generic/tsrc/documents/tsrc/working-papers/working-paper-90.pdf

Macnicol, J. (1987) In Pursuit of the Underclass. *Journal of Social Policy* 16: 293–318.

Madaleno, M. (2012) Time-Banking Offers Hope to the Dispossessed Youth of Europe. Available at: http://www.newstatesman.com/blogs/economics/2012/08/time-banking-offers-hope-dispossessed-youth-europe

Malpass, P. and Mullins, D. (2002) Local Authority Housing Stock Transfer in the UK: From Local Initiative to National Policy. *Housing Studies* 17: 673–686.

Mandelson, P. and Liddle, R. (1996) *The Blair Revolution: Can New Labour Deliver?*, London: Faber and Faber Limited.

Marmot, M. (2010) *Fair Society, Healthy Lives: The Marmot Review*, London: University College London.

Martin, S. and Webb, A. (2009) 'Citizen-Centred' Public Services: Contestability without Consumer-Driven Competition? *Public Money & Management* 29: 123–130.

Marx, K. (1974) *Economic and Philosophic Manuscripts of 1844*, London: Lawrence & Wishart.

Mauss, M. (1950) *The Gift*, London: Routledge.

May, J., Cloke, P. and Johnsen, S. (2005) Re-Phasing Neoliberalism: New Labour and Britain's Crisis of Street Homelessness. *Antipode* 37: 703–730.

McGee, S. (2014) Why You Should Care About Bitcoin: Digital Currency Is Here to Stay. Available at: http://www.theguardian.com/money/us-money-blog/2014/apr/09/why-bitcoins-matter-digital-currency-future

McKenzie, K., Whitley, R.O.B. and Weich, S. (2002) Social Capital and Mental Health. *The British Journal of Psychiatry* 181: 280–283.

McKillop, D.G. and Wilson, J.O.S. (2003) Credit Unions in Britain: A Time for Change. *Public Money and Management* 23: 119–123.

McLeod, J. and Thomson, R. (2009) *Researching Social Change*, London: Sage.

Mead, L. (1986) *Beyond Entitlement: The Social Obligations of Citizenship*, New York, NY: The Free Press.

Milbourne, L. (2013) *Voluntary Sector in Transition: Hard Times or New Opportunities?*, Bristol: The Policy Press.

Millar, R. and Hall, K. (2012) Social Return on Investment (SROI) and Performance Measurement. *Public Management Review* 15: 923–941.

Miller, E.J. (2008) Both Borrowers and Lenders: Time Banks and the Aged in Japan. Unpublished PhD Thesis, Australian National University.

Miller, K. (2005) *Communication Theories*, New York, NY: McGraw Hill.

Mohaupt, S. (2009) Review Article: Resilience and Social Exclusion. *Social Policy & Society* 8: 63–71.

Mooney, G. and Fyfe, N. (2006) New Labour and Community Protests: The Case of the Govanhill Swimming Pool Campaign, Glasgow. *Local Economy* 21: 136–150.

Morgan, G. (1988) *Images of Organization*, London: Sage.

Morris, D. and Gilchrist, A. (no date) Communities Connected: Inclusion, Participation and Common Purpose. Available at: http://www.thersa.org/__data/assets/pdf_file/0011/518924/RSA_Communities-Connected-AW_181011.pdf

Morris, K. (2013a) Troubled Families: Vulnerable Families' Experiences of Multiple Service Use. *Child & Family Social Work* 18: 198–206.

Morris, N. (2013b) David Cameron Insists That Squeeze on Public-Sector Spending Is Permanent. *The Independent* 11th November 2013.

Mowbray M. (2005) Community capacity building or state opportunism? *Community Development Journal* 40: 255-264.

Murray, C. (1990) *The Emerging British Underclass*, London: IEA Health and Welfare Unit.

Naughton-Doe, R. (2011a) Delivering the Big Society: Time Banks and Co-Production in Public Services. Presented at *Contestations and Continuations: Health and Welfare in the Big Society*, Cardiff: Cardiff University.

Naughton-Doe, R. (2011b) Time Banking in Social Housing. *International Journal of Community Currency* 15: D73–76.

Needham, C. (2003) *Citizen-Consumers: New Labour's Marketplace Democracy*, London: The Catalyst Forum.

NESTA (2012) Innovation in Giving Fund Makes First Investments. Available at: http://www.nesta.org.uk/press_releases/assets/features/innovation_in_giving_fund_makes_first_investments

New Economics Foundation (2004a) *Co-Production Works! The Win:Win of Involving Local People in Public Services*, London: NEF.

New Economics Foundation (2004b) *Exploring Co-Production: An Overview of Past, Present and Future*, London: NEF.

New Economics Foundation (2007) *Unintended Consequences: How the Efficiency Agenda Erodes Local Public Services and a New Public Benefit Model to Restore Them*, London: NEF.

New Economics Foundation (2008a) *Co-Production: A Manifesto for Growing the Core Economy*, London: NEF.

New Economics Foundation (2008b) Memorandum from the New Economics Foundation. Available at: http://www.publications.parliament.uk/pa/cm200708/cmselect/cmpubadm/408/408we18.htm

New Economics Foundation (2008c) *The New Wealth of Time: How Timebanking Helps People Build Better Public Services*, London: NEF.

New Economics Foundation (2008d) *Triple Crunch*, London: NEF.

New Economics Foundation (2009) *A Bit Rich*, London: NEF.

Nie, N.H., Junn, J. and Stehlik-Barry, K. (1996) *Education and Democratic Citizenship in America*, Chicago, IL: The University of Chicago Press.

Norris, F.H., Stevens, S.P., Pfefferbaum, B., Wyche, K.F and Pfefferbaum, R.L. (2008) Community Resilience as a Metaphor, Theory, Set of Capacities, and Strategy for Disaster Readiness. *American Journal of Community Psychology* 41: 127–150.

Norris, F.H., Tracy, M. and Galea, S. (2009) Looking for Resilience: Understanding the Longitudinal Trajectories of Responses to Stress. *Social Science & Medicine* 68: 2190–2198.

North, P. (2003) Time Banks – Learning the Lessons from LETS. *Local Economy* 18: 267–270.

North, P. (2005) Scaling Alternative Economic Practices? Some Lessons from Alternative Currencies. *Transactions of the Institute of British Geographers* 30: 221–233.

North, P. (2006a) *Alternative Currency Movements as a Challenge to Globalisation? A Case Study of Manchester's Local Currency Networks*, Hants: Ashgate Publishing Ltd.

North, P. (2006b) Constructing Civil Society? Green Money in Transition Hungary. *Review of International Political Economy* 13: 28–52.

North, P. (2007) *Money and Liberation: The Micropolitics of Alternative Currency Movements*, Minneapolis, MN: University of Minnesota Press.

North, P. (2010a) Alternative Currency Networks as Utopian Practice. In: L. Leonard and J. Barry (eds) *Global Ecological Politics*, Bingley: Emerald Group Publishing Limited.

North, P. (2010b) *Local Money: How to Make It Happen in Your Community*, Dartington: Green Books.

North, P. (2011) Geographies and Utopias of Cameron's Big Society. *Social & Cultural Geography* 12: 817–827.

North, P. and Longhurst, N. (2013) Grassroots Localisation? The Scalar Potential of and Limits of the 'Transition' Approach to Climate Change and Resource Constraint. *Urban Studies* 50: 1423–1438.

Nowotny, H. (1992) Time and Social Theory. *Time & Society* 1: 421–454.

O'Connor, J. (1998) *Natural Causes: Essays in Ecological Marxism*, New York, NY: The Guildford Press.

Oechsle, M. and Geissler, B. (2003) Between Paid Work and Private Commitments. *Time & Society* 12: 79–98.

Offe, C. (1992) A Non-Productivist Design for Social Policies. In: J. Feris and R. Page (eds) *Social Policy in Transition: Anglo-German Perspective in the New European Community*, Aldershot: Avebury, pp 87–105.

Offe, C. and Heinze, R.G. (1992) *Beyond Employment: Time, Work and the Informal Economy*, Cambridge: Polity Press.

Omran, A.R. (1971) The Epidemiological Transition: A Theory of the Epidemiology of Population Change. *The Milbank Memorial Fund Quarterly* 49: 509–538.

O'Neill, M. and Williams, G. (2004) Developing Community and Agency Engagement in an Action Research Study in South Wales. *Journal of Critical Public Health* 14: 37–47.

O'Rourke, R. (2008) *Transition Towns: Ecotopia Emerging? The Role of Civil Society in Escaping Carbon Lock-In*, London: The London School of Economics & Political Science, Geography & Environment Department, 60.

Ostrom, E. (1997) Crossing the Great Divide: Co-Production Synergy and Development. In: P. Evans (ed) *State–Society Synergy: Government and Social Capital in Development*, University of California International and Area Studies Digital Collection, Research Series #94, California, CA: California University. Available at: http://repositories.cdlib.org/uciaspubs/research/94

Ould-Ahmed, P. (2010) Can a Community Currency Be Independent of the State Currency? A Case Study of the Credito in Argentina (1995ÿ–ÿ2008). *Environment and Planning A* 42: 1346–1364.

Ozanne, L.K. (2010) Learning to Exchange Time: Benefits and Obstacles to Time Banking. *International Journal of Community Currency* 14: 1–16.

Pacione, M. (1997) Local Exchange Trading Systems as a Response to the Globalisation of Capitalism. *Urban Studies* 34: 1179–1199.

Papadopoulos, T. and Roumpakis, A. (2012) The Greek Welfare State in the Age of Austerity: Anti-Social Policy and the Politico-Economic Crisis. In: M. Kilkey, G. Ramia and K. Farnsworth (eds) *Social Policy Review 24: Analysis and Debate in Social Policy, 2012*, Bristol: The Policy Press, pp 205–230.

Parker, S. (2007a) The Co-Production Paradox. In: S. Parker and N. Gallagher (eds) *The Collaborative State*, London: Demos, pp 176–187.

Parker, S. (2007b) Participation: A New Operating System for Public Services. In: S. Creasy (ed) *Participation Nation: Reconnecting Citizens to the Public Realm*, London: Involve, pp 103–112.

Parker, S. and Heapy, J. (2006) The Journey to the Interface: How Public Service Design Can Connect Users to Reform. Demos. Available at: http://www.demos.co.uk/publications/thejourneytotheinterface

Parks, R.B., Baker, P.C., Kiser, L., Oakerson, R., Ostrom, E., Ostrom, V., Percy, S. L., Vandivort M. B., Whitaker, G. P. and Wilson, R. (1981) Consumers as Coproducers of Public Services: Some Economic and Institutional Considerations. *Policy Studies Journal* 9: 1001–1011.

Pascall, G. (2012) *Gender Equality in the Welfare State?*, Bristol: The Policy Press.

Peacock, M.S. (2006) The Moral Economy of Parallel Currencies: An Analysis of Local Exchange Trading Systems. *American Journal of Economics and Sociology* 65: 1059–1083.

Pearson, R. (2003) Argentina's Barter Network: New Currency for New Times? *Bulletin of Latin American Research* 22: 214–230.

Peck, J. (2004) Geography and Public Policy: Constructions of Neoliberalism. *Progress in Human Geography* 28: 392–405.

Peck, J. and Theodore, N. (2012) Reanimating Neoliberalism: Process Geographies of Neoliberalisation. *Social Anthropology* 20: 177–185.

Peck, J. and Tickell, A. (2002) Neoliberalizing Space. *Antipode* 34: 380–404.

Pemberton, S.A. (2015) *Harmful Societies: Understanding Social Harm.* Bristol: Policy Press.

Pemberton, S. and Mason, J. (2008) Co-Production and Sure Start Children's Centres: Reflecting Upon Users' Perspectives and Implications for Service Delivery, Planning and Evaluation. *Social Policy & Society* 8: 13–24.

Percy, S.L. (1984) Citizen Participation in the Coproduction of Urban Services. *Urban Affairs Quarterly* 19: 431–446.

Percy, S.L, Kiser, L. and Parks, R.B. (1980) *Citizen Coproduction: A Neglected Dimension of Public Service Delivery*, Bloomington, IN: Indiana University.

Pestoff, V. (2006) Citizens and Co-production of Welfare Services: Childcare in Eight European Countries. *Public Management Review* 8: 503–519.

Piachaud, D. (1984) *Round About Fifty Hours a Week: The Time Costs of Children*, London: Child Poverty Action Group.

Piachaud, D. (2008) Time and Money. In: J. Strelitz and R. Lister (eds) *Why Money Matters: Family Income, Poverty and Children's Lives*, London: Save the Children.

Pierson, C. (2006) *Beyond the Welfare State? The New Political Economy of Welfare*, Cambridge: Polity Press.

Pierson, P. (2002) Coping with Permanent Austerity: Welfare State Restructuring in Affluent Democracies. *Revue française de sociologie* 43: 369–406.

Pithouse, A. and Williamson, H. (1997) *Engaging the User in Welfare Services*, Birmingham: Venture Press.

Pollock, A.M. and Price, D. (2011) The Final Frontier: The UK's New Coalition Government Turns the English National Health Service Over to the Global Health Care Market. *Health Sociology Review* 20: 294–305.

Poortinga, W. (2012) Community Resilience and Health: The Role of Bonding, Bridging and Linking Aspects of Social Capital. *Health and Place* 18: 286–295.

Powell, K.H. and Dalton, M.M. (2003) Co-Production, Service Exchange Networks, and Social Capital. *The Social Policy Journal* 2: 89–106.

Powell, M. (1999a) Introduction. In: M. Powell (ed) *New Labour, New Welfare State?*, Bristol: The Policy Press, pp 1–27.

Powell, M. (1999b) *New Labour, New Welfare State?*, Bristol: The Policy Press.

Powell, M. (2000) New Labour and the Third Way in the British Welfare State: A New and Distinctive Approach? *Critical Social Policy* 20: 39–60.

Powell, M. (2002) *Evaluating New Labour's Welfare Reforms*, Bristol: The Policy Press.

Powell, M. (2008) *Modernising the Welfare State: The Blair Legacy*, Bristol: The Policy Press.

Powell, M. and Hewitt, M. (1998) The End of the Welfare State? *Social Policy & Administration* 32: 1–13.

Powell, M. and Miller, R. (2014) Framing Privatisation in the English National Health Service. *Journal of Social Policy* 43 (3): 575-594

Powell, M. and Moon, G. (2001) Health Action Zones: The 'Third Way' of a New Area-Based Policy? *Health & Social Care in the Community* 9: 43–50.

Prentis, D. (2007) Experts and Navigators: Public Services in a Participatory Society. In: S. Creasy (ed) *Participation Nation: Reconnecting Citizens to the Public Realm*, London: Involve, pp 113–119.

Purnell, J. and Cooke, G. (2010) *We Mean Power: Ideas for the Future of the Left*, London: Demos.

Putnam, R.D. (2001) *Bowling Alone*, New York, NY: Simon & Schuster Paperbacks.

Ranelagh, J. (1991) *Thatcher's People: An Insider's Account of the Politics, the Power, and the Personalities*, London: HarperCollins.

Rawnsley, A. (2001) *Servants of the People: The Inside Story of New Labour*, London: Penguin.

Raybeck, D. (1992) The Coconut-Shell Clock. *Time & Society* 1: 323–340.

Rees, J. (2014) Beyond the Impasse: 'Independence Under Threat' or a Progressive Public Service Synergy between the Public and 'Third' Sectors? Social Policy Association Conference, Sheffield.

Rees, J., Taylor, R. and Damm, C. (2013) Does Sector Matter? Understanding the Experiences of Providers in the Work Programme. TSRC. Available at: http://base-uk.org/sites/base-uk.org/files/news/13-02/tsrc.pdf

Reisch, L.A. (2001) Time and Wealth: The Role of Time and Temporalities for Sustainable Patterns of Consumption. *Time & Society* 10: 367–385.

Rich, R.C. (1981) Interaction of the Voluntary and Governmental Sectors: Toward an Understanding of the Coproduction of Municipal Services. *Administration & Society* 13: 59–76.

Richey, S. (2007) Manufacturing Trust: Community Currencies and the Creation of Social Capital. *Political Behavior* 29: 69–88.

Robinson, J.P. and Godbey, G. (1997) *Time for Life: The Surprising Ways Americans Use Their Time*, Pennsylvania, PA: The Pennsylvania State University Press.

Rodgers, J. (2013) Bristol Pound Is Just One Example of What Local Currencies Can Achieve. Available at: http://www.guardian.co.uk/local-government-network/2013/jun/17/bristol-pound-local-currencies

Rose, N. (1999) *Powers and Freedom: Reframing Political Thought*, Cambridge: Cambridge University Press.

Rosenstock, I.M., Strecher, V.J. and Becker, M.H. (1988) Social Learning Theory and the Health Belief Model. *Health Education & Behavior* 15: 175–183.

Rowlingson, K. and McKay, S. (2012) *Wealth and the Wealthy: Exploring and Tackling Inequalities between Rich and Poor*, Bristol: The Policy Press.

Ruskin, J. (1862) *'Unto This Last': Four Essays on the First Principles of Political Economy*, London: Smith Elder.

Russell, B. (2004) *In Praise of Idleness*, London: Routledge.

Rutherford, J. (2007) New Labour, the Market State, and the End of Welfare. *Soundings* 36: 40–55.

Ryan, L. (2014) Outsourcing and the Voluntary Sector. Available at: http://www.independentaction.net/wp-content/uploads/2014/06/Outsourcing-and-the-Voluntary-Sector-final.pdf

Savage, S.P. and Robins, L. (1990) *Public Policy under Thatcher*, Hampshire: Palgrave Macmillan.

Schiffman, J. (1991) 'Fight the Power': Two Groups Mobilize for Peace. In: M. Burawoy, A. Burton, A. Arnett Ferguson K.J. Fox, J. Gamson, N. Gartrell, L. Hurst, C. Kurzman, L. Salzinger, J. Schiffman and S. Ui (eds) *Ethnography Unbound: Power and Resistance in the Modern Metropolis*, Berkeley, CA, and Oxford: University of California Press, pp 58–79.

Schmueker, K. and Lodge, G. (2010) *Devolution in Practice 2010*, London: IPPR.

Schumacher, E.F. (1974) *Small Is Beautiful: A Study of Economics as if People Mattered*, London: Abacus.

Schutz, A. and Sandy, G.M. (2011) *Collective Action for Social Change: An Introduction to Community Organizing* New York: Palgrave Macmillan.

Scott-Cato, M. and Hillier, J. (2010) How Could We Study Climate-Related Social Innovation? Applying Deleuzean Philosophy to Transition Towns. *Environmental Politics* 19: 869–887.

Sennett, R. and Cobb, J. (1993) *The Hidden Injuries of Class*, New York, NY: W.W. Norton.

Sevenhuijsen, S. (1998) *Citizenship and the Ethics of Care: Feminist Considerations on Justice, Morality, and Politics*, London: Routledge.

Seyfang, G. (2001a) Community Currencies: Small Change for a Green Economy. *Environment and Planning A* 33: 975–996.

Seyfang, G. (2001b) Money That Makes a Change: Community Currencies, North and South. *Gender and Development* 9: 60–69.

Seyfang, G. (2003a) Growing Cohesive Communities One Favour at a Time: Social Exclusion, Active Citizenship and Time Banks. *International Journal of Urban and Regional Research* 27: 699–706.

Seyfang, G. (2003b) 'With a Little Help from My Friends.' Evaluating Time Bank as a Tool for Community Self-Help. *Local Economy* 18: 257–264.

Seyfang, G. (2004a) *Bartering for a Better Future? Community Currencies and Sustainable Consumption*. Working Paper - Centre for Social and Economic Research on the Global Environment http://www.cserge.ac.uk/user/7/publications

Seyfang, G. (2004b) Time Banks: Rewarding Community Self-Help in the Inner City? *Community Development Journal* 39: 62–71.

Seyfang, G. (2004c) Working Outside the Box: Community Currencies, Time Banks and Social Inclusion. *Journal of Social Policy* 33: 49–71.

Seyfang, G. (2006a) Sustainable Consumption, the New Economics and Community Currencies: Developing New Institutions for Environmental Governance. *Regional Studies* 40: 781–791.

Seyfang, G. (2006b) *Time Banks and the Social Economy: Exploring the U.K. Policy Context* Working Paper - Centre for Social and Economic Research on the Global Environment http://www.cserge.ac.uk/user/7/publications

Seyfang, G. and Longhurst, N. (2013a) Desperately Seeking Niches: Grassroots Innovations and Niche Development in the Community Currency Field. *Global Environmental Change* 23: 881–891.

Seyfang, G. and Longhurst, N. (2013b) Growing Green Money? Mapping Community Currencies for Sustainable Development. *Ecological Economics* 86: 65–77.

Seyfang, G. and Pearson, R. (2000) Time for Change: International Experience in Community Currencies. *Development* 43: 56–60.

Seyfang, G. and Smith, K. (2002) *Using Time Banking for Neighbourhood Renewal and Community Capacity Building*, London: New Economics Foundation.

Shah, A. and Samb, P. (2011) Time Banking Is More Than Money for Women in Senegal. Available at: https://openknowledge.worldbank.org/bitstream/handle/10986/10431/652800BRI0IFC000Banking0Angana0Shah.pdf?sequence=1

Shapely, P. (2011) Civil Society, Class and Locality: Tenant Groups in Post-War Britain. In: M. Hilton and J. McKay (eds) *The Ages of Voluntarism: How We Got to the Big Society*, Oxford: Oxford University Press, pp 94–113.

Shildrick, T., MacDonald, R., Webster, C. and Garthwaite, K. (2012) *Poverty and Insecurity: Life in Low-Pay, No-Pay Britain*, Bristol: The Policy Press.

Simmel, G. (1900) *The Philosophy of Money*, Oxon: Routledge.

Simmel, G. (1964) Faithfulness and Gratitude. In: K.H. Wolff (ed) *The Sociology of Georg Simmel*, London: Collier-Macmillan, pp 379–395.

Simon, M. (2003) A Fair Share of Health Care: Time Banks and Health. Available at: http://www.timebanking.org/documents/Publications/A-Fair-Share-of-Health-Care.pdf

Sinfield, A. (2011) Credit Crunch, Inequality and Social Policy. In: K. Farnsworth and Z. Irving (eds) *Social Policy in Challenging Times: Economic Crisis and Welfare Systems*, Bristol: The Policy Press, pp 65–80.

Sloam, J. (2012) 'Rejuvenating Democracy?' Young People and the 'Big Society' Project. *Parliamentary Affairs* 65: 90–114.

Smith, A. (2011) Community-Led Urban Transitions and Resilience: Performing Transition Towns in a City. In: H. Bulkeley, V.C. Broto, M. Hodson and S. Marvin (eds) *Cities and Low Carbon Transitions*, London: Routledge, pp 159–177.

Smith, K. (2010) Research, Policy and Funding: Academic Treadmills and the Squeeze on Intellectual Spaces. *The British Journal of Sociology* 61: 176–195.

Smith, M., Holbrook, A., Lyons, K., Macneil, J., Forster, D., Clement, N. and Freeman, M. (2013) Evaluation of the NSW Volunteering Strategy 2012–13 Final Report: Timebanking Trial. Available at: http://www.volunteering.nsw.gov.au/about-us/evaluation-and-research

Social Exclusion Unit (1999) *PAT 9: Community Self Help, Social Exclusion Unit*, London: Cabinet Office.

Soper, K. (2008) Alternative Hedonism, Cultural Theory and the Role of Aesthetic Revisioning. *Cultural Studies* 22: 567–587.

Sotiropoulou, I. (2012) Economic Activity Without Official Currency in Greece: The ★ Hypothesis. *International Journal of Community Currency Research* 16: 70–79.

Southerton, D. (2003) Squeezing Time. *Time & Society* 12: 5–25.

Stafford, J. (2012) Recession, Resilience, Resources and Relationships. *Voluntary Sector Review* 3: 257–263.

Stears, M. (2011) Everyday Democracy. Available at: http://www.ippr.org/images/media/files/publication/2011/09/everyday-democracy-110922_7993.pdf

Stone, D. (1999) Learning Lessons and Transferring Policy Across Time, Space and Disciplines. *Politics* 19: 51–59.

Stone, D. (2000) Non-Governmental Policy Transfer: The Strategies of Independent Policy Institutes. *Governance: An International Journal of Policy and Administration* 10: 45–62.

Sullivan, M. and Drakeford, M. (2011) Post-Devolution Health Policy in Wales. In: C. Williams (ed) *Social Policy for Social Welfare Practice in a Devolved Wales*, Birmingham: Venture Press, pp 35–48.

Szreter, S. and Woolcock, M. (2004) Health by Association? Social Capital, Social Theory, and the Political Economy of Public Health. *International Journal of Epidemiology* 33: 650–667.

Tawney, R.H. (1921) *The Acquisitive Society*, Charleston, SC: Bibliobazaar.

Taylor, I. (2000) New Labour and the Enabling State. *Health and Social Care in the Community* 8: 372–379.

Taylor, M. (2011) Community Organising and the Big Society: Is Saul Alinsky Turning in His Grave? *Voluntary Sector Review* 2: 257–264.

Taylor, P.J. (2012) Transition Towns and World Cities: Towards Green Networks of Cities. *Local Environment* 17: 495–508.

Taylor-Gooby, P. (2002) The Silver Age of the Welfare State: Perspectives on Resilience. *Journal of Social Policy* 31: 597–621.

Taylor-Gooby, P. and Stoker, G. (2011) The Coalition Programme: A New Vision for Britain or Politics as Usual? *The Political Quarterly* 82: 4–15.

Teater, B. and Baldwin, M. (2012) *Social Work in the Community*, Bristol: The Policy Press.

Terese Soder, N. (2008) Community Currency: An Approach to Economic Sustainability in Out Local Bioregion. *International Journal of Community Currency Research* 12: 24–52.

Testart, A. (1998) Uncertainties and the 'Obligation to Reciprocate': A Critique of Mauss. In: W. James and N.J. Allen (eds) *Marcel Mauss: A Centenary Tribute*, New York, NY: Berhahn Books.

Thaler, R. and Sustein, D. (2009) *Nudge: Improving Decisions About Health, Wealth and Happiness*, London: Penguin Books.

Thompson, E.P. (1967) Time, Work-Discipline, and Industrial Capitalism. *Past & Present* 38: 56–97.

Titmuss, R.M. (1997) *The Gift Relationship: From Human Blood to Social Policy*, New York: New Press.

Torry, R.M. (2012) Is There a Faith Sector? *Voluntary Sector Review* 3: 111–117.

Townsend, P. (1976) *Sociology and Social Policy*, Middlesex: Penguin Education.

Turner, A. (2009) Mansion House Speech. Available at: http://www.fsa.gov.uk/pages/Library/Communication/Speeches/2009/0922_at.shtml

Ungar, M. (2004) A Constructionist Discourse on Resilience. *Youth and Society* 35: 341–365.

Urry, J. (1994) Time, Leisure and Social Identity. *Time & Society* 3: 131–149.

Utting, D. (2009) *Contemporary Social Evils*, Bristol: The Policy Press.

Van Parijs, P. (2009) Joseph Rowntree Foundation Lecture – Basic Income and Social Justice: Why Philosophers Disagree. Available at: http://www.jrf.org.uk/publications/basic-income-social-justice

Waine, B. (1991) *The Rhetoric of Independence: The Ideology and Practice of Social Policy in Thatcher's Britain*, Oxford: Berg Publishers Limited.

Walker, G. and Burningham, K. (2011) Flood Risk, Vulnerability and Environmental Justice: Evidence and Evaluation of Inequality in a UK Context. *Critical Social Policy* 31: 216–240.

Wallerstein, N. and Duran, B. (2006) Using Community-Based Participatory Research to Address Health Disparities. *Health Promotion Practice* 7: 312–323.

Ward, C. (1996) *Social Policy: An Anarchist Response*, London: Freedom Press.

Warne, T. and Lawrence, K. (2009) *The Salford Time Banking Evaluation: A Report for Unlimited Potential, Formally Known as the Community Health Action Partnership*, Salford: The University of Salford.

Wearden, G. and Elliott, L. (2013) Angela Merkel Tells Davos Austerity Must Continue. *The Guardian* 24ᵗʰ January 2013.

Weber, M. (1992) *The Protestant Ethic and the Spirit of Capitalism*, London: Routledge.

Weiss, L. (1998) *The Myth of the Powerless State*, Cambridge: Polity.

Welsh Assembly Government (2006) *Beyond Boundaries: Citizen Centred Local Services for Wales*, Cardiff: Welsh Assembly Government.

Welsh Assembly Government (2008a) *Designed to Add Value*, Cardiff: Welsh Assembly Government.

Welsh Assembly Government (2008b) *The Third Dimension*, Cardiff: Welsh Assembly Government.

Westenholz, A. (2006) Identity, Times and Work. *Time & Society* 15: 33–55.

Whitaker, G.P. (1980) Co-Production: Citizen Participation in Service Delivery. *Public Administration Review* May/June: 240–246.

Whitehead, F. (2010a) Local Currencies by Design. Available at: http://www.guardian.co.uk/society/gallery/2010/sep/21/local-currencies-brixton-pound

Whitehead, F. (2010b) Will the Brixton Pound Stick Around? Available at: http://www.guardian.co.uk/society/2010/sep/21/brixton-pound-local-currency

Whitty, G. (1997) Creating Quasi-Markets in Education: A Review of Recent Research on Parental Choice and School Autonomy in Three Countries. *Review of Research in Education* 22: 3–47.

Wiggan, J. (2011) Something Old and Blue, or Red, Bold and New? Welfare Reform and the Coalition Government. In: C. Holden, M. Kilkey and G. Ramia (eds) *Social Policy Review 23: Analysis and Debate in Social Policy, 2011*, Bristol: The Policy Press, pp 25–43.

Wilbert, C. and White, D.F. (2011) *Autonomy, Solidarity, Possibility: The Colin Ward Reader*, Edinburgh: AK Press.

Wilding, P. (1986) *In Defence of the Welfare State*, Manchester: Manchester University Press.

Wilding, P. (1992) The British Welfare State: Thatcherism's Enduring Legacy. *Policy & Politics* 20: 201–212.

Wilkinson, R.G. (1996) *Unhealthy Societies: The Afflictions of Inequality*, London: Routledge.

Wilkinson, R.G. (1997) Comment: Income, Inequality and Social Cohesion. *American Journal of Public Health* 87: 1504–1506.

Wilkinson, R.G. and Pickett, K.E. (2007) The Problems of Relative Deprivation: Why Some Societies Do Better Than Others. *Social Science and Medicine* 65: 1965–1978.

Williams, C.C. (1996) Local Currencies and Community Development: An Evaluation of Green Dollar Exchanges in New Zealand. *Community Development Journal* 31: 319–329.

Williams, C.C. (2008) Repaying Favours: Unravelling the Nature of Community Exchange in an English Locality. *Community Development Journal* 44: 488–499.

Williams, C.C. (2011) Socio-Spatial Variations in Community Self-Help: A Total Social Organisation of Labour Perspective. *Social Policy and Society* 10: 365–378.

Williams, C.C. and Windebank, J. (2001a) Beyond Profit-Motivated Exchange: Some Lessons from the Study of Paid Informal Work. *European Urban and Regional Studies* 8: 49–61.

Williams, C.C. and Windebank, J. (2001b) Paid Informal Work: A Barrier to Social Inclusion? *Transfer: European Review of Labour and Research* 1: 25–40.

Williams, C.C., Aldridge, T. and Tooke, J. (2003) Alternative Exchange Spaces. In: A. Leyshon, R. Lee and C.C. Williams (eds) *Alternative Economic Spaces*, London: Sage, pp 151–167.

Williams, F. (1989) *Social Policy: A Critical Introduction*, Cambridge: Blackwell.

Wilson, R. and Bloomfield, J. (2011) *Building the Good Society: A New Form of Progressive Politics*, London: Compass.

Wright, S., Marston, G. and McDonald, C. (2011) The Role of Non-profit Organizations in the Mixed Economy of Welfare-to-Work in the UK and Australia. *Social Policy & Administration* 45: 299–318.

Wright Mills, C. (1959) *The Sociological Imagination*, Oxford: Oxford University Press.

Zakus, J.D. and Lysack, C.L. (1998) Revisiting Community Participation. *Health Policy and Planning* 13: 1–12.

Zelizer, V. (1994) *The Social Meaning of Money*, New York, NY: Basic Books.

Zelizer, V. (2005) Missing Monies: Comment on Nigel Dodd, 'Reinventing Monies in Europe'. *Economy and Society* 34: 584–588.

Zucchermaglio, C. and Talamo, A. (2000) The Social Construction of Work Times. *Time & Society* 9: 205–222.

Index